Domination through Law

Kilombo: International Relations and Colonial Questions

Series Editors: Mustapha K. Pasha, Aberystwyth University, Meera Sabaratnam, SOAS University of London, and Robbie Shilliam, Queen Mary University of London

This is the first series to mark out a dedicated space for advanced critical inquiry into colonial questions across International Relations. The ethos of this book series is reflected by the bricolage constituency of Kilombos – settlements of African slaves, rebels and indigenous peoples in South America who became self-determining political communities that retrieved and renovated the social practices of its diverse constituencies while being confronted by colonial forces. The series embraces a multitude of methods and approaches, theoretical and empirical scholarship, alongside historical and contemporary concerns. Publishing innovative and top-quality peer-reviewed scholarship, Kilombo enquires into the shifting principles of colonial rule that inform global governance and investigates the contestation of these principles by diverse peoples across the globe. It critically re-interprets popular concepts, narratives and approaches in the field of IR by reference to the "colonial question" and, in doing so, the book series opens up new vistas from which to address the key political questions of our time

Titles in the Series

Meanings of Bandung: Postcolonial Orders and Decolonial Visions
Edited by Quỳnh N. Phạm and Robbie Shilliam
Politics of the African Anticolonial Archive
Edited by Shiera S. el-Malik and Isaac A. Kamola
Asylum after Empire: Colonial Legacies in the Politics of Asylum Seeking
Lucy Mayblin
Decolonizing Intervention: International Statebuilding in Mozambique
Meera Sabaratnam
*Global Development and Colonial Power: German Development Policy at Home and
    Abroad*
Daniel Bendix
The Postcolonial African State in Transition: Stateness and Modes of Sovereignty
Amy Niang
South Africa, Race and the Making of International Relations
Vineet Thakur and Peter Vale
Postcolonial Governmentalities: Rationalities, Violences and Contestations
Edited by Terri-Anne Teo and Elisa Wynne-Hughes
*Beyond the Master's Tools? Decolonizing Knowledge Orders, Research Methods and
    Teaching*
Edited by Daniel Bendix, Franziska Müller and Aram Ziai
*Creative Presence: Settler Colonialism, Indigenous Self-Determination and Decolonial
    Artwork*
Emily Merson
Domination through Law: The Internationalization of Legal Norms in Postcolonial Africa
Mohamed Sesay

Domination through Law

The Internationalization of Legal Norms in Postcolonial Africa

Mohamed Sesay

ROWMAN & LITTLEFIELD

Lanham • Boulder • New York • London

Published by Rowman & Littlefield
An imprint of The Rowman & Littlefield Publishing Group, Inc.
4501 Forbes Boulevard, Suite 200, Lanham, Maryland 20706, USA
www.rowman.com

6 Tinworth Street, London SE11 5AL, United Kingdom

British Library Cataloguing in Publication Data

A catalogue record for this book is available from the British Library

ISBN: HB 978-1-5381-4631-6

Library of Congress Cataloging-in-Publication Data Is Available

Library of Congress Control Number: 2020946912

ISBN 978-1-5381-4631-6 (cloth)
ISBN 978-1-5381-4997-3 (pbk)
ISBN 978-1-5381-4632-3 (electronic)

Contents

**PART II: COLONIAL LEGACIES AND CONTEMPORARY
LEGAL RECONSTRUCTIONS   85**

Acknowledgments

This study would not have been accomplished without the steadfast support and assistance of many people, to whom I owe a deep sense of gratitude.

First, as this book is a product of my doctoral research, I would like to express sincere thanks to Dr. Rex Brynen, my program supervisor. I can hardly find the right words to describe the extent to which you have motivated and guided me as a young scholar since the beginning of my PhD studies to the completion of my dissertation. Thanks so much for having an unwavering confidence in me, reflected in your insightful comments on my work as well as encouraging thoughts during our meetings. You are simply the best and I would remain forever grateful. Similarly, I extend profound gratitude to my proposal and dissertation committee members including Dr. Khalid Medani, Dr. Maria Popova, and Dr. John Galaty who provided very helpful feedback on this project. Other professors have been very supportive to me in many ways during this academic journey. In particular, I am indebted to Dr. Catherine Lu, whom I always turned to for academic and moral support. You have been always willing to assist me formulate my own ideas including being a member of my proposal committee and post-doc co-supervisor, but it is your kindness in the midst of such support that greatly impacted my time at McGill. To Dr. Megan Bradley, also at McGill, I deeply appreciate your support and mentorship as my post-doc co-supervisor and senior research colleague.

Generous funding for this research was offered through the Social Science and Humanities Research Council's Vanier Canada Graduate Scholarship, McGill's Graduate Student Travel Award, and the Department of Political Science. I am deeply thankful for these grants because they enabled me to concentrate on my studies, to undertake a six-month fieldwork in Sierra Leone and Liberia, and to devote sufficient time in thesis writing. The preliminary version of this manuscript was written during my post-doc fellowship with the Research Group on Global Justice of the Yan P. Lin Center for the Study of Freedom & Global Orders in the Ancient & Modern Worlds. Many thanks to the center and members such as Dr. Catherine Lu, Dr. Yves Winter, Dr. Megan Bradley, Dr. Jacob Levy, and Dr. Arash Abizadeh for your generous financial support and collegiality. The author and publisher would like to thank the Faculty of Liberal Arts and Professional Studies, York University for the financial support it provided to this work. I also want to thank the GCRF Gender, Justice and Security Hub which enabled this accomplishment. There is a long list of colleagues including Dr. Kirsten Ainley, Dr. Eric Wiebelhaus-Brahm, Dr. Rebekka Friedman, Dr. Uwafiokun Idemudia, Dr. Merouan Mekouar, Dr. Ozgun Tupak, Dr. Mary Goitom, Dr. Pablo Idahosa, Dr. Sylvia Bawa, Dr. Nathanael Ojong, Nelson Camilo Sanchez and many others who shared their ideas and motivated me during this process. I remain particularly grateful to Professor Chandra Sriram who was the external examiner of my dissertation and mentor. The publication of this manuscript would not have been possible without the constructive and insightful feedback of reviewers as well as the generous and excellent guidance of the series editors and professional staff at Rowman and Littlefield International.

During my fieldwork, I benefited immensely from the gracious support of a host of institutions and individuals. In Sierra Leone, I am particularly obliged to Mr. Simeon Koroma, Director of Timap for Justice, which is a leading paralegal service provider in the country. Thanks for your insightful guidance into my fieldwork, for granting me access to an office space in Makeni Town, as well as allowing me to interact with your paralegals through interviews and informal conversations in many forums. I extend gratitude to Mr. Abu Brima of the Network Movement for Justice and Development for allowing his organization to host me in a similar way in Koidu Town. For leaders of Partners in Conflict Transformation (PICOT), I treasure the enlightened contributions of Paul Koroma, Maxwell Kemokia, and Ibrahim Sesay. Apart from sharing their personal experiences with me, building relationships with these leaders enabled me to participate in three important dialogue conferences organized for paramount chiefs and other traditional authorities in Sierra Leone. I am also highly appreciative of the hospitality of paramount chiefs whose chiefdoms I visited, James Sawo-Koroma of Freetown, and MP Saa Emmerson Lamina of Koidu. In Liberia, the research assistance of Sarah Sumo is greatly appreciated.

Finally, the ultimate source of emotional strength for this study comes from my loving family in Freetown and friends in Canada. My father did not live long enough to see me earn even my first degree, but his deepest desire to educate his children remains with me to date. To my mom, thank you so much for the countless sacrifices and silent prayers for me. It gives me greatest joy to make you proud through this accomplishment. To Alpha, Isatu, and my other siblings, your moral encouragement has been invaluable throughout this journey. A special word of appreciation to Dr. Paula Brook, my closest mentor and guardian. Lastly, I am deeply indebted to my dearest Juliet, for your love, prayers, commitment, and long patience with me while studying abroad.

Chapter 1

Introduction

When I graduated from the University of Sierra Leone with my first degree in 2004, I was among the first team of research assistants working on a part-time basis for a local think tank, the Centre for Development and Security Analysis, based in the capital Freetown. From then to 2010 when I left for graduate school abroad, the civil wars in Sierra Leone and Liberia had ended and both countries were embarking on rebuilding the rule of law mainly through legal internationalization, that is, exportation of legal institutions, norms, and rules from advanced domestic jurisdictions to weak ones (Beaulac 2012). Rebuilding the rule of law, which included transitional justice, law reform, and justice sector development, had also emerged as central to the international community's new emphasis on post-conflict peacebuilding and reconstruction. Participating in research projects and facilitating several meetings at the center, I had an opportunity to interact with many stakeholders—including expatriates, politicians, diplomats, human rights advocates, judicial officials, legal professionals, peacekeepers, intellectuals, consultants, researchers—who often shaped both the policies and practices of reform.[1] But the real impact of millions of dollars of international efforts to transfer the rule of law's ethical assumptions, legal models, and institutional forms on preexisting social life in these countries was never clear to me. Moreover, I wondered who benefited from legal internationalization and why, despite many emancipatory promises by reformers, the fundamental structures of injustice and inequality remained unaddressed.

After reading extensively about realist, liberal, neoliberal, and critical peacebuilding perspectives, these questions still needed empirical answers when I returned to Sierra Leone and Liberia five years later in 2014 to conduct fieldwork for my doctoral dissertation. After more than a decade of reform efforts, most people I interviewed in both countries expressed a deep sense of dissatisfaction and disappointment about post-conflict rule of law reforms. Even those who were enthusiastically involved in international efforts seemed puzzled that reform programs mostly ended up restoring and strengthening the same structures of power and material accumulation that precipitated violent conflict in the first place. Although everyone acknowledged that relative political stability had been reinstated, the perception that both countries missed an opportunity to carry out fundamental structural transformation necessary for an equitable, just, and inclusive society was widespread. In fact, every participant appeared concerned that rule of law reforms may have reproduced earlier forms of unequal power relations and domination that reformers promised to destabilize and dismantle.

In Monrovia, when I asked one founding member of the Movement for Justice in Africa (MOJA) about his experience with the rehabilitated formal justice system, he candidly replied that "there is no justice for the poor here" and then described the "reality of what [they] have as an injustice system— a system that perpetuates injustice."[2] He also considers the "fundamental reason why [Liberia] is in a mess" as due to the fact that "its educational system trains people to be more American than Americans themselves."[3] This disjuncture between reform and everyday realities was expressed not just by educated people in Monrovia and Freetown. In Gorama-Kono Chiefdom of Eastern Sierra Leone, whose modern structures only include a police outpost, local court facilities, and chiefdom council, a small-scale businesswoman told me that "I have never taken a case to the local court or police."[4] When I asked why, she added that "I don't take someone to court because doing so brings enmity into the community."[5]

Not peculiar to Sierra Leone and Liberia, this phenomenon has confounded rule of law promotion, particularly in the context of contemporary peace-building and statebuilding where most international efforts have been concentrated since the early 1990s. From Iraq, Afghanistan, Bosnia, East Timor, Colombia, Sri Lanka to the Democratic Republic of Congo and Uganda, the empirical record has consistently and overwhelmingly indicated that international efforts to restructure domestic jurisdictions have failed to significantly improve governance around the world.[6] One study shows that "traditional systems are the primary—if not the sole—means of dispute resolution for 80 to 90 percent of the population" in war-torn countries (Isser et al. 2011, 325). Although most of these traditional mechanisms lack official status and are relatively flawed, they continue as the forum of choice for the majority population in regions like Africa while formal justice systems remain the least accessible and legitimate of state institutions (Isser et al. 2011; Logan 2013; UNDP et al. 2012; Wojkowska 2006).[7] Published by the World Justice Project (WJP), the 2020 Rule of Law index even notes that "more countries declined than improved in overall rule of law performance for a third year in a row, continuing a negative slide toward weakening and stagnating the rule of law around the world" (WJP 2020).

Given the centrality of legal and judicial reforms in the field of post-conflict peacebuilding and statebuilding, many have devoted attention to the performance and legitimacy challenges confronting international rule of law promotion. For neoliberal institutionalists, the rule of law project is directly linked to processes of political and economic liberalization implemented to both legitimate war-torn societies as liberal-democratic polities and restructure them to be reintegrated into the global neoliberal economy. From this perspective, scholars and practitioners have been concerned about the failures of legal internationalization, with prominent explanations focusing on lack of coordination and harmonization among interveners, insensitivity to the politics of reform, lack of local participation and ownership, and opposing conceptions of the rule of law (Carothers 1998, 2006; Donias 2012; Mani 1998; Mansfield and Snyder 2005; Newman et al. 2009; Richmond and Franks 2009). For instance, Fukuyama (2010) argues that the two challenges associated with rule of law promotion abroad are (i) the huge infrastructure, human, and physical capital needed to construct legal systems; and (ii) the time needed to get buy-in from local communities whose cultures are different from liberal democracies. But these analyses are often preoccupied with factors that affect the (in)efficient operationalization of global normative and institutional frameworks rather than interrogating the frameworks themselves.

Trying to make sense of these challenges, one of the first peer-reviewed articles drawn from my dissertation argues that rule of law reforms in post-conflict environments fail because transplanted legal norms and institutions are hijacked by dominant actors who have been historically privileged by unequal sociolegal and economic structures (Sesay 2019). This book further explores and advances this claim by arguing that rule of law promotion as social domination has been, historically, core to international efforts. Aimed at troubling the benign characterization of contemporary rule of law promotion, the book posits that international efforts, even when well intentioned, often end up reinforcing social domination in economies, polities, and societies. Rule of law promotion as a means of social domination, it argues, disproportionately favors actors who have the requisite socioeconomic capabilities and political influence at the expense of those who lack the resources to use the state legal system. It goes on to contend that externally supported rule of law development that stresses standardization, formalization, and centralization of legal structures has only succeeded in entrenching a state-based system that is highly elitist, centralized, and designed for the application of formal English law. Rather than reducing domination, fear, indignity, and disorder as reformers and scholars often anticipate, these built-in biases in rule of law programs have succeeded in restoring and strengthening the dominant ruling class and reconstituting its relationship with global capital.

In interrogating this relationship between rule of law promotion and social domination, the book conceptually distinguishes between structural, social, and cost-related modes of inequality. Structurally, international efforts to (re) build the rule of law maintain, if not expand, the historical disparity between a small elite class (including the educated, economically well-off, and politically connected) and those of low socioeconomic status. Although this structural disparity dates to the colonial statebuilding project, the relationship is reinforced by current efforts to reestablish the modern state system through formal-legalism and narrow technocracy which depoliticize social justice concerns. In addition, institutional requirements such as legal expertise, professional rules, official language of the system, formal protocols, and standard operating procedures do not only protect privileges of the dominant class but also mount structural barriers against equal access to English law.

In terms of social and cost inequities, rule of law promotion reinforces domination by concentrating the power to allocate social values in the hands of a small class of professionals who are largely drawn from the established segment of society and whose legal tradition and judicial culture mirror society's elite interests. Alongside de jure processes that codify legal identity and exclusion, social inequality is solidified in a de facto manner by routine practices which determine what values can be accommodated in the state system, which normative orders can be officially recognized, who has legal standing in the system, and what kinds of remedies are available. In reinforcing inequality through imposition of user cost, the issue is not simply that increasing formalization and standardization increases the fee for navigating the state system, but that the material and social costs of doing so are unevenly distributed based on one's socioeconomic status. Legal formalism underwrites the individualism and liberalism embedded in capitalist mode of production at the expense of welfare and distributive justice while the system continues to produce indigents who cannot defend themselves. The combined effect of structural, social, and cost-related inequality wrought by rule of law internationalization is usually distrust, which ironically leaves the system dominated by actors with the requisite education, connections, and resources.

This is not to say that the rule of law as a concept for organizing socioeconomic and political order is inherently bad. After all, the rule of law is not an exclusively Western concept, even if its globalized normative and legal framework originated from European societies, which were among the first to institutionalize modern secular law (Fukuyama 2010). For instance, the customary practice of destoolment among the Akyem people of Ghana, as in many precolonial traditional African societies, has been described as "an equivalent to presidential impeachment and conviction, the ultimate humiliation a community could bring on a recalcitrant chief" (Banfo 2002, 149). The Hebrew Bible and Talmud of Judaism, the Roman Twelve Tables, the early church decretals and canons, the Sunna and *Hadith* of Islam, and the Vedas and *Shastras* of Hinduism are all illustrative of a core rule of law tenet—supremacy of the law (Fukuyama 2010).

The point though is that promotion of international rule of law has become a project so steeped in coloniality that, instead of living up to its emancipatory objectives, its imported technologies and institutions are often appropriated to reinforce structural violence on those it promises to help. International rule of law promotion is deeply embedded in coloniality because the legal institutions and norms transplanted into the Global South emerged from legal superimposition, Eurocentrism, and doctrinal legality that often end up reinforcing hierarchical social orders in global affairs and domestic jurisdictions. The project is legal superimposition because the modern law being globalized originally emerged from Euro-American imperialism and colonization, historical processes that subordinated the legal and normative structures of non-Western societies to "superior" standards. Superimposition requires Eurocentrism as a cultural and discursive frame that equates legal development to a superior West just as legal underdevelopment is attributed to the primitiveness and premodernity of the non-West. Constituting the link between knowledge and power is doctrinal legality, a strand of scientific positivism that allows the notion of technocratic neutrality to obfuscate ideologically motivated domination and depoliticize historical struggles for social justice within non-Western societies and in their relations with dominant powers.

The superimposition, Eurocentrism, and doctrinal legality of English law were never challenged at the formal end of colonialism. Rather these colonially established characteristics have become enduring legacies found useful for maintaining the political economy of the neoliberal world order and protecting the privileges of ruling elites in domestic jurisdictions. The comparative study of Sierra Leone and Liberia is illustrative of this active connection between the past and present as both countries can be described as a product of historical and contemporary legal (re)construction. What is today the modern state of Liberia is "an offshoot of slavery and the anti-slave trade movement of the nineteenth century" which partly led to the "emergence of pro-American colonial interests in exploring back-to-Africa schemes" (Liberia TRC Report 2009, 98). Its establishment must be linked to the American Colonization Society (ACS) which, after receiving $100,000 from the US government, was founded "to establish a colony in Africa to take free people of color residing in the United States to Africa or such other places as Congress may deem expedient" (Rev. Robert Findley, delegate to the ACS conference, Liberia TRC Report

2009, 100). Americo-Liberian domination, which lasted from 1822 when the first batches of repatriated Africans arrived in Monrovia to 1980 when the first indigenous leader seized state power, was underwritten by a Euro-American legal system, Western civilization, and Christianity (Sawyer 1992). In neighboring Sierra Leone, the modern state is equally a product of the anti–slave trade movement and British colonialism. Sierra Leone's capital Freetown was "purchased" from indigenous rulers in 1787 as home to resettle "freed" slaves, following the abolition of the transatlantic slave trade. While the Krios were the minority descendants from liberated Africans during the period of colonial rule (1808–1961), their close association with the colonial state accorded them an opportunity to access formal education and take disproportionate advantage of the English law (Alie 1990).

At independence in April 1961, Sierra Leone's educated protectorate elite assumed political power over the Krios just as the 1980 military coup in Liberia ended Americo-Liberian political hegemony. However, the colonial mode of state power and accumulation continued and the connection between settler-colonial rule and political violence in both countries persisted.[8] The Liberian Truth and Reconciliation Commission (TRC) report notes that "central to understanding the socio-political conflict and its degeneration into armed conflict is the choice made by the early leadership of Liberia," a choice to impose Euro-American civilization on the indigenous population (Liberia TRC Report 2009, 72). Likewise, Sierra Leone's TRC report (2004) identifies the colonial creation of a two-nation state with separate development policies and legal systems as among the underlying causes of the armed conflict. When the decade-long civil war in each country came to an end in the early 2000s, postwar reconstruction was carried out mostly under the legal tutelage of the same Euro-American powers that established their modern state systems—the United Kingdom in Sierra Leone and the United States in Liberia. While problem-solving studies about the legitimacy and efficacy of these interventions abound, a historical and comparative analysis that explores the interlinkages between settler-colonial rule, postcolonial authoritarianism, political violence, and post-conflict peacebuilding remains rare.[9]

REBUILDING THE RULE OF LAW IN AFRICA

In a seminal volume on peacebuilding in Africa, Sriram and colleagues (2011) link challenges to rebuilding the rule of law to an entrenched postcolonial governance culture and institutional weaknesses rooted in personalistic one-party rule that followed independence.[10] For them, reforms fail because African leaders have long relied on coercive control, patronage, clientelism, and personalized transactions to monopolize power and the economy, rather than through a functioning bureaucracy or an independent legal system (Sriram et al. 2011). This explanation of reform impasse resonates with the literature on state failure and neopatrimonialism, two related concepts which, as Wai maintains, have "held a totalitarian grip on the interpretation of the continent's postcolonial sociopolitical realities" (2012, 28).

The term "state collapse" or "failed state" is often employed either to depict the statebuilding project in Africa as an abysmal failure or to portray state institutions as chronically weak and vulnerable to societal capture (or both). It is postulated that most postcolonial African states have reneged in their roles as intangible symbols of national identity and authoritative institutions for the allocation of public values (Bratton 2004; Fawole and Ukeje 2005). Regarding symbols of sovereign authority, many states are identified with their inability to guarantee security for a populated territory and failure to command and conduct public affairs (Villalon and Huxtable 1998). Some argue that "the state no longer receives supports from, nor exercises control over its people, and it no longer is even the target of demands because its people know it is incapable of providing supplies" (Zartman 1995, 5). Others characterize the African state as "an empty shell" (Chabal and Daloz 1999), "a lame Leviathan" (Callaghy 1987), "juridical but not empirical" (Jackson and Rosberg 1982), "omnipresent but . . . hardly omnipotent" (Chazan 1988), "excessively authoritarian in disguise of being inadequately authoritative" (Mazrui 1983), and "a shadow state" at the disposal of local barons and warlords (Reno 1997, 2001).

Like state collapse, the concept of neopatrimonialism is frequently used to portray not only current capacity deficits plaguing the postcolonial state but also its irrevocable destiny. Using the analogy of "an empty shell" Chabal and Daloz (1999) contend that the postcolonial state is both vacuous and ineffectual. They stress that apart from the "deficit in professional competence, the institutionalization of state apparatus has never been in the interest of African elites" who prefer institutional weakness and inefficiency to sustain their clientelist networks and patron-client relations (1999, 14). Alluding to why genuine reform is both necessary and improbable, Van de Walle (2001) notes that weak institutional capacity has become so endogenous to the political system that elites have found low state capacity quite useful to even precipitate it, further advancing their previous argument that the neopatrimonial logic provides essential operating codes for African politics (Bratton and Van de Walle 1997). After arguing that weak institutionalization in Africa is a political practice, Chabal and Daloz conclude that "while petty corruption is usually despised by the population at large, there is often recognition that the elites' much more significant abuse of power serves a larger and more legitimate 'moral' purpose" (1999, 159). Against this backdrop, Sriram and colleagues see Africa as a preeminent target for rebuilding the rule of law not because of clientelism and patronage that are everywhere but because large swathes of the continent are experiencing "the type of intensive neopatrimo-nialism, if not pathological neopatrimonialism" (2011, 2).

In Africa, rebuilding the rule of law is also advocated as part of the deep-seated concern in the international community about the ability of non-state traditional and informal justice systems to operate according to international standards of due process and human rights. For instance, Kofi Annan called for "due regard to indigenous and informal traditions for administering jus-tice, to help them to continue their often-vital role and to do so in conformity with both international standards and local tradition" (2004, 13). While the UN now realizes that these systems are popular among majority populations in Africa, pressure is being exerted on member states to ensure that these sys-tems adhere to international procedural and substantive justice norms (UNDP et al. 2012). In terms of procedure, their adjudication methods must be consis-tent with due process and objective rules that ensure certainty, accountability, and equality. Normatively, informal mechanisms must respect substantive rules that define the rights of vulnerable groups as opposed to stipulating the rules by which those rights and duties are established (Kerrigan et al. 2012). To this end, the UNHRC requires all states to ensure that traditional, religious, or cultural attitudes are not used to justify violation of women's rights to equality before the law and equal enjoyment of all covenant rights such as those enshrined in the CEDAW.[11] Emphasizing these human rights safeguards is based on sometimes well-founded concerns that customary and indigenous mechanisms in war-torn societies may have been coerced by powerful local elites, involved inhumane treatments of offenders, and are ill-equipped to handle criminal cases and inter-communal disputes, and gener-ally discriminatory toward women and youth (Richards 1996, 2005; Kerrigan 2012; Pulver 2011; Wojkowska 2006).

In this context, where personalized exchange and bypassing the law is perceived as acceptable normal behavior, Sriram and colleagues argue that "many elements of rule of law are not being re-institutionalized but rather are being instituted for the first time" (2011, 2). Given widespread belief that "institutional atrophy precipitates conflict and disrupts the body politic" (Kieh 2007, 25), a vast array of public institutions is being (re)constituted to conduct the business of the state and market efficaciously. Largely drawn from Western experiences of neoliberal institutionalism, emphasis is on the effective functioning of a rational body of rules that requires separation of public and private spheres and redeeming the state from the clutches of pat-rimonial and personal rule. Rather than being regulated by the caprices of individuals rulers, the ideal is an impersonal entity sustained by inter-insti-tutional relationships revolving around power distribution and competition. Beyond capacity building, the state is to be reoriented to reflect the prin-ciples of public transparency and accountability. Unsurprisingly, premium is placed on security and justice sector reform, constitutional reviews, transitional justice, public service reform, conduct of free and credible elections, and the establishment of oversight institutions, such as parliament and civil society.

But, contrary to the view that legal norms were being reinstituted for the first time, the rule of law has historically been, and continues to be, used to reconstruct modern African states since colonial times (McBride 2016). In fact, whereas these reconstruction efforts have done very little to improve the efficacy and legitimacy of many African states, the ruling class in many countries has managed to consolidate power in congruence with these reforms. Moreover, the contemporary discourse about political violence and postwar reconstruction tends to vindicate external actors by ignoring their role in creating the perceived state failure and chaos in Africa. Largely missing from this analysis of African crises are the destabilization of the continent during colonial rule and the numerous ways that international liberalization policies have contributed to weakening of the capacity of African states. The dominant narrative characterizes Africa as suffering a huge rule of law deficit when in fact the modern law is usually invoked to legitimate colonial and postcolonial despotism, capitalist exploitation of resources, and social control (Prempeh 2013). These silences not only recreate Africa as an object of intervention but also justify reforms that seek to bring post-conflict countries into conformity with international legal standards (Abrahamsen 2009).

The persistence of these conditions therefore requires deeper historical and empirical examination of the relationship between colonial rule, postcolonial authoritarianism, and post-conflict peacebuilding and statebuilding in Africa. Such analysis must focus not only on the underlying problems of state formation in Africa but also on the extent to which popular analytical concepts and legitimating discourses have become an obfuscation of the empirical realities that underpin multiple legitimacy crises in the continent and beyond. It must devote attention to local sources of legitimacy/ authority and the roles of informal political institutions to examine the relationship between entrenched historical legacies, present (re)construction efforts, and the socioeconomic and political realities of Africans. Rather than taking their social relevance and desirability for granted, we also need to ask whether the Westphalian state model, market economy, and liberal-democratic values are appropriate forms of social order in Africa today. In terms of the legitimating narratives, one must wonder why the governance crisis is persistently being framed as postcolonial when states in Africa, since their colonial founding, "have never approached a Weberian ideal, nor even resembled European approximations to that intellectual construct" (Tull 2003, 430).

PROBLEM-SOLVING PEACEBUILDING
AND THE RULE OF LAW

Although largely oriented toward a positivist problem-solving and rationalist epistemology, the conventional peacebuilding literature is beginning to move beyond questions about the (in)efficiency of liberal solutions to examining dilemmas and contradictions that result in adverse consequences in the context of post-conflict peacebuilding and statebuilding. One such internal contradiction is the fact that "building peace implies the strengthening or (re)construction of the state, yet the liberal economic/social policies that are promoted arguably undermine state capacity" (Newman 2009, 41). Another concern is about how to create incentives for political forces to process their interest within representative institutions while undertaking economic reforms that inevitably engender a deterioration of the material conditions of these groups (Mansfield and Snyder 2005; Newman et al. 2009). In response to these dilemmas, Paris (2004) posits an "institutionalization before liberalisation" framework that prioritizes the building of state institutions that in turn provide the parameters needed for peaceful political and economic competition. Likewise, others have argued that even though competitive markets are essential, the state and political institutions should be reorganized—not necessarily reduced—to mitigate the risk of social disintegration that accompanies market reforms (Mansfield and Snyder 2005).

It must be stressed that these scholars do acknowledge that the neoliberal order is in deep trouble and, in fact, the lofty exuberance that accompanied post–Cold War liberal internationalism and legal globalization seems to have been tempered down.[12] But even realists, who share a similar rationalist ontology, expect powerful states to appropriate the rhetoric of liberal values and human rights only if such an approach legitimizes their intervention into weaker states in pursuit of strategic security interests (Chandler 2007). Unlike their liberal counterpart, realists make no pretense in arguing that the construction of a neoliberal order both legitimizes intervention and requires "interventionary" practices to expand the international "zone of peace" (Chandler 2007). Prioritizing limited or victor's peace, they also disagree with liberals on whether a broader conception of peace aimed at addressing structural conditions of war is a feasible or a desirable objective. In terms of international law, realists see legal concepts and arguments as post hoc rationalization of decisions taken on other strategic grounds such as geopolitics or the global economy (Trubek and Esser 1989). They dismiss the autonomy of international criminal justice institutions as a dangerous precedent and maintain that states have prerogative over war and peace, an argument often used to explain the refusal of the United States to ratify the Rome Statute which established the International Criminal Court (ICC) and heightened hostility toward the Court (Kissinger 2005). Realist conceptualization of international law as ephemeral "had its basis in the failure of the dominant legalistic-moralistic approach to prevent the Second World War" (Chimni 2017, 64).

However, this book posits that the problem-solving scholarship, which takes the social world as given and is interested in policy solutions, continues to be underpinned by the following core assumptions. Firstly, and linked to the notion of a post–Cold War "new world order," legal globalization is still considered a contemporary phenomenon separable from a distinct colonial past, with an emphasis on new technocracy, professionalism, formalization, and standardization of rules. Distinguished from Euro-American imperialism and historical colonialism, this idea holds that contemporary rule of law promotion can be carried out as an ideologically neutral project outside the self-serving interest of dominant actors in the core and periphery. Secondly, and perhaps a corollary of the first, it is believed that all adverse effects of legal globalization are either unintended consequences or pathological distortions of an otherwise well-intentioned and benign project. According to this assumption, whereas the rule of law may fail to achieve emancipatory goals in recipient countries, those failures are attributable solely to its operationalization, the behavior of reformers, and attitude of recipients. Thirdly, it is assumed that postcolonial and war-torn societies have broken down because they lack rule of law institutions and consequently recommend restoration or *de novo* construction of functional legal and judicial systems as remedy (Marshall 2014).

The net effect of these untroubled assumptions is that international rule of law promotion continues to have intuitive appeal to many policymakers and practitioners as solutions to the world's troubles (Carothers 1998, 2010). Just as about half-century ago when E. P. Thompson described the rule of law as "a cultural achievement of universal significance," its promoters today consider its legal and normative framework as "an unqualified human good" desired by every society (1975, 265). Political and legal theorists like Krygier (2011) see rule of law principles as developed in advanced democracies as quintessential for (i) reduction in domination, (ii) reduction in fear, (iii) elimination of indignity, and (iv) eradication of confusion everywhere. To date, both elements of the rule of law as stipulated by the UN have traction within the policy world: (i) the procedural element that stresses publicity of law, equal application, and independent adjudication; and (ii) the substantive component that provides content to the formal requirements in accordance to international human rights norms and standards of fairness (Sriram et al. 2011). As Fukuyama (2010) stresses, Western liberals want to see that law acts as a check on arbitrary executive power and its content resembles their cultural values. In operationalizing the concept, however, most reformers have focused almost exclusively on its positivist and procedural dimensions, insisting that (i) law is publicly promulgated and widely accessible; (ii) law is enforced in a predictable and consistent way; (iii) law is not subject to frequent convulsive and sudden changes; and (iv) law is effectively enforced by government (Trebilock and Daniels 2008).

In the UN system, eighteen out of twenty-eight UN peacekeeping missions currently include an explicit mandate to support rule of law institutions and there have been thirteen resolutions by the Security Council and seventeen reports by the Secretary-General on (re)building the rule of law in war-to-peace transitions.[13] While I was conducting this research, the Rule of Law Coordination and Resource Group (ROLCRG), made up of nine UN entities and supervised by the Deputy Secretary-General, was being constituted as an attempt to coordinate efforts and mobilize resources within the UN.[14] The UN Peacebuilding Commission brings together relevant actors and marshals resources within and outside the UN system to rebuild the rule of law in war-torn societies. Whereas development organizations such as the United Nations Development Programme (UNDP), the World Bank, and the International Monetary Fund have always been interested in rule of law promotion, the OECD (Organisation for Economic Cooperation and Development) now articulates legal and judicial development as a central plank in humanitarian interventions.[15] For USAID, the rule of law is indispensable for validating and maintaining the social contract post-conflict as it (i) provides stable social order necessary for democracy, (ii) protects property rights adequately and consistently, and (iii) guarantees expression of basic human and civil rights (USAID 2008).

What neoliberal institutionalists and reformers are slow to realize though is that many countries in the Global South are prone to political violence and despotism because of the availability, rather than the paucity, of modern law and its rule of law institutions (Massoud 2014, 2015; McBride 2016). They consider failures as a pathological distortion of what rule of law reform is supposed to achieve when in fact those results are a realization of the underlying, even if often unstated, objectives for the top-down imposition of legal norms and institutions on people. Many do not realize that "it is [even] a mistake to hope that the proliferation of laws will save us from the tyranny of men" when such laws only "create more government agents with power over their fellows" to enforce law and order rather than justice (Constant 2003, 65). That legislations are stable, prospective, and publicly announced do not make them any less discriminatory or preclude them from becoming an effective tool of social domination. Similarly, rule of law promoters have devoted little attention to ruling class interest in unequal societies, which is often about using the authority of the state "to restrain, inspect, monitor, discipline, and punish" the behavior of subjects in "a domain brought under the purview of law" (Sharon 2016, 131). If the rule of law can be likened to the proverbial double-edged sword, the sharper edge is "for social control, maintaining authority, preserving social order, and punishing rebellious acts that threaten such order" rather than placing institutional limits on arbitrary exercise of power or defending human rights (Waller 2018, 2).

In addition to taking issue with the assumptions, this book departs from the neoliberal scholarship for its normative commitment to rehabilitating rule of law programs as part of the broader agenda to "save liberal peace" (Paris 2010). In terms of economic liberalization, what is at stake, for this traditional literature, concerns not whether the market and democracy deserve a legitimate place in post-conflict environments, but what constitutes an appropriate balance between state and market. Equally, Fukuyama (2010) recommends a sequencing rule of law approach that prioritizes incremental institution-building over the disruptive cultural content of law which would take time to be normatively grounded in societal values. Building procedural infrastructure (through formal codes, computerized dockets, bar associations, efficient courtrooms, etc.) may be less disruptive than transforming customary and religious cultures into modern liberal ones, he suggests.

Without questioning the normative premises of liberal frameworks, the objective of such problem-solving explanations is better integration of, and efficacy in, the constitutive components of liberal peacebuilding (Richmond and Franks 2009). Besides, this idea of sequencing and ordering the same liberal institutions in ways that will result in optimal outcomes often leaves that normative scaffolding upon which rule of law promotion is based unchallenged (Donias 2012). Sriram and others even warn that recalibrating liberal peacebuilding "may entail the same imposition of international preferences and is likely to favor official structures and elites over civil society" (Sriram et al. 2011, 2). Whether reformers prioritize statebuilding over liberalization or vice versa, post-conflict reconstruction remains largely under international tutelage just as the legal colonization project and if liberalization can undermine institutionalization of the state so too is statebuilding antithetical to the liberal objectives so desired.

Building on the work of Sriram and others, this book's overall rationale is to transcend neoliberal problem-solving analyses by calling into question the very justificatory foundations upon which rule of law promotion is based. It views rebuilding the rule of law and its adjacent concepts such as "failed state" as the contemporary version of the law and colonization project that legitimated imperial and colonial ventures from the partitioning of Africa, Euro-American imperialism, to neocolonial relations in the post–Cold War era. New narratives about failed states that justify the need for reconstruction under international legal tutelage are no different from the legitimating discourses about legal colonization if they bestow upon the same Euro-American powers, which established colonial states, an image of contemporary peacebuilders intervening to resolve problems perceived as entirely postcolonial. Similarly, it is continuation of legal colonization when architects of the global economy, who promoted macroeconomic policies that largely undermined postcolonial economies, are authorized to reconstruct the same neoliberal order that has historically troubled many African countries. Legal domination is reenacted when, in representing and legitimating these interventions, rule of law promotion stresses formal-technocratic principles that de-historicize and internalize political conflicts in ways that absolve Western powers of any responsibility for the structural conditions that (re)produce violence. As outlined briefly below, the perspective developed in this book is indebted to the critical peacebuilding literature but also draws from diverse critical legal studies to connect legal globalization and legal colonialism in the context of post-conflict peacebuilding and statebuilding.

CRITICAL PEACEBUILDING, COLONIALITY, AND LAW

Recently, the critical peacebuilding literature has turned to the local as an effort to both criticize dominant frameworks and acknowledge the agency, needs, and priorities of people in recipient countries. In particular, critical scholars have challenged the appropriateness and quality of liberal peacebuilding, arguing that its "assumed universality" is "the promotion of what are essentially Western values," with the "international community" serving to placate fears of Western hegemony (Stammes 2016, 229).[16] Duffield and Hewitt (2009) make this point by drawing stark parallels between current technologies of humanitarian interventions and the nineteenth-century techniques of colonial governmentality, arguing that both old *mission civilisatrice* and contemporary interventionism depend on a veneer of liberal justification to control others. Beyond the veneer of routine and neutral technocracy, Mac Ginty argues, the liberal framework has become "highly political in that it favors 'solutions' that originate from, and perpetuate, particular ideological stances" (2012, 288). Stammes affirms that "the construction of liberal democracies and stable states contributes to the smooth functioning of the current world order, thereby maintaining its particular distribution of power and wealth, ignoring those threatened by its very existence" (2016, 231).

Among the staunchest critics of the liberal peace project and its neoliberal statebuilding framework is Richmond, who categorically claims that such an intervention "fails to promote peace" because "it produces and normalizes political and social inequalities both in the international order of states and within society" (2015, 8). Focused on microlevel practices and everyday dynamics, some works have raised the fundamental question of why many progressive interventions that have been formulated precisely to emancipate vulnerable populations often end up producing an opposite outcome (Autesserre 2007, 2010, 2014). Irrespective of the ideological character of interventions,

Autesserre (2014) warns, there are adverse consequences of imposing foreign ways of doing and thinking at the expense of local knowledge, expertise, and methods of peacemaking. Others have examined the material pressures, mundane organizational rules, and rigid bureaucratic culture at the operational level as sources of pathology (Cooley and Ron 2002; Denney 2013, 2014; Massoud 2015). Apart from exposing the power asymmetry and status quo bias of liberal peacebuilding, the critical peacebuilding literature has also demonstrated how the diffusion of liberal-democratic norms is shaped by the action, challenges, and resistance posed by actors in recipient countries (Björkdahl and Gusic 2015; Mac Ginty 2011; Richmond 2012).

The few authors who concentrate on the nexus between law and liberal governance in war-torn societies have warned that "rule of law reformers must learn the lesson of colonialism, lest they perpetuate a new imperialism" (Pimentel 2010, 1), defined as "trampling on local customs" in favour of "higher standards of justice, human rights, or the rule of law" (4). For Hamoudi, the rule of law promotion project is "often a thinly disguised form of legal orientalism" that has not yet fully embraced the reality of legal pluralism (2014, 136), while Chalmers (2019) focuses on the "mythology of modern law" as central to rule of law promotion. Drawing from criticisms of the pre–Cold War law and development projects, Park (2008) argues that ethnocentrism, cultural reification, and legal centralism are among the most troubling aspects of international rule of law promotion today. Those writing about rebuilding the rule of law in the aftermath of foreign military intervention have argued that the imposition of legal norms and institutions on non-Western societies is nothing short of "new imperialism" (Stromseth et al. 2006). Expressing this concern, Brooks insists that war-torn societies "must put up with some of the worst aspects of imperialism (culturally insensitive occupying armies that drive up prices, distort local economies, and push through ham-handed 'reforms') with few of imperialism's benefits" (2003, 2283).

This book concurs with these critical views in terms of their ability to interrogate the deeper legitimacy crisis confronting contemporary peacebuilding and statebuilding to which the rule of law is central. But it further argues that, beyond the issues of bad interveners, bad recipients, and bad peacebuilding operations, the fundamental problem is that the legal norms and institutions transported into war-torn societies are themselves hegemonic instruments better suited to reproduce oppressive and hierarchical social orders than to dismantle them in postcolonial environments (Gathi 2019). As with law and colonialism, within the very promises of liberal governance lie the seeds of both domination and resistance, depending on who has the social standing to fill the content of transported rule of law institutions and instruments. This argument is consistent with Sabaratnam who argues that international "interventions fail—and keep failing—because they are constituted through structural relations of colonial difference which intimately shape their conception, operation, and effects" (2017, 4). Also, this is an interpretation of modern law that focuses on "identifying and scandalising forms of rule, influence, control, exploitation, exclusion, inequality, or violence which obscure colonial structures, all the while enabling their continuing propagation and consolidation" (Dann and Hanschamann 2012, 124). From this perspective, when the transplantation of law under international tutelage persistently fails to achieve purported emancipatory objectives, we ought to focus attention on other unstated objectives that may have been realized rather than concluding that a policy failure has occurred.

To formulate this postcolonial rule of law critique, the book draws from Marxist-inspired scholars who have been preoccupied with "efforts to theorize the role of law in the production and transformation of capitalist hegemony" (Trubek and Esser 1989, 26). According to this social critique, the law as a cultural and institutional artefact is "part of the economic superstructure adapting itself to the necessities of an infrastructure of productive forces and productive relations" (Thompson 1975, 259). Structuralists assume that law is no more than class relations translated into legal institutions and discourses to mask and mystify the reality of social inequality and hegemony (Mattei and Nader 2008; Thompson 1975). They also hold a deeper ideological theory of law that views legal doctrine as "simply an unqualified restatement of capitalist values and ideals, directly transmitted to all members of society, and operated mechanically to constitute all citizens as compliant subjects" (Hunt 1985, In Trubek and Esser 1989, 27). Based on this assumption, legal ideology has an unalterable logic of control that "becomes a powerful tool for exploring the relationship between 'the law,' legal subjects, and social relations" (Hunt 1985, 16). When associated to human subjectivity, legal discourses are not merely external mechanisms of regulation but constitutive of identities, social relations, and lived experiences, transforming human and social entities into bearers of rights and duties (Mattei and Nader 2008; Trubek and Esser 1989).

Nonetheless, while there are structural and ideological dimensions of international law, rule of law promotion in the Global South has a distinct racial history and politics that is not preordained simply by class struggle. Most countries in the Global South were subjected to colonialism and are currently entangled in complex neocolonial relations with former colonial powers and the global financial architecture that cannot be reducible to the universalism of scientific materialism theorized by Marxist-inspired scholars. Fixation on ahistorical structuralism as well as binary class categorization can only provide a partial portrait of the unequal relations between the Global North and South, ignoring particularly the complex reconfigurations that have emerged over time. But paying attention to the significance of historical colonialism in the evolution and development of law, a postcolonial perspective enables us to relax (not abandon) the dogmatism that is inherent in structural explanations (Chimni 2017). Also, whereas structural theory focuses on macro-level analysis to explain the relationship between legal ideology and capitalism, there is need to account for multiple and localized spaces of contestation, conflict, and compromises (Lu 2017).

Furthermore, the role of legal ideology and the nature of its relationship with economic and political interests—whether in reinforcing or challenging existing social relations—must be open to empirical examination rather than assumed (Trubek and Esser 1989). It is an agenda for empirical social science to "seek to describe the ideologies of law and legal reform prevalent in policy circles today and to explain their production, transmission, persistence, or effect by relating them to the underlying structure of institutional and social relations in which they are situated" (Trubek and Esser 1989, 28). Beneath the smooth surface of legal reasoning and judicial pronouncement, we need to empirically assess how law resonates with social, economic, and political struggles in historical and contemporary circumstances. In this regard, Hunt recommends that "the nature of the relationship between reality and its ideological representation should be 'the problem' or 'object of analysis' without prejudgment as to the way in which the relationship can be captured or portrayed" (1985, 21). His argument is born out of concern that "the materiality of law—that is to say, law's real impact on real people and real relations—tend to be ignored" by structuralists (1985, 26). Stressing that colonial structures may have transformed the very nature of modern and international law, legal anthropologist Merry also notes that

> Understanding the complicated role of law in colonialism—as a mode of coercion, a form of social transformation, and discourse of power developed by dominant groups but also open to seizure by subordinates—is helpful in making sense of the dynamics of globalisation and the expansion of the rule of law today. (Merry 2003, 578)

Therefore, this book advances a postcolonial theory of rule of law promotion that problematizes international law not only as an ideological project with material consequences but also as a material project itself (Eslava and Pahuja 2012). Its analysis of the relationship between historical colonialism and present-day neoliberalism systematically teases out patterns of ideological continuity and disjuncture (see chapter 2 for details) while paying close attention to the material practices that affect real social relations in the Global South. The book argues that whereas rule of law promotion has increasingly been professionalized and standardized, the underlying objectives to promote neoliberal economic growth, subordinate indigenous legal systems, and advancing ruling interests remain the enduring legacies of legal colonialism. This materialist conceptualization sees "international law as inseparable from the production, organization and re-organization of our material world as well as from our political, economic and social realities" (Eslava 2017, 80). Fleshed out in the history of legal development in Africa (chapter 3) as well as the empirical chapters on Sierra Leone and Liberia, the book is attentive to multiple conjunctural relations, that is, the intersection of spaces between the historical and contemporary, structural and agential, macro- and microlevel, and formal and informal dynamics of law.

Empirically, the book differentiates three spheres of legal internationalization, each focusing on a specific postcolonial context within which societies experience rule of law development as reinforcing dominant and unequal power relations. The first focuses on local economies to argue that promoting the rule of law opens pre-industrial societies to global capital, which profits the capitalist class at the expense of the majority population who depend on the informal economy for their livelihood. Specifically, rule of law internationalization facilitates "good business governance" in the formal economy while ignoring the corresponding dispute resolution needs of an informal sector reproduced by dominant neoliberal economic practices. The second examines the local politics of rule of law reforms to argue that governments have often appropriated legal and judicial instruments to consolidate power instead of placing limits on dominant rule. Whereas this politicization of the rule of law is not the same as the complicity of law in repressive regimes, it posits that legal institutions and tools transplanted from outside are still being used to consolidate state authority and delegitimize political opponents. The third deals with communal settings where indigenous and customary structures remain relevant to collective survival. The problem addressed here is that the rule of law (which is based on an adversarial English legal tradition) undermines local norms of justice that are focused more on bringing to bear noncoercive social pressures and incentives to induce conformity to communal rules and norms in line with customary laws of reconciliation and restoration of social order. In each setting, the English law not only reinforces structural, social, and cost-related inequities but also allows the global/local collaboration necessary for corporate capitalism, statebuilding projects, and hierarchical social orders to thrive.

As noted, the postcolonial critique developed in this book does not entirely preclude the use of law for counterhegemonic or emancipatory purposes, even by the weak. In fact, "if law is evidently partial and unjust, then it will mask nothing, legitimate nothing, and contribute nothing to any class's hegemony," which makes its consequences plainly counterproductive (Thompson 1975, 263). It is even expected that some rule of law promoters outside and within post-conflict societies might be genuinely committed to empowerment and emancipatory objectives on behalf of those marginalized by dominant state, market, and social structures. The main point remains that whatever goodness is associated with this dubious altruism, there is a corresponding harm, or it is purposefully allowed to legitimate an objectionable goal. In other words, allowing some semblance of goodness in (post)coloniality, while seemingly inconsistent with the book's overall proposition, is not contradictory if the ultimate goal or outcome remains to reinforce domination. In this duplicitous rule of law discourse and practice, the ruling class sometimes may even acquiesce to reforms that promise to emancipate the oppressed but, beneath this veneer of morality and change, transplanted legal instruments are the arena in which dominant actors validate unequal relations of power. Without structural transformation to dislodge rule of law's superimposition, Eurocentrism, and doctrinal legality, these intermittent counterhegemonic legal reforms do very little to alter the underlying logic of domination and even detract attention from the political project of structural change.

RESEARCHING HETEROGENOUS SETTINGS OF WEST AFRICA

From the lofty standpoint of international law and international relations (IR), one can find out very little about how legal globalization has reconstituted places, subjects, and modalities of governance in post-conflict countries. For Sierra Leone and Liberia, keeping such an imaginary distance between international law and the everyday realities at the local level is unhelpful for the following reasons. Initially, both countries exemplify Mamdani's concept of the "bifurcated state" as they have maintained dual legal regimes crucial to local governance of peripheral territories. While Sierra Leone inherited from indirect rule British common law alongside customary law, in Liberia a separate legal justice system based on the common law was meant to protect the privileges of minority settlers against the indigenous majority population (Lubkemann et al. 2011). Moreover, legal dichotomy has been perpetuated in both countries by successor regimes in order to discriminate the distribution of citizenship rights and funnel local resources into ethno-clientelist networks in exchange for loyalty. Here, national governments must demonstrate dual commitment to upholding international rule of law standards and at the same time protecting the interest of a ruling class whose survival often rests on close patrimonial connection with traditional authorities. Operating a donor-dependent economy constrains national governments to succumb to some demands for liberal reforms in the same way as enhancing internal revenue mobilization requires opening the domestic economy through market reforms. Yet national elites must balance commitment to institutionalize the rule of law and protection of their local ruling coalition whose support remains vital to their political survival and domestic power base.

Additionally, if international law is understood as material practice, then its real impact must be found on the bodies, livelihood, and everyday spaces of local communities away from national capitals. In fact, while international law is negotiated at the global center and ratified by states, the authors and entrepreneurs of global legal and normative frameworks routinely portray their efforts as on behalf of ordinary people (Eslava and Pahuja 2012). Although legal professionals and bureaucrats are increasingly incorporated in the dense lattice of horizontal and vertical networks described by Ann-Marie Slaughter (2004) as the new conduit for legal globalization, it is not uncommon in both countries for human rights activists to bypass state authorities and deal directly with civil society groups. From the structural adjustment programs of the 1980s to postwar efforts to encourage foreign direct investment, the social impacts of liberal macroeconomic policies promoted by the World Bank and the IMF are mostly visible on ordinary living conditions as demonstrated by the fact that almost all recent organized protests against the corporate world have taken place in rural communities that host agribusinesses and mining operations.

These everyday realities mean that international law in Sierra Leone and Liberia "cannot be conceptualized simply in terms of a restricted body of norms or situated only in bureaucratic and institutional environments beyond daily life" (Eslava and Pahuja 2012, 217). It requires a mixed methodology that allows us to move beyond the ideological project to capture the material life of international law as well as its encounters with people in unconventional and heterogenous spaces. This move enables us to "examine practices within and beyond international law's traditional historical confines, modes of self-representation, and sites of enactment and performance" (Eslava and Pahuja 2012, 217; Eslava 2017; Gathi 2019). In Sierra Leone and Liberia, these unconventional spaces of the international are located at the subnational level, where authority is linked to multiple, often overlapping, sources of legitimacy ranging from traditional, colonial, to postcolonial modern legal systems.

Moreover, many researchers have argued that building formal institutions and infrastructure in both countries remains a crucial challenge (Isser et al. 2009; Sriram 2011). State-constituted institutions are not robust enough to enable efficient delivery of public goods and services, to build civic trust, or to enhance accountability between state and citizens. Rather, informal institutions and practices rooted in relation-based networks and social forms of governance are prominent. For instance, one study notes that "most rural Sierra Leoneans, who live under social forms of governance embodied in customary law and chiefs," continue to "have few regular or substantive encounters with formal institutions and agents of the state" (Brown et al. 2005, 12). In both countries, the majority population live under customary law and resolve their disputes through traditional justice mechanisms (Alie 2012; Alterman et al. 2002; Fanthorpe and Sesay 2009; Lubkemann et al. 2011; PICOT 2014). Applying the concept of customary sociality in Sierra Leone, Fanthorpe contends that traditional customs, while deficient, "still serve as a defence against the putative realm of politics and sociality where loyalty and trust are at the disposal of the highest bidder" (2005, 45). As in Liberia, it is argued that the vast majority of Sierra Leoneans obtain primary rights of residence, land use, legal claims, and political representation as subjects of chiefdoms rather than as citizens of the state (Fanthorpe and Sesay 2009; Isser et al. 2009).

Such complexity makes both countries suitable for applying a subnational method for empirical data collection and analysis, which Snyder defines as "a regionally differentiated perspective that highlights variation across subnational units in a country" to construct controlled comparison and "explain the dynamic interconnections among the levels and regions of a political system" (Snyder 2001, 100). Sierra Leone and Liberia are also instrumental cases not because of their intrinsic value but because of their potential to provide insight into a general problem beyond a particular case narrative (Stake 1995). To collect data for an in-depth, contextualized, and fine-grained analysis of cases, I conducted six months of fieldwork that included participant observation of formal courts, local courts, and chief barrays (palaver huts) as well as in-depth interviews and archival research (Stakes 1995). Undertaken from February to August 2014, I observed the proceedings of two high courts, three magistrate courts, four local courts, and six local chief barrays, and conducted approximately two hundred in-depth interviews in four regional districts of Sierra Leone and two counties of Liberia. In addition to judicial officials and traditional authorities, approximately sixty ordinary residents who have used multiple forums to seek justice in these local chiefdoms and peri-urban Freetown were also interviewed, using a semi-structured questionnaire with open-ended questions.

These sites were selected as a representative sample of important ethnoregional divisions, disparity in economic development, local administrative structure, and concentration of state authority. The capital cities of Freetown and Monrovia (Montserrado County) represented the seat of central bureaucratic and judicial power. Originally settlements for freed slaves from North America (who became Krios in Freetown and Americo-Liberians in Monrovia), the majority population in these urban centers are now people of indigenous-rural origins who migrated as internally displaced persons or in search of better socioeconomic opportunities. Districts that have historically been neglected due to poor physical conditions and inequitable state policies included Bombali and Kono in northeastern Sierra Leone and Krahn homeland of Grand Geddeh County in Liberia. Such regions tend to be highly traditional with institutions of chieftaincy, secret societies, and spiritual authorities playing a crucial role in maintaining social order. Sierra Leone's southern district of Moyamba represented districts that are rural yet have been a provincial focal point for state and donor policies.

Although these locations were chosen based on the researcher's ability to purposefully and intentionally select sites for an in-depth exploration of the central phenomenon, they all display different dimensions of the phenomenon, a core purposive sampling requirement (Cresswell 2008; Patton 1990). In each district, representatives of each layer of traditional authority—from paramount chiefs, tribal heads, to village heads—were interviewed, totaling twenty-eight paramount chiefs, chiefdom speakers, and tribal heads; twenty-five section chiefs; ten town/village heads, and twelve women/youth leaders. As table 1.1 illustrates, the selection of respondents also reflected the dual nature of local administration in that parallel traditional authority structures (linked to precolonial rule) operate alongside the state system. To avoid a dominant local elite perspective, I also interviewed separately at least fifteen ordinary residents in each district considering their diverse socioeconomic status and the multiple forums through which they seek justice.

Table 1.1   Postcolonial Authority Structure

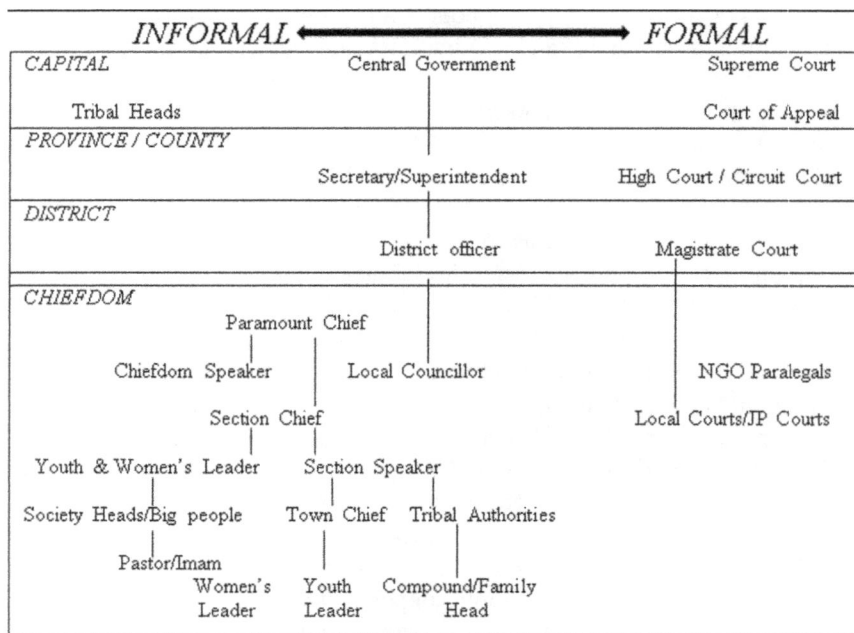

INFORMAL ◄────────────────────► *FORMAL*		
CAPITAL Central Government		Supreme Court
Tribal Heads		Court of Appeal
PROVINCE / COUNTY		
	Secretary/Superintendent	High Court / Circuit Court
DISTRICT		
	District officer	Magistrate Court
CHIEFDOM Paramount Chief		
Chiefdom Speaker Local Councillor		NGO Paralegals
Section Chief		Local Courts/JP Courts
Youth & Women's Leader Section Speaker		
Society Heads/Big people Town Chief Tribal Authorities		
Pastor/Imam		
Women's Youth Compound/Family Leader Leader Head		

Source: Adapted from R. E. Manning, World Bank (2009).

For information on formal implementation of justice reform and expert opinion on the justice landscape in Sierra Leone and Liberia, the following policymakers, legal professionals, and practitioners were also interviewed: lawyers, judges and magistrates, human rights activists, customary law officers, local government administrators, local court staff, and representatives of donor agencies. A key source of relevant information on primary justice systems were community-based paralegals of four local NGOs: Timap for Justice, Network Movement for Justice and Development, Center for Democracy and Human Rights, and Justice and Peace Commission. In most cases, respondents would be identified as someone in a formal or informal position of authority (judge, local chief, paralegal). Where participants were initially unknown, it was necessary to use a "snowball" technique whereby I asked a respondent to identify another source of importance to interview (e.g., a paramount chief suggested his speaker or section chief, who in turn recommended town/village heads).

Another primary source of data was national and provincial archives. The national record departments in Freetown and Monrovia house original source materials such as chronicles, memos, letters, newspapers, colonial ordinances, official government documents, and transcripts of speeches. For documents on postwar reform policies and legislations, government ministries in charge of local governance and the justice sector were useful. These documents include acts of parliament, position papers, reports of consultative processes, policy briefs, project reports, training manuals, internal memos, and so on. In some instances, these documents are available upon official request, but in most cases informal connections and good rapport with officeholders opened the door to access. Provincial archives were not easily accessible as some had been destroyed by war and others neglected for long. However, many traditional authorities have personal copies of important administrative documents and local historical records that were made available to the investigator. Another set of records accessible in rural areas were local court case catalogues, which, although not comprehensive for systematic analysis, gave an indication of the frequency and nature of disputes reported to the state-constituted court system.

As a Sierra Leonean, my knowledge of the sociocultural settings and ability to communicate in some local languages proved useful. For instance, while recruitment protocols and forms approved by my university's Research Ethics Board sufficed to access educated elites and urban residents, knowledge of customary protocols and symbols was crucial for interaction in rural communities. My affiliation with local NGOs that organized regular community dialogue meetings helped to build trust as I was sometimes perceived as working for these organizations or as an intern. In one such meetings held on May 14, 2014, I volunteered to take minutes of a small gathering to discuss issues related to access to justice in a local chiefdom. Being abroad for a while, there was the tendency to be regarded as a "JC" (just came) in the local setting, an African associated with Western civilization, wealth, and power. But I guarded against that impression by being in the company of paralegals (who carry with them similar research instruments). Using local dialects, hanging out in *attire bases* (coffee shops), and commuting via local transportation (e.g., *poda poda, okada*) also helped to make me "ordinary" in the field. The use of multi-methods provides opportunity to triangulate information from different sources, an important procedure to identify and rule out distorted information and biased interpretation.

STRUCTURE OF THE BOOK

To enable a systematic integration of historical and contemporary analyses of legal development in Africa, the remainder of this book is organized into two parts, comprising six chapters. Part I, which revisits the relationship between the rule of law and coloniality, has two chapters. The first, which is chapter 2, is a theoretical component with the sole objective of laying out a postcolonial rule of law critique. It stresses how historical superimposition, Eurocentrism, and doctrinal legalism favor social domination rather than emancipation. It also indicates the structural, social, and cost-related mechanisms that inextricably link rule of law promotion to modern statebuilding, neoliberal capitalism, and cultural imperialism in the context of post-conflict reconstruction. Chapter 3 presents a genealogy of legal development in Africa from colonial to postcolonial times, interrogating both the common law tradition introduced by British colonial indirect rule and its civil law counterpart used mainly by France under the policy of assimilation. While recognizing that contemporary international law and development are largely framed by British/American legal traditions, the chapter equally focuses on the Napoleonic codes and *état de droit* inherited by Francophone Africa to understand whether they have similar implications. In addition to laying the foundation for the selection of cases, the historical background points to the colonial legacies underpinning the legal reconfiguration of local economies, polities, and societies in Africa today.

Part II, which comprises three chapters, uses historical and empirical materials to explore the relationship between legal colonialism and legal globalization in the context of post-conflict reconstruction in Sierra Leone and Liberia, focusing on three specific contexts in which rule of law promotion is experienced as reinforcing domination: the economy, politics, and society. The first, chapter 4, devotes attention to the nexus between rule of law and political power to examine why legal and judicial development in undemocratic settings tends to reinforce hierarchical and unequal power relations. It illustrates that continuation of politics by legal means is largely a settler-colonial legacy in postcolonial and transitional societies, reinforced paradoxically by the idea that rule of law internationalization is ideologically neutral. This chapter argues that transitional governments usually welcome justice sector reform not because they want the sector to be independent but because they need it to "professionally" maintain regime security. While the chapter does not dispute the fact that rebuilding the rule of law is often intended to place institutional limits on power, it insists that the ruling class in postcolonial settings can carefully appropriate legal and judicial mechanisms, which have benefited from international reform efforts, as an instrument to consolidate power. In terms of efforts to restructure traditional authority structures, this chapter argues that while those efforts are consistent with global standards, the key to reform is the shifting local balance of power and control over local resources.

Chapter 5 draws from legal and judicial reform programs in post-conflict Sierra Leone and Liberia to examine why the rule of law tends to favor neoliberal market economics, who benefits from this formal-legalism, and its impact on the informal economy that accounts for the survival and livelihood of the majority population in sub-Saharan Africa. The chapter uses the current scramble for large-scale land acquisition in both countries to argue that macroeconomic policies which open local economies end up promoting multinational agribusinesses and mining at the expense of preexisting livelihood sources. It demonstrates, for instance, that small-scale farmers who lack a codified legal basis of their land claims usually lose titleship to rich and powerful elites using the rule of law to secure the displacement of people with customary land rights. Another argument in this chapter is that whereas economic integration brings local workers into the global value chain, they often lack the knowledge or resources to navigate sophisticated judicial systems to protect their rights. Making a connection between neoliberal economic growth and the informal sector, it argues that whereas informality is a product of Africa's growing formal economy (which relies on corporate outsourcing and subcontracting), (re)building the rule of law often criminalizes informal employment, making ordinary people vulnerable to the punitive arm of the state.

Chapter 6, on the relationship between the rule of law and social order, focuses on questions of cultural compatibility between global and local norms in both countries. But instead of reifying an essentialized notion of local values, the chapter asserts that introduction of state-centric international standards destabilizes dispute resolution norms that are vital for survival in local socioeconomic environments. The core argument is that the common law tradition (which stresses adversarial litigation processes, best handled by a trained lawyer) undermines local norms of reconciliatory dispute resolution that are crucial for preserving informal trust networks and group solidarity required for collective survival in poor socioeconomic conditions. In addition to the adversarial and punitive nature of litigation, the chapter analyzes social and cost-related barriers that militate against equal access to justice, including English language, formal rules of court, and court fees, all disproportionately affecting people of low socioeconomic status. In these settings, the chapter stresses that standardization, legalization, and formalization of the administration of justice have entrenched a state-based justice system that is ill-suited for providing affordable, timely, and socially relevant justice for the majority population.

Chapter 7, which is summary and conclusion, synthesizes insights garnered from the case studies of Sierra Leone and Liberia. In doing so, it reiterates not only a connection between colonial and contemporary rule of law promotion but also the adverse consequences of imposing dominant standards on postcolonial economies, politics, and societies. Then the chapter re-emphasizes that these consequences have been, and continue to be, produced because modern law remains embedded in legal superimposition, Eurocentrism, and doctrinal legality. Finally, the book concludes with some reflections on what the comparative analysis of Liberia and Sierra Leone means for decolonizing rule of law promotion, as both a normative principle and a practical intervention in the Global South.

NOTES

1. Among our first studies was a Mano River Security Perception Survey conducted in 2005 and funded by the Institute of African Studies, Hamburg, Germany. Then in 2007 we undertook perhaps one of the earliest nationwide studies on the impact of the truth commission in Sierra Leone. It was a year-long research project titled "The Impact of Sierra Leone's Truth and Reconciliation Commission on the Prevention of Torture and Organized Violence in Selected Communities in Sierra Leone," funded by the Rehabilitation and Research Center for Torture Victims (RCT), Denmark, 2007–2008. I was involved in facilitating six updates, seven roundtables, eight student debates, and five newsletters on peace, security, and development issues (CEDSA 2005–2009).

2. Author's interview, professional economist and political activist, Monrovia, July 26, 2014.

3. Author's interview, professional economist and political activist, Monrovia, July 26, 2014.

4. Author's interview, small-scale businesswoman, Eastern Province, Sierra Leone, May 31, 2014.

5. Author's interview, small-scale businesswoman, Eastern Province, Sierra Leone, May 31, 2014.

6. For this debate, see Barnhizer and Barnhizer (2009), Blair et al. (2019), Brooks (2003), Chandler (2004, 2006), Fukuyama (2010), Grenfell (2013), Haggard and Tiede (2014), Isser et al. (2009, 2011), Kristjansdotter et al. (2012), Mani (1998), Marshall (2014), Park (2008), Rajagopal (2008), Sesay (2019), Sriram (blessed memory) et al. (2011), Stromseth et al. (2006), Trebilock and Daniels (2008).

7. In this book, the terms "traditional" and "customary" are used interchangeably to mean a practice of considerable duration while "indigenous" refers to a locally-inspired practice. (Mac Ginty 2008).

8. In this book, the concept of settler-colonialism refers specifically to the settlement of a predominantly non-white population in Africa (blacks, mulattos, etc.) (Galli and Ronnback 2020).

9. The few exceptions include Wai (2012, 2014, 2015), Dyck (2013), Chalmers (2015, 2017, 2019).

10. I would like to acknowledge here that Chandra Sriram, who sadly passed away in 2019, was the external examiner of my dissertation from which this book is drawn.

11. CEDAW is the 1979 Convention on the Elimination of All Forms of Discrimination against Women. It is an apt example of the substantive human rights concerns customary justice systems are now expected to address.

12. Among the optimistic scholarship are Fukuyama (1992), Ikenberry (2011), Slaughter (1997, 2004).

13. Boutros Boutros-Ghali, "An Agenda for Peace: Preventive Diplomacy, Peacemaking and Peacekeeping," United Nations Report, 1992; Lakhdar Brahimi, "Comprehensive Review of the Whole Question of Peacekeeping Operations in all their Aspects," UN Report, August 2000; Thomas F. Keating and Andy W. Knight, *Building Sustainable Peace* (New York: UN University Press, 2004).

14. The UN agencies comprising ROLCRG are the UNDP, Department for Peacekeeping Operations, Department for Political Affairs, Office of the High Commissioner for Human Rights, Office of Legal Affairs, United Nations High Commission for Refugees, UNICEF, United Nations Office of Drugs and Crime, and UN Women.

15. Department for International Development, "Building the State and Securing the Peace," Policy Paper, DFID 2009, p. 15; OECD, "Building Peaceful States and Societies," Practice Paper, 2010; Organization of Economic Cooperation and Development, "Principles for Good International Engagement in Fragile States and Situations," *OECD Journal on Development*, 9, 3 (2009): 61–148; World Bank, *Conflict, Security, and Development* (World Development Report 2011); United Nations, "Transforming Our World: The 2030 Agenda for Sustainable Development," UN Sustainable Development Goals.

16. Scholars who have contributed to this critical perspective include Autesserre (2007, 2010, 2013, 2914), Björkdahl and Gusic (2015), Donias (2012), Chandler (2010), Chandler and Richmond (2015), Mac Ginty (2008, 2010, 2012), Mac Ginty and Richmond (2013), Richmond (2009, 2012), Stammes (2016), and Young (2016).

Part I

THE RULE OF LAW AND COLONIALITY REVISITED

Chapter 2

The Coloniality of the Rule of Law

Among other things I introduced in chapter 1 is the core argument of this book, that is, rule of law promotion as social domination. I also mentioned that my contention draws strongly from the critical scholarly tradition—particularly the postcolonial literature in IR—in contrast to the problem-solving analyses that characterize the liberal peacebuilding and international law scholarship. As indicated, the post/neocolonial critique presented in this book takes serious issue with the legal and normative frameworks themselves rather than their operationalization as the point of analytical departure to interpret why rule of law promotion in conflict-affected societies often fails. What the present chapter does is to construct and develop this critique, focusing on the mechanisms through which modern law serves as multiple forms of oppression and their reenactment through contemporary legal globalization. While the first section is grounded in the sociological and political history of international law, what follows situates legal colonization within the context of contemporary peacebuilding and statebuilding. This section theorizes the centrality of law to post-conflict reconstruction and international security but its primary purpose is to serve as an analytical interlocutor between legal colonization and legal globalization. The last section illustrates how the structural, social, and cost-related legacies of legal colonization continue to determine who benefits from modern law in the state system, neoliberal economy, and social order. In other words, the chapter uses a postcolonial perspective to establish the legal discourses and structures that "have outlived the formal end of colonial rule and continue to exert strong influence today in politics, economics, and culture" (Dann and Hanschmann 2012, 124).

INTERNATIONAL LAW, IMPERIALISM,
AND COLONIZATION

From the postcolonial IR scholarship, law and colonization studies, sociole-gal studies, to third world approaches to international law, three explanations account for the relationship between modern law and colonization. Firstly, this law is a superimposition in terms of its intellectual heritage, philo-sophical traditions, core concepts, and ordering techniques and principles.[1] Although often theorized by (neo)liberal institutionalists as the quintessential normative and institutional framework for promoting rationality, moder-nity, and progress, the modern law arose in large part from Euro-American imperialism, which resulted in the "spread and expansion of industrial and commercial capitalism," as well as in European colonialism, which led to the territorial annexation and occupation of the non-Western world (Gathi 2006, 1013). Imperialism introduced modern rules of property, torts, and contract prior to formal control of non-Western territories while colonialism transmit-ted rules of acquisition of territory, including statehood and sovereignty. In addition to enabling and facilitating the subjugation of non-Western nations, international law evolved essentially as an effort to absolve Euro-American powers of any liability and accountability for historical injustices related to imperial and colonial exploitation of non-Western peoples and resources (Anghie 2005; Grovogui 1996; Mattie and Nader 2017).

Emphasizing this inextricable nexus between international law and colo-nial international relations, Anghie argues that the concept of sovereignty represents an attempt "to create a legal system that could account for relations between the European and non-European worlds" as an encounter between unequal legally constituted subjects (Anghie 2005, 3). While European pow-ers presented themselves as sovereign states with control over a demarcated territory, political community, and functional government, the absence of sovereignty elsewhere according to the Westphalian standard became the basis for subjugating other nations to European rule (Anghie 2005). Known elsewhere as the *mission civilisatrice*, the idea was that the construction of international society necessitated the extension and universalization of a European concept into regions which the modern law declared *tera nul-lius* (unoccupied lands) and granted Europeans the rights of first possession (Benton 2001, 2002; Comaroff 2003; Graziadei 2019; Tomlins 2001). Then an individualistic property right concept, diametrically opposed to traditional and indigenous ownership, was universalized not only to render communal land tenure incompatible to "modernity" but also to allow white settlers to dispossess the indigenous population (Bennet 2019).

Additionally, law gave European states the rights to demand hospital-ity from, and engage in trade with, non-Western peoples as well as to use force to implement "treaties of friendship" and impose remedies whenever indigenous insubordination arose (Anghie 2005). Such commitment to an imperial conception of the international informed "the attendant law-making processes" in the post-World War II era that "authorised and perpetuated its Eurocentric foundation, frustrating the [equal] participation, and limiting the power of non-European states" (Otto 1996, 338). It is also "evident in statutes and judicial opinions that have sought to preserve by legal and economic means the privileges that the former colonial powers would have had to forfeit after genuine self-determination" (Grovogui 1996, 6).

At stake here is the inextricable link between international law and relations wherein the modern law serves to rationalize the military-industrial complex and the economic supremacy of specifically the Euro-American powers vis-à-vis the rest of the world (Hoffman 1977; Smith 2000). As Acharya and Buzan contend, the main ideas of these frameworks are "deeply rooted in the particularities and peculiarities of European history, the rise of the West to world power, and the imposition of its own political structure unto the rest of the world" (2007, 293). Apart from the fact that foundational international law and relations texts are rooted in Western classical traditions, the way the mainstream IR discourses emerged and became framed is reflective of values and interest central to the West (Shilliam 2011). For instance, obsession with the state as a central actor in the international arena stems from what Acharya and Buzan (2007) call the "Westphalian straightjacket," a reference to the 1648 treaty of Westphalia that culminated in the emergence of the modern nation-state system as primarily a European foreign policy issue. Furthermore, orthodox theories "speak [mostly] for the status-quo great powers and the maintenance of their dominant role in the international system/society" (Acharya and Buzan 2007, 290). Bandyopadhyaya (1982) similarly argues that visualizing foreign policy as the exercise of power in an essentially Hobbesian world justifies the use of power politics to achieve foreign policy objectives. Thus, these theories can assume the role of functional ideology, reinforcing the existing international order and the dominance of Western powers. Referring to concepts such as balance of power, hegemonic stability, or liberal-democratic peace, Acharya and Buzan (2007) contest that mainstream approaches construct the international system they purport to theorize.

This is an understanding of law and theory not as mere narrative accompaniment to colonial structures established by expansionist wars and cultural encounters but as an intellectual project deeply involved in "issues of the political economy of imperialism, the cultural practices of differentiation, the uses of violence, or excessive exploitation of natural resources that have accompanied the expansion of the international legal order" (Eslava and Pahuja 2012, 199; also Chanock 1985; Gathi 2006; McBride 2016; Merry 2003). In terms of enabling pacification and governmentality, the English law (i) appealed to particular legal sensibilities through which "empty territories" were mapped and transformed; (ii) provided the legal instruments for property rights, entitlements, labor relations, and contract entered into by Europeans; (iii) instituted colonial knowledge as a taken-for-granted gestalt for studying the social world; and (iv) defined the nature of colonial subjects as the racialized and tribalized other (Benton 2001; Comaroff 2001; Shamir and Hackers 2001; Tomlins 2001).

Meanwhile, the colonial justice system introduced "civilised judicial procedures" to deal with customary and indigenous laws, "forcibly incorporated indigenous dispute resolution into the colonial state at the lowest levels of its hierarchy of courts," and "statutorily criminalized cultural practices deemed primitive and dangerous" (Comaroff 2001, 306; Merry 2003; Benton 2002). As Acharya and Buzan assert, it is through imperial contacts that local traditions of thought in the developing world were overwhelmed and other people disrupted from their historical trajectory into the Western intellectual frame. For these scholars, this also partly explains why mainstream paradigms have been expanded and remained robust in the non-Western world even when they are now being contested in the West. The dominant discourses rode on the back of Western powers to "imprint on minds and practices of the non-Western world their own understanding of world politics" (Acharya and Buzan 2007, 294).

Secondly, the very identity of modern law, which requires differentiating universal legal cultures from their particularistic counterparts, is rooted in Eurocentrism. From this perspective, Eurocentrism is not just about the fact that foundational legal concepts and traditions are profoundly entrenched in the European (more generally, Western) intellectual movement. It is also about the disequilibrium that emerges "when the persistence of European attitudes gives rise to distortion in the comprehension of the non-European or prevents appreciation of the merits of non-European laws" on their own terms (Glenn 2019, 434). What Mamdani (1996) calls "history by analogy," the non-European is reduced to a residual category, lacking an independent conceptual existence and analytical content, which can be achieved only in relation to a superior category—the European. According to this dubious distinction, one set of experiences is considered universal and normal on its own terms, whereas another is regarded as residual or deviant, "not in terms of what it is but with reference to what it is not" (Mamdani 1996, 9).

Referring to the Eurocentrism of international law, some have argued that "its ethical tenets flow from a Judaeo-Christian tradition" (Kahn 1999, cited in Kelsall 2009, 9) while others focus on the fact that "its standards of evidence are rooted in a European scientific worldview and enlightenment philosophy" (Kelsell 2009, 9). Mohammed Bedjaoui, who was a former president of the International Court of Justice, notes that "classic international law consists of a set of rules with a geographical basis (European), a religious-ethical inspiration (Christian), an economic motivation (mercantilist), and political aim which is imperialist" (Bedjaoui 1985, cited in Kelsall 2009, 148). This is so because "the historically contingent process of European development" allowed the region to take the lead as the first civilization to experience codification, legal specialization, institutional autonomy, and a correspondence between law and social norms as Fukuyama (2010) claims. At the same time, the expansion and universalization of these cultural practices require a legitimating discourse that incorporates notions of civilizational hierarchy, natural evolution, and racialized progressivism (Merry 2003).

The literature on law and colonization notes that legal cultures "were simultaneously languages of practices, symbolic and ritual systems, abstract principles to produce social orders, citizenship and subjects, and immanent material realities" precisely because they constituted the entire colonial world (Comaroff 2001, 310). According to this argument, the "civilising mission" by imperial Europe was rationalized in the name of "humane and enlightened universalism" whereas colonization legally justified "itself by sustaining the premodernity of overseas subjects" whom it constantly "tribalised, ethnicized, and racialised" (Comaroff 2001, 307). This technique of binary construction echoes Benton who sees jurisdictional disputes "as a defining feature of the [colonial] legal order" as "they intersected clearly with, and helped to shape the developing discourse about cultural, ethnic, and racial differences in the Americas" (Benton 2001, 375). For Anghie (2005) there is a dynamic of cultural difference, a primordial dichotomy between the civilized and uncivilized which international lawyers must uphold, even while continually developing legal doctrines and techniques for overcoming it. Others assert that the "civilising process made headway by introducing routinised and bureaucratised forms of organising social life in a way that simultaneously worked to restructure native consciousness and to ensure an effective command and control colonial apparatus" (Shamir and Hacker 2001, 436).

This ethnocentrism of international law and relations has silenced other bodies of knowledge that may have been relevant to the development of both disciplines and accorded an epistemic advantage to Western scholarship. It also created from the outset a binary divide that privileges Western scholarship as scientific (credible) knowledge and the "other" as inferior or common sense (Fricker 2007). The former became the standard by which other forms of knowledge were to be measured before being accepted into the formal canons of both fields. According to Fricker (2007) this is a form of testimonial injustice and it creates a credibility deficit in which the [West] uses its epistemic position to deflate the credibility of other narratives. For Shilliam, the question of hegemony in IR relates centrally to the West being regarded as the universal standard of civilization—an assumption that "relegated all other peoples and cultures in the world to an object of enquiry rather than thinking subject of and on modernity" (2011, 3). The obsession with behavioralism and rational choice approaches especially has done little to correct this deficit; rather, it reinforces the epistemic privilege of Western academics as enunciators of knowledge.

In taxonomy of law or comparative legal history, which is an intellectual effort to group legal traditions and systems into families with comparable characteristics, this ethnocentric attitude toward the non-European is equally glaring.[2] For instance, most seminal works prioritize European civil, common, and socialist traditions as the main legal families, and then relegate all other laws of the world into a fourth category, often described as Other conceptions of social order (David 1950; Merryman and Perez-Perdomo 2019; Tetley 2000). In one study, the authors group Hindu, Muslim, Far East, Black Africa, and Malagasy Republic as "Other families" either because their law is framed differently from Western conception or because their social relations are governed by other extralegal means (David and Brierley 1968). In fact, the very concept of legal families or traditions has built-in biases that give a preferential treatment to Western concepts of law and legal systems. As Glenn observes, "Western legal traditions are the only ones of the world which have developed the concept of legal system as opposed to simply living according to law" and the project of national codification aligns only with the Westphalian conception of the nation-state (Glenn 2019, 435). Regardless, in Global South regions like Africa , "European laws—whether French, English, Portuguese, Belgian, or Roman-Dutch—have constituted the basic laws of the land," the ideal to which other laws are expected to conform or apply as a matter of deviance (Bennett 2019, 657).

The temporal and spatial distancing of the non-Western world, even though it is inextricably linked to the West, serves a social purpose. Spatially, when the domestic sphere of sameness is considered distinct and different from what lies beyond its boundaries of sovereignty, it leads to "deferral of genuine recognition, exploring and engagement of difference" (Blaney and Inayatullah 2004, 44). Temporality, which is demarcation of the evolution of history, justifies imposition of Western models of development and rationality over alternatives in other parts of the world as indicated by the current international political economy and wave of neoliberal doctrines (see below). Together, both techniques enable the use of ordering nomenclatures not only to shape and influence the identity of people but also to establish the non-Western World as an object of intervention. They legitimize interventions that seek to control, adapt, and reshape the structures, practices, and ways of life of non-Western people (Abrahamsen 2009, 116). Instead of recognizing the possibilities of an overlap of "self" and "other," boundaries are rigidly drawn, carefully policed, and mapped into difference between good and evil

(Abrahamsen 2009; Barkawi and Laffey 2006; Blaney and Inayatullah 2004; Dunn 2003). Thus, for Said (1978), the real power of the West resides not in its massive economic development and technical advances but rather in its power to define, represent, and theorize—the power of discourse. The West's claim to knowledge has enabled it to appropriate and control the past, present, and future of the non-West (Said 1978).

Thirdly, there is the notion of legal science, with its doctrine of "logical rationality," "system building," and "formal-legality" as well as abstract principles of "scientism, conceptualism, and purism" (Merryman and Perez-Perdomo 2019, 68; Meierhenrich 2000). This doctrine, which underpins the construction of dominant legal systems, has long rested on the "assumption that the materials of law (statutes, regulations, and customary rules) can be seen as naturally occurring phenomenon or data," and "legal scientists can discover inherent principles and relationships just as the physical scientist discovers natural laws" (Merryman and Perez-Perdomo 2019, 67). Embraced mostly by positivist Euro-American legal scholars and jurists, the assumption is premised on the following foundational claims: (i) law is a central framework for social organization, interaction, and governance; (ii) law is a neutral process, committed to rational optimization of collective action at reduced transactional cost; and (iii) legal scholarship is an authoritative voice that represents the neutrality and rationality of law (Trubek and Esser 1989). Together, these claims "purport to separate the legal from the political both in terms of institutionalisation and justification for decision-making" (Chanock 2001, 511). Legal decisions, according to this paradigm, are the dictate of legal rules and doctrines that determine rights and entitlement separately from substantive considerations, and to accomplish this, lawyers must operate "primarily with reference to the intellectual concerns raised in statutory documents, authoritative court decisions, and learned treaties" (Chanock 2001, 512).

At the heart of legal rationalism is Max Weber's analytical distinction between law's legality and legitimacy and his argument that the function of law centers around its legality that need not be legitimate. Weber posits that "norms and institutions are legal when they display functional competence based on reason," which is a requirement separate from the need to make law legitimate—a synthesis of morality and legality (cited in Meierhenrich 2000, 24). Akin to Weber's notion of logical rationalism is legal positivism, a philosophy of law that provided primary jurisprudential resources to jurists in the late eighteenth to early nineteenth centuries when the philosophy of natural law fell out of favor in international law. While natural law is premised on human reason, positivist law asserts that international law applies only to sovereign states, with the Western construction of that order considered the point of reference. Positivism led to the claim that inherently ethnocentric exercises, such as distinguishing between civilized and uncivilized nations, can be undertaken scientifically by "doctrines devised for the purpose of defining, identifying, and categorising the uncivilised" (Anghie 1999, 4). Another element of positivism is the assumption that the state has prerogative over all legal and regulatory institutions, meaning that "legal and non-legal norms must be clearly distinguished, and legal norms must have overriding authority" not only to administer law but also to reflect the state's sovereign will (Bennett 2019, 674; Anghie 1999).

However, legal professionals are "ideological captives of their eras" in that dominant values are "concealed behind a façade of ideological neutrality" (Merryman and Perez-Perdomo 2019, 67). In addition to "ignoring the constant play of class and interest behind law's neutral façade," defending scientific positivism for a discipline that is socially embedded in society "obscures the fragile foundations of legal scholarship itself" (Trubek and Esser 1989, 8). It is this way that "European jurisprudence embodies and perpetuates nineteenth century liberalism, locking in a selected set of assumptions and values and locking out all others" as uncivilized (Merryman and Perez-Perdomo 2019, 67). Thus, law became a "post hoc rationalisation of decisions taken on grounds other than those deployed on the surface of legal argument and influenced by forces other than those of law" (Trubek and Esser 1989, 9). In addition to institutional structures that regulate social interaction, any conception of law is constitutive of socially defined interest as well as its ideological and normative underpinnings (Mattei and Nader 2008; Meierhenrich 2000; Thompson 1975). Furthermore, legal formalism allows the ruling class to "emphasise compliance with the form of 'civilized' behaviour rather than the substance of social justice" and equality (Merry 2003, 571). This tenuous separation between law and politics is a strategy that protects the sanctity of law, even when produced within unjust structures and influenced by discourses of discrimination. As European powers attempted to establish authority without electoral consent, "legality became the preeminent signifier of state legitimacy and 'civilisation,' the term that united politics and morality" (Hussain 2003, 4).

There are intermediate positions within legal hierarchy, meaning that acquisition of the superior European legal standards draws an "uncivilized" closer to its superior counterparts, albeit this assimilation does not suggest attainment of civilizational symmetry. Also, counterhegemonic possibilities can arise from the most oppressive colonial legalities, providing an opportunity for subaltern people to mobilize legal instruments and cultures for their own course as legal anthropology and sociolegal studies have stressed (Comaroff 2001; Massoud 2013, 2014; Merry 2003). In fact, colonial administrations maintained or "reinvented" preexisting legal institutions to preserve social order whereas "conquered and colonised groups sought, in turn, to respond to the imposition of law in ways that included accommodation, advocacy, subtle delegitimisation, and outright rebellion" (Benton 2003, 3). In some regions, "the creation of law, like the 'invention of tradition' or construction of 'tribe,' was always a joint enterprise in which [local] agents played a leading and often determining role as interpreters of both law and language" (Waller 2018, 2). Arguing that law is not simply an instrument of class oppression, Thompson (1975) suggests that some degree of consent and legitimacy needs to be manufactured for it to become an effective means of control.

Nonetheless, law as a vehicle for colonial governmentality cannot be equated with law as a subversive anti-colonial tool. That the English law emerged fundamentally to provide a universal script for governance rather than human rights explains why the principles of constitutionalism and liberalism were consolidated in Europe at the very historic moment colonialism and imperialism flourished (Glenn 2019; Zolo 2007). Perhaps the greatest irony in liberal thought, whereas the rule of law was established to restrain the internal sovereignty of modern European nation-states, it left their external sovereignty intact and coexisted with colonial and imperialistic foreign policies designed to impose unrestrained power on other peoples (Zolo 2007). Conceptualizing this tension inherent to colonial rule of law, Hussain defines the construction of colonial lawful rule as a form of governmentality that "lays claim to legitimacy through law but is literally full of rules that hierarchicalise, bureaucratise, mediate, and channel power" (Hussain 2003, 32). Chalmers's "mythology of modern law" is an argument about how "the rule of law purports to act in the name of the world's people while denying their laws and how those laws rule" (Chalmers 2019, 980). This version of the rule of law, which came to be redefined as protection of the state rather than people, is "inextricably connected to inegalitarian global institutions and power dynamics" even if "offered as the corrective to these same dysfunctions" (McBride 2016, 4). As a "compulsory gospel which admits no dissent and no disobedience," it makes sense that colonial administrations believed that their law represented "the sum and substance" of what they have to teach their colonized subjects (Fitzjames Stephen 1875, cited in Hussain 2003, 4).

These explanations—superimposition, Eurocentrism, and doctrinal legality—indicate that international and modern law arose in large part to facilitate the acquisition of non-Western territories, to ensure that non-Western peoples conform to European cultural standards of morality, and to guarantee commerce and commercial activities that disproportionately benefit Euro-American markets. Moreover, this is an interpretation of the deep and critical place of coloniality in the genealogy of law, an exercise that denies the acoustic and artificial separation between the past and present to capture legal transmission, continuity, and ruptures across time and space. This analytical maneuver is premised on the assumption that "the past, far from being gone, is constantly being retrieved as a source or rationalisation of present

obligations" (Orford 2013, 175). It is a view of the history of legal development that does not conform to a linear progressive narrative in which order
overcomes chaos, liberalism trumps despotism, decolonization ends inequality, and colonized peoples eventually enjoy the rights of self-determination
as Langer's (1986) "Farewell to Empire" assumes. Rather, this view insists
that the so-called liberal progressivism carries within it an enduring legacy of
repression in the same way that the new world order "retains the subordinate
and dependent positions of Global South elites to their former colonial powers and to multilateral capital interests" (Gathi 2019, 25).

This emphasis on continuity amid disjuncture relates to Nobles's (1974)
analysis of the relationship between political and scientific colonialism, that
is, the parallels between the exploitation of social scientists and the political
and economic extraction by colonists. He argues that "to exploit data from
a country or community to one's own country or community for processing
into manufactured goods is no different than exporting raw materials and
wealth from a colony for the purpose of processing into manufactured goods"
(Nobles 1974, 15). According to him, the most powerful tool and single most
effective technique of the social scientist is "its conception and formulation as
the standard by which all peoples of the world are to be understood" (1974,
16). Although his analysis focuses on the psychological investigation of the
black man, his intelligence, and self-conception, Nobles's understanding
of scientific colonialism, which has continued long after the formal end of
political colonialism, applies to the power of the legal profession to reproduce unequal subjects of international law today. Just as the philosophical
thinking, guiding principles, and ethical assumptions continue to shape the
psychologist view of the non-European so too is the field of modern law still
inherently ethnocentric in its worldviews and traditions.

Lastly, this reconstruction of legal history is based on a conception of
historical context that is not frozen in time and geographical space. Here,
the larger context constitutes superimposition, Eurocentrism, and doctrinal
legality, which have outlived the formal end of historical colonialism and
continue to reproduce the knowledge/power relations needed to uphold
hierarchical social structures between and within nations. The focus is on
the systemic, structural, and discursive forces that continue to influence the
conception, meaning, and application of new legal regimes, thereby ensuring
the privileges and entitlements of those who have been historically favored
by colonial-era laws. But beyond structural understanding, this historical
reconstruction enables us to dispel the notion that non-Western peoples are
simply innocent victims of the dark side of international law to account for
the place and role of the local ruling class, including its connection to former
colonial powers and global capital. When contemporary rule of law promotion is framed as essential for statebuilding, economic liberalization, and

democratization (as illustrated below), the colonial history of legal development reminds us to look beyond the veneer of untroubled reformism for unstated, but no less, powerful drivers, including the ruling class and global capital. Knowing this history enables us to understand that the formal end of colonialism was mostly a transition to contemporary forms of structural domination in global affairs and among citizens with historically differential access to rights, freedom, and justice (Otto 1996).

RULE OF LAW, STATEBUILDING, PEACEBUILDING

Today, international efforts to restructure domestic jurisdictions focus mostly on conflict and post-conflict situations as well as the context of long-term development (Beaulac 2012). In war-torn societies, these efforts are further divided into two components: implementation of transitional justice (TJ) and strengthening national justice systems and institutions. The genealogy of TJ has often been linked to the two post–World War II International Military Tribunals established in Nuremburg and Tokyo by the Allied powers and then to the Third Wave democratization in Latin America and Eastern Europe following the disintegration of the Soviet Union. TJ has been a "field of activity and inquiry that focuses on how societies address legacies of past human rights abuses in an effort to combat impunity and advance reconciliation" (International Center for Transitional Justice 2006, 4). TJ activities are operationalized by a set of judicial and non-judicial mechanisms designed to redress the effects of atrocity crimes committed in civil wars or by repressive authoritarian regimes, and they include those aimed at retributive justice such as war crimes trials and lustration (Akhavan 2001; Ferencz 1998; Kritz 1996; Orentlicher 1991) as well as those intended to foster restorative justice, including truth commissions, reparations, memorials, and human rights institutions (Hayner 2007; Tietel 2000).

With globalization of communication, education, and socialization technologies, "the speed and intensity of the circulation of legal ideas and symbols have also increased exponentially since the early twentieth century" (Merry 2003, 589). Slaughter even anticipates "a disaggregated world order" in which "national government institutions, rather than unitary states or a supranational bureaucracy, are the primary norm-producing actors connected by an increasingly dense lattice of horizontal and vertical networks" (Slaughter 2004, 166). A parallel development is the growing number of norm entrepreneurs, from influential individuals to transnational human rights movements, which use advocacy and expert knowledge to embark on moral proselytism and pressure (Acharya 2004, 2009). By one count, the major international TJ advocacy organizations include Human Rights Watch (International Justice Program), Amnesty International (Campaign for International Justice),

International Center for Transitional Justice (ICTJ), Center for Justice and Accountability (CJA), Open Society Justice Initiative Institute, and Coalition for the International Criminal Court (Subotić 2012). With enough funding, professional staff, and international visibility, these non-state actors "can set the tone of the TJ debate and create and recreate TJ templates or a menu of TJ options from which states may choose" (Subotić 2012, 108).

Although TJ mechanisms are temporally demarcated and mandated, they are expected to promote a rule of law culture beyond their official mandates of holding human rights violators accountable, documenting such violations, and restoring the dignity of victims. As Mendez argues, "the pursuit of retrospective justice is deemed an urgent task in transitional societies as it highlights the fundamental character of the new order based on the rule of law" (Mendez 1997, 1). In fact, while attempts to confront past injustices remain crucially important, the attention of practitioners, including the UN, has now shifted to the legacy of TJ mechanisms. Focusing on hybrid tribunals, the UN High Commissioner for Human Rights (UNHCHR) defines this legacy as "the lasting impact on bolstering the rule of law in a particular society, by conducting effective trials to contribute to ending impunity while also strengthening domestic judicial capacity" (UNHCHR 2008, 4). Legacy is what war-crime tribunals can bequeath to post-conflict societies beyond just convictions, acquittals, and brick and mortar, according to O'Neill (2003). If the physical infrastructure left behind constitutes the hardware part of TJ legacies, the software relates to "policies and processes that help to ensure the domestic system operates more effectively and efficiently, consistent with its international human rights obligations" (UNHCR 2008, 2).

Beyond the transitional justice phase, activities to strengthen national justice focus on the justice sector, comprising two interrelated aspects as well: legal reform and justice sector development. Law reform in war-torn countries aims to bring their laws and legal institutions into compliance with rule of law principles and international human rights norms and standards.[3] "Where laws are outdated, reform efforts should ensure that existing laws are modernized, that obsolete or anomalous provisions are repealed, and that new laws meet changing social needs. Law reform efforts also aim to dispel legal chaos and to simplify the legal framework" (UNODC 2011, 61). Normally, the reform process begins with a review of applicable international and domestic laws to assess which violations of international human rights norms and criminal standards should be considered as well as whether the laws are laconic or ambiguous. In terms of good governance, the drafting of a new constitution is with the objective of reestablishing constitutionalism that connotes a government defined, regulated, and limited by law (Ndulo 2011). These processes are implemented because legal reformers believe that the preexisting legal framework may be the product of postcolonial authoritarian rule, layers of overlapping and conflicting laws, or war-time governance by rebel groups or military dictators (Ndulo 2011; UNODC 2011).

Efforts to restore and strengthen the justice sector often focus on the judiciary, police, prison services, and other law enforcement institutions of the post-conflict state.[4] Regaining public confidence in these institutions and the justice sector as a whole, for the UN and its related partners, requires a substantial and comprehensive institutional strengthening to include capacity-building, vetting, and formal oversight. In war-torn countries, capacity development means equipping institutions with the human and material resources necessary to perform their functions as well as the administrative and management capacity to deploy these resources effectively. Usually capacity-building begins with quick impact projects to support the rebuilding of court infrastructure and law enforcement facilities that have been destroyed by war or fallen into disrepair. Training assistance is intended to impart skills, knowledge, and tools so that local institutions can provide efficient and effective services that are responsive to the need of vulnerable populations in the post-conflict contexts.[5] To this end, the UN has developed a large supply of training manuals, courses and modules, guidance materials, and judicial doctrines to facilitate rule of law engagement in field missions.[6] Other capacity development initiatives include financial and technical support for judicial training programs to train law enforcement agencies on command responsibility, investigations, and accountability, and how to deal with gender-based violence and juvenile justice. Technical assistance in capacity-building consists of support to court case management, information technology systems, and operations to ensure efficient administration of justice.

Vetting, recruitment, and promotion are aspects of institutional strengthening in these countries aimed at gradually replacing personnel implicated in the outgoing regime and corruption with a new breed of local actors. "Vetting currently serving judicial officials to determine their suitability for continuing office is seen as a natural link between transitional justice and long-term institutional reform" (UNHCR 2008, 34). It is a process intended to ensure that those officials are held accountable for past actions and at the same time deny them an opportunity to repeat such misconduct. Often undertaken with the supervision of civilian peacekeepers, vetting procedures "scrutinize the qualification and past performances of judicial personnel to ensure they have the requisite professional integrity and have not been complicit in past human rights violations or crimes against humanity" (UNHCR 2008, 6). After or while vetting is being carried out, a widespread national recruitment drive is usually launched to bring in new professionals into the justice system. The new recruitment system is to introduce a "new ethos of service in which recruitment and promotion should be based on objective criteria not nepotism or political favoritism" (UNODC 2011, 79). New measures are intended not only to promote fair and transparent criteria but also to reflect ethnic, racial, and gender diversity.

For the judiciary, procedures for appointment and promotion are intended to achieve institutional and financial autonomy. Therefore, conditions of services are designed to promote "an appropriate appointment procedure, security of tenure, which the executive cannot adversely affect" (Ndulo 2011, 98). To avoid (or minimize) the temptation of dispensing justice to the highest bidder or most influential, judges are to be adequately remunerated—although the introduction of international remuneration standards by donor-supported projects often brings heavy burden on national governments to maintain such pay standards long-term. In the interest of ensuring socio-ethnic diversity, judicial appointments may be influenced by the need to be politically correct in post-conflict restructuring. Yet, it is crucial that candidates are competent persons with a track record of professional conduct and integrity germane for building public trust in the judiciary (UNODC 2011).

Oversight and discipline aim to ensure that justice sector institutions operate transparently with integrity and are held accountable to rules of standards of conduct (DPKO and OHCHR 2011). While capacity development may be geared toward effective performance, internal and external accountability mechanisms are necessary to ensure that enforcement agencies are disciplined and secure public trust. With regard to the police and correctional services, internal measures include the development of professional codes of ethics that specify what acceptable and unacceptable conduct is. Also put in place is an incentive system that rewards ethical behavior and punishes corruption and abusive practices. "Internal disciplinary mechanisms, if fair and objective," are expected "to encourage good behavior since they directly influence an officer's career" (UNHCR 2008, 33). Programmers anticipate that "performance assessment would go into personnel files which then affect promotions, transfers, raises, assignments, and opportunities for further training and skills enhancement" (UNODC 2011, 78). Such information also becomes useful for generating policy changes and recommendations as well as adaptation in training and incentive structure. A direct corollary to such an internal mechanism is that the public needs to know what the complaint procedures are and have confidence in them as transparent forum of redress (UNHCR 2008).

Equally, codes of judicial ethics are established to define the parameters of public expectations of judicial conduct. Codes of ethics set service standards for judicial personnel and may require them to disclose their assets as check against potential corruption. Strengthening independent oversight of the judiciary also means setting up formal accountability mechanisms such as judicial service commissions as well as judicial reviews and inspections through the courts (UNODC 2011, 78). Relevant independent bodies may include commissions of inquiry, human rights commissions, or ombudspersons who investigate complaints relating to the miscarriage of justice against members of the public. By assisting people to navigate the justice system, paralegal and human rights NGOs are seen as potential watchdogs to expose corrupt practices. With these oversight mechanisms operational, coupled with the enhanced institutional capacity of justice sector institutions, rule of law programming is anticipated to create the conducive environment for security, development, accountability, and, above all, increased access to justice in war-torn and developing countries.

For neoliberal institutionalist, rebuilding the rule of law is inextricably linked to the wholesale transfer of institutions for the promotion of democracy, market-based economy, and modern statebuilding in countries torn apart by political conflict (Richmond 2004, 2008; Newman 2009).

This pervasive faith in the emancipatory power of legal-rational institutions dates to the 1990s when *An Agenda for Peace* shifted from terminating armed conflict to a broader conception aimed at strengthening and solidifying peace in order to avoid a relapse into violent conflict (Boutros-Ghali 1992; Brahimi 2000). This broader use of the term also indicates that peacebuilding ought to address the underlying structural causes of conflict by embarking on institutional reforms crucial to the cultivation of a culture of accountability and good governance (Keating and Knight 2004). In a report on peacebuilding in the aftermath of conflict, the UN Secretary-General states that "advancing the extension of state authority and rebuilding state institutions is crucial to the sustainability of peace in two respects: (i) reducing incentive for violent conflict, and (ii) strengthening a state's resilience in the face of possible renewed violence" (UNSG 2014, 10). Renewed emphasis on statebuilding is also not unconnected from the post–Washington Consensus on states' role in development, growing attention to human security, and a post-9/11 concern about weak states becoming safe haven for global terrorism and other transnational organized crimes (OECD 2009).[7]

In the neoliberal institutionalist literature, reliance on statebuilding to consolidate peace and prevent a recurrence of violent conflict has been labeled "statebuilding as peacebuilding" and at the core of this approach is an attempt to re-establish the *social contract* in war-torn societies (Paris and Sisk 2009; Richmond and Franks 2009). According to Richmond (2011), the "liberal peace" is based on an expectation of a post-conflict social contract between citizens and their leaders within the framework of human rights and democratic norms. "The social contract entails a consensual relationship between state institutions, government, and its peoples, in which the latter defer some of their freedoms in return for resources and security provided by the state" (Richmond 2011, 44). "Where the state has the will and capacity to deliver its functions, meet public expectations and uphold its obligations to protect human rights, the population is more willing to pay taxes, accept the state's monopoly on the legitimate use of force and comply with rules and regulations" (DFID 2009, 15). In other words, the state is expected to demonstrate a minimum level of functionality and will to provide these basic functions, including safeguarding the human rights of their populations. In return, citizens have obligations to the state to pay taxes, accept the state's monopoly on coercive force, and other curtailments of their freedom (DFID 2010).

For neoliberal reformers, the contract is expected to establish rules of the game, "focusing particularly on issues such as defining the mutual rights and obligations of state and society, negotiation how public resources should be allocated, and establishing different modes of representation and accountability" (DFID 2009, 15)—and as such constitutes the fundamental source of state resilience (OECD 2009). This growing preeminence of institutions—rules of the game and the organizations that frame and enforce them—as a crucial element of peacebuilding is clearly reflected in the 2011 World Development Report on the theme of conflict, security, and development. This report attributes recurrence of violent conflict in the developing world to weak state capacity and paucity of legitimate institutions. Weak security and defense capacities undercut states' ability to mitigate stresses that may induce organized violence, including armed threats posed by rebel or organized criminal groups. A group contemplating the use of political or criminal violence, the report notes, is likely to find that option feasible knowing that the country's security forces have inadequate intelligence and coercive capacity to counteract such a move (also DFID 2010). The report thus concludes that countries with the weakest institutional legitimacy are the most prone to instability and the least able to respond to internal and external shocks. Similarly, while acknowledging that institutions alone cannot guarantee peace, Paris and Sisk (2009) argue that "without adequate attention to statebuilding, war-torn states would be less likely to escape the multiple and mutually reinforcing traps of violence and underdevelopment" (Paris and Sisk 2009, 3).

But as elaborated below, when viewed from the postcolonial perspective established above, this statebuilding as peacebuilding model is almost legal colonialism déjà vu under the guise of ideologically neutral legal reconstruction.

FROM LEGAL COLONIZATION TO
LEGAL GLOBALIZATION

Initially, the idea of state reconstruction was based on a specific set of legitimating narratives that historically and ideologically obscure the problems confronting conflict-affected countries through concepts such as "state collapse," "state failure," or "state disintegration." These concepts, the standard representation of political violence in the Global South today, "have often been used to obfuscate analysis of the failure of statebuilding as a post-imperial project while still reinforcing the widespread obsession that links institutional failure with underdeveloped societies" (Eslava and Pahuja 2012, 212). As a reenactment of coloniality in international law, the state failure narrative effectively dehistoricizes and internalizes interpretation of political violence as a postcolonial phenomenon that can be resolved by rebuilding the rule of law. It spatially and temporally separates "ungoverned spaces" from the West without exploring their creation as part of Euro-American domination in the past and present (Fair 1993). According to Abrahamsen (2009), orthodox IR understanding of North-South relations re-echoes colonial discourses when they depict non-Western states as failed or failing, descending helplessly and inevitably into anarchy and violence. This replay of colonial imagery establishes failed states as abnormal, deficient, and lacking and reinforces the image of the West as democratic, rational, and morally superior. Yet Dunn (2003) notes that an understanding of the current conflict in the Great Lakes region of Africa requires an appreciation of how Western discourses of a "barbaric" and "chaotic" Congo have shaped international response and policies in the region. For Inayatullah and Blaney (2004), it reinforces, rather than challenges, the interpretation of difference as a dangerous aberration from norms of stability, safety, and order.

Likewise, TJ is usually framed as a temporal framework focused on atrocity crimes committed by postcolonial authoritarian regimes and in civil wars, while long-term reform efforts are devoted toward restoration and strengthening of the state justice system. As a field of study and practice, the endgame of TJ is to a large extent restoration and legitimation of the post-conflict state, even if the political conflict in question is precisely about the illegitimacy of that state. Focused on the settler-colonies, Jung argues that Western governments' "attempt to use of TJ to draw a line through history and legitimate present policy" continues to deny indigenous communities their rights to self-determination and control over their homeland (Jung 2011, 218). For him, a TJ framework designed to reassert the sovereignty and legal authority of a settler government silences the competing claims to sovereignty and legal authority that define the identity and historical struggle of indigenous peoples (Jung 2011). This argument is affirmed by other critical TJ scholars like Maddison and Shephard who assert that "efforts to divorce the notion of transition from concerns with historical injustices" constitute ideological obfuscation intended to mask the structural inequalities inherent in present-day settler societies (Maddison and Shephard 2014, 254). Sitze argues that transitional justice mechanisms not only fail as miracle-making processes but often end up "reiterating the forms of colonial sovereignty and governmentality" (2013, 251).

Extensively discussed in the next chapter, restoration and strengthening of the national justice system in post-conflict societies is also a reenactment of the colonial imposition of the Westphalian state system on non-Western societies during the formative years of international law. "By enforcing nation-statehood upon diverse communities and multiple identities, international citizenship requires becoming civilised according to European standards which involves succumbing to modern techniques of governmentality" (Otto 1996, 342). But in addition to an ideological commitment to the modern state, Euro-American powers who support efforts to rebuild the rule of law may be motivated by the following strategic and political objectives. While they are in part responsible for the establishment of colonial states, the state collapse, transition, and restoration narratives provide these powers plausible legal deniability just as legal colonization did in the age of empire. As Wai cogently argues, the term "state failure" obscures understanding of statehood as an "unfinished political project" with questions about "citizenship and political membership" arising from the attempt of colonial masters to "hastily and arbitrarily force multiethnic societies into states that were intended to serve the interests of the colonial masters who created them" (Wai 2012, 34). Where international law authorizes foreign intervention and peacebuilding into war-torn societies, it transforms and represents Euro-American powers as models of liberal-democratic governance, even though these were the same powers at the forefront of imperial and colonial projects that led to colonial states and remain exponents of many illegal interventionist wars today.

Another strategic political objective, crystalized by the post-9/11 foreign policies of many Western states, is confinement of law and order problems within postcolonial states before they become transnational threats. This concern has been framed as the "security-development" nexus, an integrative framework that regards justice and security as essential prerequisites for development, operationally meshing together, via the rule of law, sectors that were traditionally seen as discrete spheres of external intervention (Hurwitz and Peake 2004; Porter et al. 2013). The security-development nexus focuses on the link between structural underdevelopment and the threat posed by state failure, intrastate conflict, and transnational organized crimes (Denney 2014; Duffield and Hewitt 2009; Keukeleire and Raube 2013). But again, attempts to domesticate these security challenges obfuscate the fact that colonial states lacked legitimacy and were externally imposed without substantive governance capacity (Jackson and Rosberg 1982). As in the colonial era, although the social contract is coerced and largely about state capacity, it suffices to contain political violence within domestic borders while the international system remains relatively stable.

Furthermore, this narrative is promoted while the rule of law has done very little to promote democratic, inclusive, and accountable governance in the international system—a system still largely run by realpolitik and shaped by the material capabilities of states (Lu 2017; Otto 1996). From international criminal justice to WTO dispute settlement rules, increasing legalization continues to have differential meaning and impact on member states. The issue is not the multiplication of legal rules and institutions in world politics; rather, it is the fact that they apply mainly with respect to the weak and well behaved instead of those whose power needs to be checked (Chimni 2006; Eslava and Pahuja 2012; Tamanaha 2004). It therefore makes strategic sense for global governance to focus on rebuilding the rule of law in domestic jurisdictions of the Global South, even if this means legal formalism without sustained commitment to ensure transparent and accountable governance. For Otto, this strategy, which "effectively circumvents questions of representation, participation, and legitimacy in the global polity," is a "successful management of a treacherous terrain to prevent democratic demands from spilling over into the international arena" (Otto 1996, 338).

This interpretation equally applies to the relationship between law and the global neoliberal economy, particularly in terms of "helping to legitimise and sustain unequal structures and processes that manifest themselves in the growing north/south divide" (Chimni 2006, 3). Perhaps the most significant aspect of global injustice—the decolonization of political power in the post–World War II era is hardly accompanied by economic independence to allow governments and peoples in the Global South to determine their development model and priorities outside foreign influence. Additionally, the restructuring of international trade and commerce provides greater space for the market to thrive in both the global economy and domestic jurisdiction at the expense of social welfare and redistributive policies that are needed to address postcolonial development challenges (Baxi 2012; Miller 2008). Implemented by international financial institutions such as the World Bank and the IMF, structural adjustment programs of the 1980s and the 1990s restructure local economies to reduce public spending, privatize state-owned industries, deregulate the market, and introduce other liberalization policies to induce private sector–led economic growth. As Hobden and Wyn Jones allege, these liberal policies benefit mostly the core because as the most "efficient producer, its goods will be cheaper anywhere in the world" (2001, 213).

It is also no secret that international financial institutions often prefer macroeconomic performance that is conducive for the private sector over social and welfare policies such as healthcare, education, food subsidy, and infrastructural development that increase public spending in developing countries (Collier et al. 2003; Hanlon 2005). As Donias notes, "the economic reform prescriptions for post-conflict states have remained embedded within the Washington consensus and broadly similar to those principles associated with structural adjustment programs in the Third World" (Donias 2011, 25).

The neoliberal economic agenda that stresses reduction in public expenditure, privatization, and fiscal constraints on fragile states have been considered unhelpful for building peace (Chua 2004; Newman 2009). Pugh argues that war results in the "collapse of market entitlements for large groups of people which makes it highly dangerous to rely exclusively on the market to allocate resources, set prices, and fix incomes" (Pugh 2005, 25). Others contend that economic liberalization, as an attempt to separate the sociopolitical sphere from the technical realm of economics, silences structural victimization that emanates from zones of conflict (Donias 2012; Richmond and Franks 2009). As Pugh notes, there are real adverse social consequences when:

> The liberal project ignores the socio-economic problems confronting war-torn societies, aggravates vulnerability to poverty and does little either to alleviate people's engagement in the shadow economies or give them a say in economic reconstruction. (2005, 25)

Additionally, "many of these rules are designed to promote corporate [interest] in efficient production abroad even as the Third World markets are being pried open for its benefit" (Chimni 2006, 10). A global financial architecture, underwritten by international law and the operations of international financial institutions, has emerged to suit the needs of transnational capital, including multinational companies, regimes of parastatals, business tycoons, and so on. Rooted in principles of liberal positivism and individualism, international law "ignores global imbalances of power, by claiming a position of neutrality and objectivity which, in reality, operate as a code for Euro-American privilege" (Otto 1996, 346). In creating these conditions for global capital to thrive, "there has emerged a transnational ruling elite with the ruling class of the Third World playing a junior role," mainly granting access to local resources and labor (Chimni 2006, 14). Within the context of state reconstruction, rebuilding the rule of law does not necessarily restore the same class of elites who succeeded colonial administrations. Reinstated rather is the formal state system as primary means of economic accumulation and power, capable of extracting local resources and labor as the economy becomes reconnected to global capital.

Focusing on TJ, Franzki and Olarte argue that "the field is value-bound not only in that it militates for (an idealised) liberal democracy, but also in that it contributes to the legitimation of the economic counterpart, i.e., market economies" (2014, 202; Miller 2008). The same can be said for international criminal justice regime that has developed laws and norms to hold individuals accountable for grave international crimes such as genocide, crimes against humanity, war crimes, and, most recently, crime of aggression, none of which is related to structural and distributive injustices in the global economy. This emphasis on violations of civil and political rights aligns with the state collapse and bad governance narrative that reduces injustices in the Global South to the inefficiency, incompetence, corruption, and moral decadence of domestic leaders. It is a narrative that absolves corporate actors, multilateral financial institutions, and the state system of any criminal responsibility for imposing neoliberal economic policies and practices that have undermined many postcolonial economies since the 1980s. Such liberal-democratic discourse is "influenced by hegemonic ways of thinking that imagine a fundamental distinction between economics and politics" (Etzioni and Mitchell 2007, 202) when in fact "economic decisions have been the source of at least as much, if not more, human sorrow and suffering as by political leaders" (201).

Regarding societal order, the superimposition, Eurocentric, and doctrinal nature of English law requires the promotion of certain legal cultures and practices in which the post-conflict state and economy can thrive. In fact, rebuilding the rule of law in war-torn societies presupposes "a set of normative commitment to the project of law itself, a commitment to the orderly and nonviolent resolution of dispute and willingness to be bound by an outcome of legal rules and processes" (Stromseth et al. 2006, 75). There is no nonsubstantive version of the rule of law because "the formalism of its central processes rests on a foundation of implicitly shared assumptions about the proper order and purpose of society" (Barnhizer and Barnhizer 2009, 34). In other words, the formal principles are themselves based on a particular set of normative beliefs of how society should be socially regulated and ordered. This explains why legal traditions in legally pluralistic societies are often hierarchically organized to subordinate customary and indigenous norms to the rule of state law (Grenfell 2013). For this reason, the international community recognizes customary and indigenous justice systems only when they operate in accordance with international rule of law and human rights standards (UN General Assembly 2012).

However, the practice of subjecting customary and indigenous systems to formal regulation and international law is indicative of a systemic problem because lawyers who engage these systems tend to have been educated exclusively in formal English law, which makes them ill-suited for this task. Apart from lacking the background and skills to grapple with contextual complexities of customary institutions, legal practitioners often use their legal training to portray non-state practices as inferior and backward. These practitioners tend to focus only on stereotypes and caricatures, including extortionist courts or inhumane practices such as witchcraft, female genital mutilation, and slavery. In fact, the widespread tendency is to misread culture, perceiving it as "the problem" and reifying a false dichotomy between culture and rights (Merry 1997). For Isser, "this built-in normative bias poses an obvious challenge facing customary systems that are not based on the international ideal rule of law premised on Western liberal democracy" (Isser 2011, 4).

Also problematic is that customary and indigenous justice institutions are subjected to the regulation of the state system, even though the formal judiciary remains comparatively far less functional and legitimate than the institutions it is meant to regulate. Where these customary and indigenous practices are considered as subject of reform, both scholars and practitioners tend to focus exclusively on how the modern state can compel them to conform to international standards (Isser 2011). The concern becomes one of commensurability, that is, accommodation of differences, which tolerates what is considered less threatening to the European conception of justice while relegating to "the world of superstition, randomness, and criminality" what "cannot be articulated on its own terms within the European frame" (Otto 1996, 338). It reduces the former colonized nations "to an evolutionary time scale that emphasises backwardness, savagery, and primitiveness," essentializing cultures that have never been homogenous or inert (Fair 1993, 12). As Hamoudi emphasizes, it takes "a mind colonised in the assumption of legal centralism" to presume that the only possible solution to abusive customary practices is to bring them under the control of state institutions that are equally abusive (2014, 143).

Furthermore, there is a built-in normative bias to exclude as unacceptable practices that do not conform to international human rights standards and norms. For Obarrio (2011), attempts to overhaul traditional institutions reflect a "tendency to view their justice mechanisms from the perspective of positivist norms associated with Western juridical concepts and [liberal] institutions" (Obarrio 2011, 24). He contends that in the broad judicial reforms implemented in Africa since the 1990s, the relationship between informal justice actors and public sector institutions has not been addressed in a manner that takes into account the central role of traditional justice mechanisms. Where efforts have been made to recognize traditional values, there has been "a clear contradictory tendency to idealize, mythologize, and generalize those values while at the same time attempting to bring in line with modern conceptions of human rights" (Obarrio 2011, 24). This means that "colonial domination was continuing, albeit in a different guise, not only by mandating the adoption of European laws and values but, also significantly, leaving global economic control with Western-dominated Bretton Woods system of financial institutions established in 1944" (Otto 1996, 343).

CONCLUSION: THE LOGIC OF DOMINATION

From Euro-American imperialism, colonialism, postcolonial structural adjustment programs to contemporary post-conflict peacebuilding and statebuilding, rule of law promotion has been a project that reinforces social domination. This outcome has prevailed across historical periods because the modern law known to the Global South is deeply colonial, demonstrated by its superimposition, Eurocentrism, and doctrinal legality. In the contemporary context of post-conflict reconstruction, this version of legal internationalization emphasizes restoration of the postcolonial state, the neoliberal economy, and a social order that enable connections between the ruling class and global capital. Analogous to the metaphorical double-edged sword, the rule of law in the context of colo-niality is inherently contradictory: alongside its sterile promises of liberalism are acute processes of domination and resistance. Here, the discourse about an egalitarian society and human rights is made possible by the same legal frame-work that prevents its substantive realization (Merry 2003).

This logic of domination, however, does not entirely preclude the use of law for counterhegemonic purposes. The point is that any "goodness" experi-enced in the context of coloniality must be largely attributed to a function of the system which allows certain changes that only end up recalibrating and legitimating the same system. As with the period of decolonization and post-conflict reconstruction, most of these seemingly emancipatory movements culminate into restoration and strengthening of the existing political struc-tures of domination because the extent of change permissible is conditioned by the prevailing legal system. As Dugard underscores, the legal order thus serves to both institutionalize social domination and obstruct radical social change by insisting that the prevailing social order can only be legitimately questioned in ways stipulated by the law (Dugard 1987). Rather than trans-formation, reform is the language of the existing system—allowing accom-modation of some changes but not as fundamental as to call the survival of the system itself into question. It is a process of self-upgrade that can produce some opportunities for the oppressed to advocate and mobilize their efforts, sometimes forcing the ruling class to acquiescence to certain demands. But overall, the state legal system legitimizes its status by simultaneously serving as the formal standards for recognizing alternative legal and normative frame-works and disciplining those considered incommensurate to its standards.

Another element of the logic of domination is a realignment of interests that complicates the simple Western/non-Western, global/local, traditional/modern, formal/informal dichotomies. Heralded by colonial rule, there is a reconfiguration of interests in preserving dominant legal traditions and systems that is about both hegemonic socialization and material accumula-tion. Beyond education and cultural assimilation of indigenous elites are interlocking material interests that globalize local needs and localize global capital. The survival of global and local ruling classes is mutually reinforcing, a relationship that re-emerged in the immediate aftermath of decolonization when the independent nation-state came to represent an educated indigenous elite closely allied to former colonial powers rather than the mass of indig-enous peoples (Otto 1996). Vested in protecting dominant legal traditions and cultures, those charged with the responsibility of interpreting and applying the law would be more devoted to defending the legal system, even if this means standing in the way of justice. As the next chapter on legal development in Africa reveals, this logic of domination explains why the majority population in Africa continues to experience rule of law reform as reinforcing social inequities long after the formal end of colonialism.

NOTES

1. While it is misleading to speak of colonial law as a homogenous law, I use this term in a singular sense to stress the core features that characterize law as an instrument of domination in the context of coloniality. While I do not dispute the fact that law can be used for counterhegemonic and anti-colonial purposes, I argue that such justice-oriented goals were peripheral to the legal colonization project. This argument is in agreement with John Comaroff who notes that acknowledgment of dissonance and tensions within the colonial legal order in no way makes imperialism any less exploitative or coercive (Comaroff 2001).

2. Although legal tradition and legal system are conceptually distinct, their relationship is crucial for understanding the history of legal development in colonial and post-colonial societies. The legal tradition brings the legal system into a cultural perspective that it partially expresses (Merryman and Perez-Perdomo 2019).

3. According to the United Nations Office on Drugs and Crime (UNODC), the following laws and regulations need to be ascertained when engaging in criminal justice reform: laws on courts and the selection, appointment, and removal of judges; laws on prosecutors and the selection, appointment, and removal of prosecutors; police laws; laws relating to legal practice in the country, including legal aid laws and laws on bar associations; relevant codes of ethics for judges, prosecutors, lawyers, and police; laws on any law reform agencies or bodies; laws on legal education; laws on non-state justice systems and the relationship between these systems and the formal State system; laws on private security providers; laws on immunities of state figures and public servants; laws on associations (including NGOs); and laws establishing special courts or transitional justice mechanisms (UNODC, *Criminal Justice Reform in Post-conflict States: A Guide for Practitioners*, developed jointly with the United States Institute of Peace, 2011).

4. While the UN's *Rule of law Tools for Post-conflict States* identifies forty-two justice sector institutions, other studies have categorized justice sector institutions and actors into (i) criminal justice delivery institutions including the police, courts, prosecution services, detention and prisons, criminal defense and lawyers; (ii) criminal justice management comprising the ministry of justice, ministry of the interior (also known as the ministry of home affairs); (iii) oversight bodies including executive, legislative, and civil society; (iv) lawmaking and law reform bodies such as law reform commissions and judicial reform commissions; (v) legal education, police, and corrections training institutions; (vi) customary and non-state justice systems; and (vii) private NGO and civil society organizations (see UNODC, *Criminal Justice*

Reform in Post-conflict States: A Guide for Practitioners, 2011; USAID *Guide to Rule of law Country Analysis: The Rule of Law Strategic Framework*, 2008).

5. Paying attention to the specific needs of vulnerable and marginalized groups means operating according to numerous international treaties and guidelines, including: the United Nations International Covenant on Civil and Political Rights and its two additional protocols; United Nations International Convention on the Elimination of All Forms of Racial Discrimination; United Nations Convention on the Elimination of All Forms of Discrimination against Women; United Nations Convention on the Rights of the Child; Optional Protocol to the Convention on the Rights of the Child on the Sale of Children, Child Prostitution and Child Pornography; United Nations Declaration of Basic Principles of Justice for Victims of Crime and Abuse of Power; United Nations Declaration on the Elimination of Violence against Women; United Nations Declaration of Human Rights of Individuals Who Are Not Nationals of the Country in Which They Live; and the United Nations Declaration on the Rights of the Child (UNODC 2011).

6. For example, see Guidance Note of the Secretary-General on UN Approach to Rule of Law Assistance, April 2008; Guidance Note of the Secretary-General on United Nations Assistance to Constitution-making Processes, June 2009; DPKO Policy Directive on Prison Support in UN Peacekeeping Operations, December 2005; DPKO Legal and Judicial Rule of Law Work in Multi-dimensional Peacekeeping Operations: Lessons Learned Study, March 2006; DPKO Primer for Justice Components in Multidimensional Peace Operations: Strengthening the Rule of Law, December 2006; DPKO Supporting National Prison Systems: Lessons Learned and Best Practices for Peacekeeping Operations, December 2005; and UNDP Global Program on Strengthening the Rule of Law in Conflict and Post-conflict Situations: Building Peace through Security and Justice, 2010.

7. According to the OECD, statebuilding must be a central objective of international assistance because "states are fragile when they lack political will or capacity to provide basic functions such as safeguarding the security and human rights of their populations" (Principle 3, OECD DAC's Ten Principles for Good International Engagement in Fragile States and Situations, 2007). Although peacebuilding and statebuilding are often viewed as coterminous, it is important to note that the two terms are not conceptually synonymous. Paris and Sisk (2009) consider statebuilding as a subcomponent of peacebuilding that calls for greater attention to strengthening governmental institutions.

Chapter 3

Legal Development in Africa

In the previous chapter I laid out the theoretical perspective and framework through which rebuilding the rule of law in war-torn societies—via transitional justice, law reform, and justice sector development—will be examined and evaluated in this book. I have conceptualized rule of law promotion in terms of both the mechanisms adopted and its centrality to domestic order and international security within the broader post-conflict peacebuilding and statebuilding agenda. Whereas the neoliberal institutionalist literature takes the desirability and objectives of legal reconstruction for granted, the post/ neocolonial critique advanced in the chapter calls into question this benign characterization, defining instead the coloniality of modern law to include its superimposition, Eurocentrism, and doctrinal legality. Stressing how these tenets have outlived the formal end of colonialism, I illustrated their continued influence on the structural, discursive, and social forces of legal globalization today, particularly in the context of post-conflict reconstruction under international legal tutelage. In addition to bringing out the underlying strategic, political, and ideological objectives of foreign intervention, the framework is useful for analyzing what reconstruction means for the local ruling class and their relationship with global capital. Another analytical utility of this post/neocolonial critique lies in its ability to transcend the veneer of liberal morality and narrow technocracy to excavate the often-unstated underlying drivers of reconstruction as they relate to the state system, neoliberal economy, and hierarchical social order.

While the critique has been constructed in abstraction, this chapter is designed to historically situate the theory within the context of legal development in Africa from nineteenth-century colonialism to the decolonization period. Considering that the trajectory of legal development may have been shaped by the continent's indigenous traditions, European colonialism, and postcolonial reconstruction, the chapter aims to integrate the critical theory with historical materials to pinpoint structural, social, and cost-related inequities specific to Africa. It focuses on both the continent's relations with European powers and the legal construction of domestic jurisdictions under the tutelage of those powers. The chapter begins with the external dimension of Africa's legal development, focusing particularly on the centrality of law in European scramble and partitioning of the continent and in delegitimizing the sovereignty of African nations. Then I present a comparative overview of the common law and civil law traditions to bring out their assumed substantive differences in ideology, procedural structures, legal and judicial cultures, and institutional practices as transplanted to Africa mainly by the British and French. What follows is a discussion of how the processes of colonial administration and law affected, and was affected by, the material realities of Africans in the economy and state-society relations. The conclusion raises some questions and issues that legal colonialism engendered and how the first generation of African leaders sought to frame and deal with them in the immediate aftermath of colonial rule.

INTERNATIONAL LAW AND THE COLONIZATION OF AFRICA

The subjugation of almost the entire African continent to European colonization was undertaken by a variety of means, ranging from diplomacy, warfare, commerce, and Christian missionary activities (Du Bois 1943).[1] However, in the process of establishing and consolidating European colonial rule over Africa, international law performed the following legitimating functions. Firstly, the European scramble and partitioning of Africa was situated within a legal discourse that considered the deprivation or nonrecognition of the sovereignty of African peoples as consistent with positivist international law that was in fact interpreted and developed to serve as colonial justification (Umozurike 1971). Among the common legal techniques adopted by European powers were flag planting, treaty-making, and European conventions that legitimized the suzerain authority of colonial administrations over African state and stateless societies (Herbst 2000). Since a treaty agreement is between entities with international personality, the Europeans at first recognized African sovereigns and then proceeded to obtain their cooperation using force, threat of force, deceit, or arrogance (Umozurike 1971). During the five years preceding the Berlin Treaty of 1884/85 on the division of Africa, the continent "witnessed an unprecedented number of such treaties euphemistically called treaties of protection" or friendship treaties (Umozurike 1971, 96).[2]

Instead of protecting African peoples, the treaties of protection were standard means to lay suzerain claims over African territories and to ward off competitive adventures from fellow colonialists. Protectorate treaties had "a certain amount of security against hostile neighbours for the colonialist would always crack down on those whose activities he disapproved but this was just a fringe benefit when compared to the loss of sovereignty" (Umozurike 1971, 100). Similarly, King Kaiser I and Chancellor Otto Von Bismarck convened the Berlin Conference of 1884/85 primarily to develop a legal framework for avoiding the risk of war as Europeans scrambled for African territories following a military encounter between French and British troops in West Africa, the sudden French invasion of Algeria, the British takeover of the Suez Canal, King Leopold's seizure of most of Central Africa, and Germany's ambition to acquire colonies of its own (Mutua 1995). Signed on February 26, 1885, Chapter 5 of the Berlin General Act required any power in possession of territories in Africa to maintain sufficient authority to administer and defend them. The so-called principle of "effective occupation" was to compel all claimants of territories in Africa to establish effective control over them, in line with the prevailing Machiavellian view of sovereignty at the time which emphasized force as the basis of all law. Other European international treaties, designed to prioritize the peace among colonialists at the expense of Africans, include the Act of Brussels of 1890, Convention De Saint-Germain-En-Laye of 1919, Treaty of Versailles of 1919, and the League of Nations Covenant of 1919. With these treaties on their side, colonialists regarded any African rebellion as a subversive act that must be put down by overwhelming brutal force as the Maji Maji wars in Tanganyika and the German–Herero war in Southwest Africa illustrate.

Secondly, as international law developed in tandem with the establishment and consolidation of colonialism in Africa, it was effectively used to strip away the legal personality of Africa, thereby reducing it to an object instead of subject of modern law. The entire continent was terra nullius, opened to the possession of European powers, and Africans lacked any subjective personality to demand redress within the international system, according to international law. Colonialism was legally defined as an exercise of effective European authority to arbitrarily redraw and impose state boundaries in Africa based solely on the short-term strategic and economic interests of imperial powers rather than those of the Africans they housed. As the law that governed relations between sovereign Christian states of Europe could not be extended to Africa, colonial decisions to cut off preexisting structures and resources like a market, streams, mountains, rivers, wells, or grazing grounds from some of the traditional users could only be considered as the necessary consequences of legal development on the continent (Mutua 1995; Umozurike 1971).

Consider, for example, that it was an exercise of legal authority when the Somali people were divided up among Ethiopia, Somalia, and Kenya; the Masai between Kenya and Tanzania; the Yurobas between Nigeria and Dahomey; the Fangs between King Leopold's Congo and French Congo; the Hausas between Nigeria and Niger; the Luos among Uganda, Kenya, and Anglo-Egyptian Sudan; to name a few (Umozurike 1971). This dehumanization and denial of subjective legal standing before international law was vivid in African interpretation of the Berlin General Act as reflected in this Lagos Observer statement at the time: "the world has, perhaps, never witnessed a robbery on so large a scale . . . Africa is helpless to prevent it" (Lagos Observer, 19 February 1885). While colonialism was massive plunder and robbery in the subjective African mind, international law denied the actualization of that subjectivity because Africa at the time was not considered as a bearer of bona fide sovereignty that must be free from external usurpation.

The denial of an African sovereign personality was also evident in the languages used in nineteenth- and early twentieth-century international law. For instance, the Europeans framed and justified most of the international treaty conventions held during this time as necessary to resolve "the African problem" or to look after the welfare of Africans in the strenuous world of international relations. The Berlin and Brussels Acts "pledged in the name of Almighty God to protect effectively the aboriginal populations of Africa and to ensure to that vast continent the benefits of peace and civilisation" (Lugard 1930, 65). Similarly, the Treaty of Versailles and Covenant of the League of Nations, which established an international trusteeship and mandate system as well as the Slavery and Forced Labour Conventions of 1926, were all paternalistically considered as an assistance from "the more advanced nations towards those not yet able to stand alone in the strenuous conditions of the modern world," conditions created by the very powers (Lugard 1930, 65). A mandate was in fact acknowledged under international law as "a territory for the performance of disinterested service for the benefit of the people themselves who were regarded as wards of civilisation" and its rationale "was that those people who were weak to stand by themselves would be tutored by more advanced nations who were best-placed to do so" (Umozurike 1971, 102).

Using Africa as a proxy arena to continue European violence by legal means and victor's justice was evident when all territories were withdrawn from Germany after its defeat in World War I: Southwest Africa became a C-mandate while Tanganyika, Ruanda-Urundi, Togo, and the Cameroons became B-mandate (only Turkish territories in the Middle East were declared A-mandate). In addition to the subordination of African societies to European paternalism, the Mandate Commission did very little to prevent colonial exploitation, apart from delegitimizing the colonial possession of a World

War I vanquished power. In fact, mandate powers not only failed to respect humane conditions stipulated by the Commission but also insisted that international law did not apply to colonial territories outside the mandate system. For example, when Southwest Africans (Namibians, brought under South Africa as mandate-C) protested excessive taxation, discriminatory laws, and infringement of land rights by the apartheid regime, they were savagely suppressed in the name of preserving the mandate system (Umozurike 1971). Such denial of African subjectivity was also evident in the writings of Western philosophers, philanthropists, humanists, theologians, anthropologists, and other social scientists who served as agents to (re)invent an image of Africa as an undifferentiated "other," a dark continent in need of European legal guidance and direction (Grovogui 1996; Mudimbe 1998; Mutua 1995; Wai 2012).

Another way that colonizers represented Africans as objects of law was to write colonial treaties in highly legalistic and technical European languages not only to obfuscate the underlying motives of such agreements but to also include clauses and loopholes that would absolve European powers of any criminal liability related to the colonial project. One aspect of this legal technology was to emphasize the superiority of written evidence over oral ones particularly when establishing colonial sovereignty over territories where communal land tenure prevailed. Mostly in settler colonies and plantation economies (discussed below), the inability of Africans to produce written documentation as evidence of land ownership was used by colonial administrations to exercise the right of alienation, that is, expropriating of land from customary landowners for public use or private development. "While it is a maxim of international law that a succeeding government should respect private property in establishing control over [people], the colonial powers found that, except in few circumstances, property was communally held and many of them assumed that such rights were too primitive to respect" (Buell 1927, 26). It was also common for treaties to make a distinction between conquest and occupation to affirm that "Africa's land surfaces and underground wealth were unknown and unexploited" before being occupied when in fact those territories fell under customary property laws. Even where the customary property rights of Africans were recognized, those rights often gave way to the colonial state which became the institutionalized representation and expression of the interests of settlers, Christian missionaries, privileged indigenous groups, and industrial capital that in turn reinforced the colonial project.

Although the languages of Europeans and Africans were mutually unintelligible, the treaties between them were usually written in European languages to conceal their legal implications from Africans. Based on the mastery of European languages, the treaties were carefully worded to give Europeans "a free hand in enforcing, altering, and discarding" them if they became an inconvenient or if colonialists wanted "to impose more onerous burdens on Africans" (Umozurike 1971, 100). For example, when a prominent Ibo ruler in Nigeria, King Jaja of Opobo, asked for the definition of the term "protection" in a treaty he was to sign, the reply from Consul Hewett of the Niger Coast Protectorate stated that:

> I write as you request with reference to the word "protection" as used in the proposed treaty that the Queen (of England) does not want to take your country or your market, but at the same time is anxious that no other nations should take them. She undertakes to extend her gracious favour and protection which will leave your country (Opoboland) still under your government. (cited in Umozurike 1971, 100)

King Jaja is described as a friend of the British who fought on their side in the Ashanti War of 1875–1876 but nonetheless critical of British firms and dishonest European brokers who abused contracts to exploit business transactions with his people. When the king pressed the issue about his trading rights under the treaty being violated, the British colonial office redefined the meaning of "protection" in a more technical language as such:

> The promotion of the welfare of natives of all these territories taken as whole by ensuring the peaceful development of trade and facilitating their intercourse with Europeans (superseded any contrary obligation). It is not to be permitted that any chief, who may happen to occupy a territory on the coast should obstruct this policy in order to benefit himself. (cited in Umozurike 1971, 100)

Thirdly, it must be stressed that in addition to extending the European state system and civilization, legal colonization in Africa was fundamentally geared toward the integration of local economies into the global capitalist order, primarily for the benefit of the colonial metropole. This centrality of capital was captured by Du Bois who argues that "the political domination which insured monopoly of raw materials to the various contending empires was predicated on the exploitation of African labour inside the continent" (Du Bois 1943, 721). As discussed, legal concepts such as alienation, freehold, and individual property rights were introduced primarily to make land accessible to settlers and businessmen who could not gain access through African communal land tenure systems. Where it was impossible to transform communal to freehold tenure, the concept of leasehold, which allowed corporate use of land for an inordinate length of time (almost amounting to permanent possession), was introduced first in Belgium Congo and then across the entire continent (Huxley 1949). Also, the prioritization of corporate interest was demonstrated even before the establishment of colonies when the governance of European possessions was entrusted in private chartered companies such as the Royal Niger Company, British East African Company, British South African Company, the German East African Company, and the Sierra Leone Company. The British East India Company, which was established in 1608, extended its jurisdiction to East African countries such as Kenya, Uganda, and Zanzibar that were yet to become fully administered British colonies (Joireman 2006).

As commercial and contractual laws were purposefully designed to serve the European industrial class, the terms of agreements were always tilted in favor of corporate actors who needed to use law to invent modern property rights in communal settings. "Treaties of commerce were concluded with African kings for valuable raw materials like rubber, palm oil, palm kernel, timber, and elephant tusks in exchange for cheap manufactured goods from European traders" (Umozurike 1971, 96). Recounting the treaty-making process with African chiefs, Lord Lugard, who is credited for establishing indirect rule, even cavalierly noted that "I have known a valuable concession purchased by the present of an old pair of boots" (cited in Umozurike 1971, 100). The close alliance between the colonial state, commerce, and Christianity was essentially about employing legal instruments to dispossess communal property owners and legitimize new claimants based on the Weberian protestant ethic. For example, this explains why the indigenes of South Africa who formed 80 percent of the population came to possess only 8 percent of the land and why the most productive land in Kenya and Rhodesia was disproportionately owned by white settlers who constituted the minority (Du Bois 1943, 723). Alluding to this alliance, Du Bois insisted that the "moral force represented" by philanthropy and Christian civilisation "would have met with greater resistance had it not been working along lines favorable to English investment and colonial profit" (Du Bios 1943, 722). Law became the common ground between English philanthropy and English imperialism because it ensured the establishment of authoritative political control that European citizens needed to generate the profits required to fund home governments and self. When calculated in taxes and revenues collected by mother country as well as the profit made by private industries, the return on governmental investment and political control was enormous (Du Bois 1943).

To be sure, the development of international law did not entirely preclude human rights issues affecting Africans during this period. One human right issue that was repeatedly highlighted by Euro-American leaders, philanthropists, humanitarian organizations, and missionary groups was the eradication of slavery and other forms of forced labor within the continent. Both the 1885 Act of Berlin and 1890 Act of Brussels were framed as an international solution to the African problem and provided "some measures to combat the Arab slave trade in East Africa and for restrictions of the arms and liquor traffic to Africa" (Buell 1927, 24). The Slavery Convention and the Forced Labor Conference were based on the report of a Slavery Committee established by the League of Nations in July 1924. The mandate system required European powers to (i) proscribe all forms of forced labor outside public works and without adequate compensation, (ii) protect natives from violation and fraud through supervision of labor recruitment and contracts, and (iii) consider native laws and customs when regulating property rights (Buell 1927). Yet, beneath the veneer of morality, the same law was used to prioritize European access to African labor and land as part of the colonial statebuilding project. Buell has argued that neither the Berlin Act nor the revised Brussels version "attacked the fundamental problems created by the entrance into the African continent of European industrialism" (Buell 1927, 24). As discussed below, "the definition of slavery limits the term to the rights of ownership in the person of the slave" to the exclusion of other conditions analogous to slavery that facilitated access to resources and labor (Lugard 1930, 66).

That the foundational legal frameworks through which Africa was integrated into the international state system remain contested and questionable does not mean that those frameworks were without effects. From the onset of the colonial statebuilding project, African states became inherently de jure constructions because "they exist by fiat of the international community, which recognizes them as sovereign whether or not they have governments capable of effectively controlling and administering" their allocated territories (Jackson 1993, cited in Ottaway 2002, 1003). Juridical, as opposed to empirical, statehood imposed on the continent was to serve as "post-imperial ordering devices" for multilateral institutions interested in freezing African states in their inherited colonial jurisdictions and blocking any post-independent movements toward self-determination (Jackson and Rosberg 1982). In terms of internal order, the incongruence between juridical authority monopolized by the state and substantive capacity to govern resulted in parallel structures that, even though lacking official legality, perform socially relevant public functions.

African international law was also to be fundamentally based on respect for the inviolability of colonially demarcated borders as enshrined in the Charter of the first continental treaty body, the Organisation of African Unity (OAU) established in 1963. Article III of the OAU Charter affirmed the sovereign equality of all member states, non-interference in domestic affairs, respect for sovereignty, peaceful settlement of disputes, and the illegitimacy of subversion, all legally prohibiting any action to undo jurisdictions inherited from colonial predecessors. In a 1964 conference, the OAU solemnly reaffirmed the organization's strict respect for the principles laid down in Article III and all member states pledged themselves to respect borders demarcated by colonial powers.

In fact, it could be argued that colonial statebuilding in Africa, contrary to the European Westphalian project, resulted in a relatively successful international accord and civility alongside internal discord and violence. Governance among African states and their relations with the international state system would become far more institutionalized than internal governance among a variety of groups that were forced to coexist because of arbitrary imperial desires rather than a political process of nation-state formation. Instead of succeeding the resolution of the native question (Mamdani 1996), the African state system raised that very question by creating a legitimacy crisis in the form of an incongruent state-society relationship with far-reaching implications affecting national citizenship, identity, and representation. As Mutua aptly argues, "the contrived and artificial citizenry of African states is at the center of this legitimacy crisis," only to be exacerbated by an unresolved, if not unresolvable, tension between nation-building and sub-national loyalty to pre-colonial ethno-political structures, as discussed below (Mutua 1995, 1144). While legal development reflected the interest and privileges of settlers—both whites and blacks—there would be no correspondence between European legal traditions and the existing social norms of indigenous Africans.[3] As Englebert affirms, this incongruence would ultimately raise the question of how to make "formal institutions endogenous to their own societies and... historically embedded [in prior] domestic social relations," a challenge that both the transplanted European civil law and common law traditions would ultimately confront (2000, 11).

EUROPEAN LEGAL TRADITIONS AND THE "NATIVE QUESTION"

In responding to the "native question" of how a foreign minority could rule over an indigenous majority (Mamdani 1996), the legal and administrative models of colonial governance converged depending on each European power's (i) conception of colonized people and (ii) vision of the colonial project (Crowther 1964). The British generally saw colonized Africans and their cultures as too different to be governed directly by European institutions and personnel and wanted to reduce the administrative cost of running colonies as much as possible. They also envisioned the colonial project as a specific mission to civilize Africans and then depart once the ability to undertake legal-rational governance had been established, especially in non-settler colonies. Operationalizing British conception of Africa and colonialism led to the establishment of an indirect system of rule or decentralized despotism, which co-opted some African traditional authority structures and practices into the British imperial project (Crowther 1964; Mamdani 1996; Young 1994). According to this administrative technique, "Great Britain generally adopted the plan of governing Africans whenever possible through their native rulers," often "accomplished by setting up a hierarchy of European officials alongside the native administration" (Whittlesey 1937, 363).

Like the British, the French and other continental European powers assumed that African cultures were uncivilized but also regarded Africans as people who wanted to be like Europeans if they were given the opportunity (Lapie 1944). Ostensibly based on the ideals of the French Revolution—liberté, égalite, and fraternité—the French colonial mission, for example, was to make Frenchmen out of Africans. In administrative terms, the French colonial project translated into a policy of assimilation that allowed "Frenchmen to occupy all the important positions, though properly trained Africans can fill subordinate posts, and in special circumstances even to become French citizens" (Whittlesey 1937, 363).

Both British indirect rule and French policy of assimilation required an operating set of legal institutions, procedures, processes, and rules to underpin administration of the colonial state, that is, a legal system. Each legal system was drawn from a legal tradition, "a set of deeply rooted, historically conditioned attitudes about the nature of law, about the role of law in society and the polity, about proper organisation and operation of a legal system, and about how or the way law is or should be made, applied, studied, perfected, and taught" (Merryman and Perez-Perdomo 2019, 2). Colonial administrations instituted legal systems which had "a vocabulary used to express concepts, rules arranged into categories, techniques for expressing rules and interpreting them" (Tetley 2000, 682). British indirect colonial rule largely aligned with the English common law tradition that stresses judicial precedent, while the French policy of assimilation became associated with the civil law tradition that was basically the Napoleonic code subdivided into five standard codes (civil, commercial, civil procedure, criminal procedure, and penal) (Merryman and Perez-Perdomo 2019).[4] Both powers also introduced statutory law, found in legislation other than civil codes, to complement the Napoleonic codes in civil law and precedents in common law jurisdictions (Tetley 2000).

In terms of originating conceptions and philosophical principles, the common law system "developed with the idea of the protection of individual rights from the state as a primary goal" to be "achieved through a particular process of investigation and decision-making" instead of the application of abstract codes (Joireman 2001, 6). This conception of common law is linked to the rule of law, a concept derived particularly from the works of A. V. Dicey (1815), an English political thinker who formulated a tripartite understanding of the concept to include supremacy of regular law, equality before such law, and constitutional protection of fundamental civil liberties.[5] Dicey used this formulation to contrast a political system governed by the rule of law with those based on the exercise of personal, arbitrary, and discretionary powers. Where rule of law prevails, "no one suffers punishment for any conduct not forbidden by law, everyman's legal rights and liabilities are determined by the ordinary courts of the realm, and individual rights become the basis on which a constitution is founded," he argued (Dicey 1815, xxxxii). Admitting that the rule of law contained in his treatise was a distinctive characteristic of the English constitution, Dicey was wary that the use of extrajudicial means to settle disputes in England was beginning to resemble the *droit administratif* of France in the seventeenth and eighteenth centuries. In agreement with other English thinkers like John Locke, Dicey was referring to an English constitutional structure that emerged from conflict between parliament and the crown, one in which the common law "became strongly associated with the idea of economic freedom and the subject's liberty from arbitrary action of the crown" (Mahoney 2001, 508). Although the origin of this tradition goes back to 1066 when Normandy conquered England, its liberal ideological foundations were mostly laid in Magna Carta of 1215 and then in the seventeenth century when judges aligned themselves with parliament and landowners to oppose the feudal prerogatives of the Stuart dynasty.

Whereas the common law arose to protect individual property rights and limit state power, the civil law tradition emerged from "the idea of the state as supreme and the role of the individual in obedience to it" (Joireman 2004, 318). Rooted in Montesquieu's separation of power theory, "one of the basic characteristics of the civil law is that the courts' main task is to apply and interpret the law contained in a code or statute to case facts" (Pejovic 2001, 9). "While security of economic rights was the motivating force in the development of the English common law, security of executive power from judicial interference was the motivating force in the post-revolution legal development that culminated in the code Napoleon" (Mahoney 2001, 509).[6] Throughout the course of European history, which was initially dominated by the Romano-Germanic power, the civil law tradition emerged as a composite of several sub-traditions with distinct origins and development, including the Romano-Germanic civil law, cannon law, commercial law, and the revolution. From the Justinian corpus of *Juris Civilis*, the Roman Catholic doctrine, and Gratian's Decretum arose the idea of codification of family law, private law, succession, criminal law, and law of procedure. Building on this notion was the Enlightenment, "a social and intellectual revolution" that became "the main source of public law in the civil law tradition" (Merryman and Perez-Perdomo 2019, 15).

Moreover, the Bourbon monarchy of eighteenth-century France, like the Stuarts of seventeenth-century England, was dealing with a social crisis that threatened the survival of the ruling establishment but which was directed at the collusion between the assembly and judiciary instead of executive power as in England (Mahoney 2001). With resentment against the power and corruption of the judiciary as part of the French Revolution, the central goal of post-revolutionary legal reform was intensification of codification to sacrifice all rights to the political ends of the state and prevent the return of government by judges (Mahoney 2001; Pejovic 2001). The assertion of the Machiavellian primacy of politics over judicial authority later translated into Napoleon's ambition to centralize power in the executive and subsequent colonial foreign policy to use law to expand and administer the empire.

With regard to institutional structures, the common and civil law traditions draw from their intellectual heritage and ideological origins to produce divergent frameworks for organizing government. In common law, judge-made precedent is core to legal development, with emphasis placed on objective procedures and processes as the source of justice in dispute resolution (Joireman 2001, 2004; Tetley 2000). Judicial independence is considered essential both to state accountability and to protection of liberty to the extent that judges have the authority to review executive action and statutory law (Joireman 2001; Mahoney 2001; Pejovic 2001). Under the common law, very little distinction is made between private and public law, the same principles of law apply to the protection of private and public property, and judges who review administrative action can enforce private rights (Mahoney 2001). This is contrary to the civil law tradition, which "assumes a larger role for the state, defers to bureaucratic decisions, and elevate collective [meaning, state's rights] over individual rights" (Mahoney 2001, 511).

Another central feature of the civil tradition is a sharp distinction between "private law (the law that governs relations between citizens) and public law (the law that governs relations between the citizens and state)" (Mahoney 2001, 512). The implication of this distinction is that public law in the civil system tends to place a lighter restraint on public officials and the civil law courts lack authority to review government action. In the absence of judicial review or judges' ability to interfere with the operation of administration, the civil law tradition has an administrative justice system authorized to review administrative decisions outside the judicial system. Insisting that courts refrain from intrusion into the pursuit of public interest, even "the strong emphasis on property and contact that characterises private law gives way to concerns for preserving the government's freedom to pursue collective ends" in the civil law system (Mahoney 2001, 512).

As to processes and procedures, the common law tradition differs from its civil law counterpart in the following respects. The common law is an "adversarial system... in which the parties to a dispute are pitted against one another in a relatively brief oral contest with the expectation that competition between the two sides will reveal the truth" (Joireman 2001, 574). In this system, lawyers and attorneys have traditionally been very active and influential in the adjudication process and, in the course of performing their defense and prosecutorial roles, an oppositional relationship between lawyers for the plaintiff and defendant is inevitable. Normally, "the plaintiff, defendant, and lawyers representing them are gathered together to present their case before a jury and judge who is expected to be an impartial arbiter of justice" (Joireman 2004, 318). At the end of the proceedings, the judge who is rather passive in the process, "decides the case according to the more convincing of competing presentations" (Pejovic 2001, 21). Alternatively, the civil law is characterized by an inquisitorial system of adjudication that relies heavily on judges to find the truth by conducting their own investigation, evidence gathering, and examination of witnesses (Joireman 2001).[7] Lawyers are rarely active in inquisitorial trials because their role is usually reduced to providing advice to their clients or the courts when called upon to do so in writing. Here, "the role of the judge is not merely to decide the case according to the stronger of competing presentations but to ascertain the definite truth and then make a just decision" based on the principle of *jura novit curia* (meaning, the court is supposed to know the law) (Pejovic 2001, 21). Where common law lawyers are guided by process and precedent, their civil law counterparts operate on the mantra of *da mihi factum, dabo tibi jus* (give me the fact, I shall give you the law).

Judicial processes and techniques also relate to the determination of fact, that is, evidence gathering and discovery methods, service of documents, their admissibility in court, and the technical processes of adjudicating them. In common law jurisdictions, there is a pre-trial search for evidence dominated by prosecutorial and defense counsels who are required to produce admissible facts and information, whether in favor of their client or to challenge the adverse party (Pejovic 2001). Often with very little intervention by the court, this process of investigation and presentation of evidence is "a private matter performed by a lawyer in accordance with prescribed procedures," regardless of whether the matter involves civil or criminal law (Pejovic 2001, 23). With regard to rules of admission, weight of evidence, and rules of court, the common law system stipulates many rules that restrict what is considered admissible in a court of law, including the requirements of authenticity, hearsay rule, and the best evidence rule (Pejovic 2001). "Matters relating to the administration of justice, procedures, evidence, and execution of judgment have, for common law lawyers, an importance equal or even superior, to substantive questions and legal rules" (Daniel and Brierley 1968, 2).

Another basic principle of common law is the examination and cross-examination of witnesses in the presence of a judge and jury, with oral testimony considered weightier than written evidence. As the cross-examination is largely a technical exercise to expose weak evidence and fallacies in your opponent's case, the counsels can prepare their clients for the hearing to avoid statements that may serve as evidence against them. They can also call in expert witnesses, appointed and paid by their client to support one side of the case and take the witness stand to be cross-examined by the opposing side. The civil law system equally places premium on evidence and admissibility but with the judge playing an active public role in collecting the required documents and information without a pre-trial discovery (Joireman 2004; Pejovic 2001). Although the system operates on rules of evidence "which determine what may be introduced as evidence and sets conditions of admissibility and weight of evidence" (Pejovic 2001, 24), these rules are relatively more flexible compared to common law. In the civil law system, written evidence supported by documentation prevails over oral testimony, preparation of witnesses by counsel is strictly forbidden, and court experts are invited only by the judge to provide highly technical knowledge and facts rather than to serve as partial witnesses as in the common law system (Fordham 2006; Pejovic 2001).

As the common and civil law traditions differ on the need to distinguish between public and private law, they diverge on whether a criminal judgment must have effect on subsequent civil proceedings when one wrongful act has both civil and criminal liabilities. The common law forbids adjudication of civil action facts by reference to a previous criminal trial because civil and criminal matters are separated and there is a difference of standard of proof for each matter (Pejovic 2001). Even if the facts of the case are identical, criminal judgments are not binding on civil courts as they are free to produce an outcome that is different from the decision of a criminal court. The plaintiff in civil cases is required to prove "a balance of probability or preponderance of evidence," while the standard of evidence in criminal cases is a much stricter "beyond a reasonable doubt" threshold (Pejovic 2001, 26). On the contrary, with few exceptions such as the rule of strict liability, criminal jurisdiction in the civil law tradition takes precedence over the civil jurisdiction (*le criminal tient le civil en l'état*) when both are dealing with the same case. According to the civil law system, it is not only that "a criminal judgement has the force of a conclusive evidence to bind the whole world" but the relationship between criminal and civil tort liabilities is such that a criminal conviction can become the basis for awarding damages in a civil tort matter (Pejovic 2001, 26). Additionally, there is no distinction in the standards of proof when adjudicating criminal and civil cases, allowing for close collaboration between civil and criminal courts in the civil law tradition.

With respect to approaches to the legal process, the main principles and rules in the civil system are usually stipulated in codes and statutes that the courts are only required to apply, meaning that the written law prevails over case law and other bodies of law (Pejovic 2001). Perhaps the continued influence of Montesquieu's separation of power theory, this approach also mean that the legislator's role is to legislate while the function of the court is mainly to apply the law (Tetley). In this system, "jurisprudence plays a secondary role to codes (which govern the law primarily in the area of private law) and statutes (which predominate in public matters)" and doctrinal guidance leaves very little room for judicial discretion (Fordham 2006, 2). In applying the law, the civil lawyer is to be guided by the logic of deductive reasoning that stresses judgment of a particular case from inferences derived from general principles and logically connected concepts contained in legal norms and legislations (Pejovic 2001).

Conversely, the judge in a common law tradition can be considered a lawmaker as case law, expressed through specific facts, constitutes the core of law to be supplemented by statutes or codes (Tetley 2000). Unlike the French who distinguish between *loi* (written statutory rules and codes) and *droit* (equivalent of law generally in English), the word "law" in the common law system applies to all legal rules, irrespective of whether its source is legislative or judicial (Tetley 2000). Also, "a lawyer in common law starts with the actual case and compares it with legal issues that have been previously dealt with by the courts, and from these relevant precedents, the binding legal rule is determined by means of induction" (Pejovic 2001, 10). Consequently, whereas civil lawyers tend to be more conceptual, systematic, and abstract in their reasoning, their counterparts in common law jurisdictions are expected to be more pragmatic and process-oriented, although the rules of *stares decisis* and *obiter dicta* ensure that only precedents relevant to the case are followed. Unlike the civil law system that tends to be "highly systematized and structured and relies on declarations of broad general principles, the common law is usually much more detailed in its prescriptions" (Tetley 2000, 283).

As indicated by the cases selected for in-depth study—Sierra Leone and Liberia—this book focuses exclusively on the Anglo-Saxon common law tradition, so the following section further examines the relationship between law and indirect colonial rule introduced in Africa by the British. At the same time, it must be underscored that, in the context of coloniality, both the civil law and common law traditions (as well as British indirect rule and French policy of assimilation) were of European origin with differences in style rather than kind. Instead of emerging organically through endogenous legal development as in Europe, both traditions became dominant legal systems in African as a result of transplantation in the context of colonial domination (Joireman 2006). As Tetley argues, "common law and civil law traditions share similar social objectives (individualism, liberalism, and individual rights) and they have in fact been joined in one single family, the Western law family, because of this functional similarity" (Tetley 2000, 701).

Rooted in superimposition, Eurocentrism, and doctrinal legality, both systems were deeply embedded in the project of legal colonization, which resulted in the construction of the modern state system, capitalist economy, and hierarchical social orders. The importation of legal doctrines, legislative models, judicial systems, legal cultures, judicial procedures, and administrative principles, even when disguised as transfer of modern technologies and expertise, was primarily to serve one imperial goal—legal colonization and subordination of non-European people. Focused on South Africa, which is an amalgam of European common and civil law traditions, Chanock argues that the "development of the legal system in the early twentieth century was crucial to the establishment and maintenance of the systems that underpinned the racist state, including control of the population, the running of the economy, and legitimation of the regime" (2001, 1). In agreement, Meierhenrich notes that "apartheid was installed not through military means but largely through the everyday work of civil administration in the 1950s" that included the promulgation of racist laws by a sovereign parliament and its administration, application, and interpretation by judges, magistrates, prosecutors, judicial officials, and lawyers (2000, 107). In performing this socializing and structuring effects, "procedures mattered a great deal" as "bureaucrats within the normative state valued predictability, stability, and efficiency as good in themselves and were genuinely impressed by the technical means that they could deploy" (Meierhenrich 2000, 108). This ensures what Chanock describes as "the existence of a legal system clearly based on the liberal forms of law at the heart of a racist and oppressive state," that is, clothing the cruelties of the everyday exercise of power in an immaculate garment of law (2001, 20). As illustrated below, in terms of dealing with the native question, the common law (which was supposed to be liberal) "shared aspiration of regulating society, resolving disputes, and meting out justice" according to European conceptions of morality, equity, and justice (Fordham 2006, 6).

THE POLITICAL ECONOMY OF THE
COMMON LAW AND INDIRECT RULE

Indirect rule, initially introduced in Nigeria by Lord Lugard, implied a form of institutional segregation in which colonial laws protected the legal status of non-natives separate from the natives whose means of legal recourse remained limited to their customary institutions.[8] In line with the common law tradition, customary law and justice systems continued to operate alongside the imported English legal structures but were limited to settling civil disputes among natives only. Criminal matters and cases between non-natives or involving natives and non-natives were the prerogative of colonial administrative officers and judges. A paradox of integration and differentiation, this move was seen as both practical and moral: "practical in the sense that European judges often could not understand the language and custom of people in the dock and moral in terms of legitimizing alien courts in the eyes of Africans" (Ibhawoh 2009, 435). Another practical dilemma of this dualism was the fact that while the colonialists could not rely upon customary law to maintain social order in protected territories, scarce resources and shortage of administrative personnel made it imprudent to rule solely by coercive means (Akuffo 2000).

Beyond administrative expediency, however, legal institutional dualism, which the common law encouraged, was also a means of conquest, subordination, and control. By assuming the role of lending official recognition to customary systems, colonial governments retained ultimate control of those systems, determining which customary law was applicable and supervising their application. Moore likens this legitimizing idea to the notion of legal evolution that placed British conception of law as "a set of clear rules and durably recorded rulings" above African legal thoughts viewed as "hopelessly muddled with little sense of the importance of evidence and proof, no appreciation of *res judicata*, and no understanding of the need for impartiality" (Moore 1992, 13). Based on this perception, colonial officers envisioned their mission as laying the foundation for a modern legal court system to eventually discipline preexisting quasi-judicial institutions in Africa.[9] Questioning the claim that describing customary law as unwritten is simply a technical legal conclusion, Snyder stresses the political implication which was that "those ideas and their social bases were subordinated to the colonial law of European origin, and therefore to the social forces whose interests the latter represented" (Snyder 1984, 36).

Colonial governments adopted numerous instruments to discipline customary law and the institutions that apply them. Among these, the most infamous was the so-called repugnancy clause that prohibited the application of customary law deemed to be inconsistent with colonial conception of natural justice, equity, and good conscience (Ibhawoh 2009; Merry 1988; Moore 1992; Obarrio 2011). Stated unequivocally in various customary court ordinances, the repugnancy principle was used to outlaw African customs deemed to be unacceptable according to colonial standards. The 1957 Local Government Memoranda of Tanganyika (now Tanzania) states that "there are some things which a British government cannot permit, since they outrage our sense of what is just or right" (1957, 25). In addition, customary laws were inadmissible if they conflicted with any formal legislation in the colonial territory. As with the repugnancy test, whenever customary law conflicted with colonial ordinances and statutes, those aspects found wanting were not only overruled but also abrogated. Allott (1984) affirms that repugnancy clauses gave the British judges and administrators the apparent power "to delete what they did not like about customary law" or to "modify substantially [the tolerable aspects] so as to bring them into line with their own ideas and institutions" (Allott 1984, 59).

Akin particularly to the colonial standard of morality at the time was the concept of the rule of law, which Moore (1992) maintains was fundamental to the British way of life and considered one of those concepts that merited transplantation into colonial territories. As the 1957 Tanganyika Ordinance stipulates, colonial officers supervising the administration of native justice were instructed to put down in writing a body of law so as to meet the requirement of certitude which is pivotal to upholding the rule of law. Instructions to insist on the rule of law when engaging customary justice systems, according to Gluckman (1969), were based in part on the widely held view that conflict resolution in Africa was based solely on occult beliefs and procedures, even though reference to supernatural power was not always the case.[10] It was also failure to recognize that some established kingdoms in precolonial Africa (e.g., the Ashanti and Barotse) had a well-formed body of law, a tribunal of traditional leaders whose decisions were often based on "forensic" evidence (Allott 1984; Joireman 2001), and that the potential of customary justice systems to resolve disputes lies in their very informality (Gluckman 1969).

Underlying these assumptions was the basic fact of Western (European) arrogance in their perception of superiority of (cultural) norms and values—translated into living standards, lifestyles, and thus an overall "civilized way of life." This was how the codification of customary law started and what became officially codified was not the rules handed down from the precolonial era but instead an historical construct of colonial encounter. "The nature of law changed as it was reshaped from a subtle and adaptable system, often unwritten to one of fixed, formal, and written rules enforced by native courts" (Merry 1991, 897). Anthropologists were occasionally commissioned to produce a handbook of traditional law and customs (Merry 1991); chiefs assumed to be loyal to the colonial administration empowered; and assessors (mostly elderly men) deemed to be versed in customary law were appointed to aid colonial officers' interpretation of customary practices (Moore 1992). In a study on native assessors, Ibhawoh notes that "assessors became exponents, interpreters, and sometimes inventors of local customs, shaping the processes and outcomes of colonial law and justice" (Ibhawoh 2009, 432).

However, codification of customary law was not an uncontested and irreversible progressive enterprise—it was highly political with competing interests not just between colonialists and the colonized but also among local interest groups and elites. Using a divide and rule strategy, the metropole rewarded traditional authorities whose interests aligned with imperial policies with more powers (including increased judicial authority) while those in opposition to colonial rule were deposed, exiled, or eliminated by colonial governments. Some accounts show that indirect rule was a response to situations where traditional authorities, whose powers were being undermined by colonial policies, threatened to withhold their support or spark off a rural rebellion (Chanock 1985). Commenting on the reduction in the number of colonial courts as well as the magistrates' sudden interests in upholding the authority of chiefs and bonds of kinship, Chanock argues that "an apparent breakdown in order beginning in the 1920s led the British to shift course, putting support behind traditional authorities" (1985, 172). Meanwhile, the emerging mission-educated elites, who opposed the increasing powers of traditional authorities and their alliance with the colonial regime, preferred formalization of customary justice as a way to reduce the authority of traditional rulers (Merry 1991). Moore also reminds us of anti-centralized movements in local communities that tried "to control their own members and do everything to manage their internal autonomy, bypassing colonial courts and settling their own affairs internally as they choose" (Moore 1992, 12). In short, "some pockets of customs and non-Western law remained and even flourished despite the efforts of colonial officials to eradicate them" (Merry 1991, 918).

A neo-Marxian reading of customary law helps to situate legal dualism within the local political economy and its connection with the global capitalist order. Marxists link the establishment of the colonial state to "the economic task of opening the pre-colonial subsistent economy for primary accumulation by the metropolitan capital as well as the development of a captive export market" (Akuffo 2006, 137). This link between the state as an instrument of imperial rule and capitalist production drew Africa into a new set of economic relations designed to the advantage of dominant economic classes of the metropolitan center and colonized territories (Cohen and Daniel 1981; Gutkind and Wallerstein 1976; Harris 1975; Merry 1991). In synch with a dual legal system, there were notionally two separate economic sectors but, in reality, the pre-capitalist economy became subsumed into the colonial market system. In this political economy, "law served to extract land from pre-colonial users and to create a wage labor force out of peasant and subsistence producers" (Merry 1991, 891). But conversely, law also became an instrument used by the colonial state and colonizers to restrain the more brutal exploitation of land and labor (Berry 1992). Whether colonial or customary, legal rules were codified in order to regulate labor contracts, land tenure, vagrancy, and to control social relations that affected production, distribution, and exchange (Merry 1991). Colonial courts were instruments for "labor discipline and tax prosecutions, enforcing new colonial regulations about work obligations, labor contracts, and property rights" (Chanock 1985, 236).

To be specific, "the possibility of cultivating cash crop for the market rather than for consumption led to enormous changes in African land tenure systems" (Allott 1984, 59). But there were different approaches to customary land law in settler and non-settler colonies (Seidman and Seidman 1984). In settler colonies (mostly in East, Central, and Southern Africa), the system of land law depended mainly on land allocation by government-appointed administrative officers and the basic thrust of the law was to establish labor reserves (Cohen and Daniel 1981). "Land laws placed constraints on the peasant's capacity to grow cash crops" so as to make labor available for European enterprises (Seidman and Seidman 1984, 53). In order to precipitate labor migration, European entrepreneurs lobbied colonial governments to adopt laws that would make life in the hinterland expensive and arduous, mainly through land reform, poll taxes, hut/head taxes, and marketing rules. Faced with hardship and the need to earn cash to pay colonial taxes in the hinterland, most male workers migrated into export enclaves to provide cheap labor as mine or plantation workers.

In non-settler colonies (mostly in West Africa), land tenure was based mainly on land allocation by traditional authorities, followed later by the introduction of the right to free alienation that made land available in the open market (Cohen and Daniel 1981). The main purpose of land law in the non-settler territories was to promote cash-crop farming, particularly the growing of cocoa, coffee, palm kernel, and raw materials needed in European industries. Before the introduction of the market economy, land holding under West African indigenous legal systems was based on the principle of communal or group ownership. But as Akuffo notes, "the colonial courts converted community-based property rights into individual rights by enforcing the alienation of communal and family land by contract" (2006, 141). Since a native subject lacked formal documentation to invoke his right against a sovereign colonial government, many European powers freely alienated land owned by indigenous people under customary law either to themselves or for settlement or commercial purposes (Buell 1927). Arguing that colonial officials used "equity as an instrument of dislocation," some describe the introduction of English conveyance forms as the basis for transforming communal ownership of land into freehold and leasehold systems in West Africa, which then made cocoa and palm oil land available for purchase in the open market (Akuffo 2006, 141; Seidman and Seidman 1984).

As with the process of codifying customary law, it is important to note that the colonial capitalist order did not succeed to wholly suppress alternative forms of economy (Merry 1991) nor was the exchange economy entirely new to Africa (Ayittey 2006). At best, the intermixture of various cultural and social structures resulted in an incomplete transformation with colonized people adopting English laws for instrumental purposes accompanied by occasional popular resistance to deflect changes considered too costly. Economic regulations were shaped not just by macrostructural processes to preserve the material interests of the metropole but also by micropolitical struggles in which emerging African elites used English law to meet their interests and needs under changing political and economic circumstances. Under such conditions, traditional authorities would equally invoke customary law as a political resource to renegotiate their status and access to resources (Chanock 1985). "The existence of [these] social spaces in which capitalism and law have been resisted and neutralized indicate that the subordination of Third World Countries to western legal forms is neither historically inevitable nor irreversible" (Merry 1991, 911).

COLONIAL LAW AND THE CREATION OF UNEQUAL STRUCTURES

Although superimposition was not without local agency, the legal systems instituted by colonial administrations reinforced structural, social, and cost-related inequities as follows. Initially, the legal system, like its administrative counterpart, was primarily introduced to deal with the legitimacy crisis created by the imposition of a modern state in Africa, rather than enabling indigenous societies to call into question the legality of that state. In the system, "a British citizen in any colony of the British Empire would expect to be a subject of British law with a reliance on British legal precedents as defined by British case law," while a British-protected person under customary law would be denied such rights (Joireman 2006, 194). Describing colonialism in Africa as globalization of English law, Ibhawoh asserts that "large-scale transfer of laws and legal institutions resulted in a dual legal system—one for the colonized and one for the colonizers, casting the latter as sole possessor of law and civility" (2009, 429). One might assume that experiences in countries colonized by continental powers would be dissimilar for the Napoleonic code was a ready-made legal instrument to create citizens who were to enjoy the rights enshrined in the civil law tradition. But in French colonies, though citizenship was extended to anyone who attained French education and civilization, "those who were not citizens operated under a different legal code than the French citizens," thereby creating the same dual legal structures that characterized British indirect rule (Joireman 2006, 194). Also, "while French colonies were seen as an extension of France" under the policy of assimilation, Africans who lived in Paris quickly "discovered that they were not 'French,'" a realization that partly led to the Negritude movement (Ahluwalia 2001, 22).

Thus, whether based on the French civil code or the British common law, transplanted legal traditions ended up creating multiple legal and social orders in a single state, what became the genesis of parallel and contradictory governance structures in Africa. In both settler and non-settler colonies, colonial legal development resulted in bifurcation of Africans as natives and non-natives, indigenes and strangers, citizens and subjects, with considerable implications for competition over citizenship rights, property rights, and upward social mobility. In addition to white settlers, Africans who drew closer to colonial powers and European civilization saw themselves as subjects of European law, whereas the indigenous population remained the object of modern law. For the British, it was a policy designed to divide and rule Africans, reinforced a by a superior English law that selected certain elements of customary law such as those related to family, marriage, divorce, inheritance, and forced labor for official recognition and endorsement. As Berry (1992) aptly argues, the colonial invention of African traditions was not out of respect for African customary law but reflective of the fact that colonialism itself had contradictory implications, including the perceived indispensability of African backwardness to industrial profit and the strategic relevance of decentralized despotism to the suppression of agrarian revolt against the colonial political economy (also Joireman 2006; Mamdani 1996). For the French, whose policy of assimilation was designed generally to make Frenchmen, differentiation in the colony could be described as a default of the failure or deceit to assimilate most Africans into French citizenship.

Socially, an overarching objective that united all European legal and administrative systems was the subordination of preexisting legal and normative orders, especially when they conflict with the imperial agenda of "effective occupation." It must be noted that "nowhere in Africa was there an institutional and cultural *tabula rasa*, particularly in the area of dispute resolution" (Joireman 2006, 193), which means the imposition of European legal traditions could be carried out only by powerful social forces. For instance, since both the adversarial and inquisitive methods of dispute resolution were of European origins, one would imagine that indigenous methods that served the majority population would prevail where indigenous law clashed with European law. But as these tensions were politically resolved based on who controlled the modern state, it was common practice to elevate the common or civil law tradition (which served only a minority of the population) to general law status, whereas indigenous/customary laws (which applied to the majority population) were relegated as inferior. As with European languages, which became official languages in all African colonies, the superimposition of European law was usually justified on the grounds that African indigenous/ customary laws are too particular when in fact both the common and civil law traditions emerged from specific Romano-Germanic cultures. Moreover, both the adversarial and acquisitive processes of adjudication were to be accorded a superior official status, while the more socially oriented procedures common to many preexisting African societies would become inferior alternative dispute resolution mechanisms.

Beyond the de jure differentiation of Africans and subordination of their social institutions, European legal systems were introduced in Africa with built-in processes and procedures that favored certain groups of citizens, namely, the educated, Christians, economic elites, and the political class. Although such discriminatory experiences were not a product of deliberate colonial policies, they created effective cost-related barriers that hindered equal access to the structures established by European law. Based on European languages, legal traditions, and cultural practices, the colonial justice system became more accessible to those who attained citizenship rights because they could navigate the system for themselves or afford an attorney to advocate on their behalf, particularly in common law colonies. Only a formally educated African or someone with the required financial resources could use the modern state institutions to claim citizenship rights, seek formal dispute resolution, or defend himself against the state. The rules of evidence, admissibility requirements, rules of court, formal investigation and presentation of evidence, and other formal processes of adjudication already served to alienate those without the social standing to demonstrate the legal competence to use the formal courts. While everybody could hire a lawyer to navigate the system, the cost of doing so (in terms of both legal fees and other expenses) was to disproportionately burden the poor, the majority of whom happened to be indigenous Africans.

Unlike the French civil law system that limited litigation practices and active involvement of lawyers, the adversarial nature of the British common law tradition would heighten the demand and cost of legal service, a concept that was hardly part of precolonial African legal and judicial practices. Manteaw (2008) has linked this problem to the fact that African lawyers called to the English Bar were trained exclusively as barristers, not as solicitors, and their legal training paid no attention to the challenges of practicing law in heterogenous countries with multiple systems of law. Compounding the issue was an attention to private practice for monetary gain, deeply rooted in the colonial policy of using legal instruments to protect the market, revenue collection, and commercial interests. Manteaw reminds us that in the absence of a significant number of African lawyers during colonial rule, the legal profession in Africa became heavily dominated by European expatriates and wealthy Asians who were more interested "in representing rich and commercial clients and litigating cases," a political economy of law that was bound to continue in postcolonial times (Manteaw 2008, 916). As in Kenya where the Indian Contract Act governed contractual arrangement until 1960, "the reliance on colonial Indian laws and procedures created a legal environment conducive for the practice of private law by lawyers, both Africans and Asians, trained in India" (Joireman 2006, 200).

Finally, legal colonization in Africa must also be interpreted as the reconstruction of a broader legal culture that encompassed more than the professional, bureaucratic, and juristic realm. It was the "creation of a more general consciousness or experience of law that is widely shared by those who inhabit a particular legal environment," a sharing that required the colonized people to undervalue their own traditions, shared beliefs, common ways of thinking in favor of a superior legal culture (Cotterrell 2019, 712). For example, the "broader public discourse about law [in South Africa] was dominated for much of the existence of the white state by an affirmation of the liberal idea of neutral law on one level, with a pragmatic acceptance of, and insistence on, the use of law to secure racial advantage" on the other (Chanock 2001, 522). This legal construction of social order is depicted by political philosopher Fitzjames Stephens who argues that

> The establishment of a system of law which regulates the most important parts of the daily lives of people constitutes in itself a moral conquest, more striking, more durable, and far more solid than the physical conquest which it renders possible. Our law is in fact the sum and substance of what we have to teach them. It is, so to speak, the gospel of the English and it is a compulsory gospel which admits no dissent and no disobedience. (cited in Hussain 2003, 4)

POSTCOLONIAL LEGAL ORDER: DISJUNCTURE OR CONTINUATION?

With most African countries gaining formal independence following World War II, what then should be the relationship between European and African (including those colonially invented) legal traditions and of what use would the colonial legal order be in the postcolonial state? These questions, which seem only a formal legal dilemma, actually raised profound political issues regarding postcolonial national identity and citizenship that were to confound the statebuilding project beyond the immediate aftermath of independence (Moore 1992). On the eve of decolonization of many African states, these questions were necessitated by a conflation of factors including both the international and domestic dimensions of the Anglo-Saxon law. For instance, whereas international law had previously denied African sovereignty, the self-determination of colonized people was being considered a right recognized by the Atlantic Charter and United Nations Organisation (Umozurike 1971). Internally, every decolonization effort (even those that required a violent liberation movement) was marked by a series of constitutional reforms to introduce elected representative assemblies, equal citizenship rights, an independent judiciary, limited terms of executive authority, and other forms of constitutionalism that were absent in the regime of colonial rule in the previous century or so.

In most independent African states, as will be closely illustrated by Sierra Leone and Liberia, indigenous elite response to these questions was both a foregone conclusion and strategic move to consolidate postcolonial power. In some countries, the "new" educated elites, who had been exposed to Western law, succeeded in taking over from colonial rule and were interested in retaining hegemonic bureaucratic and political institutions left behind by their white counterparts. Preference for maintaining the dominance of colonial legal structures, even though they alienated the majority population at the time, was not because traditional legal systems had been completely compromised or non-existent. Rather, it was primarily because the modern elites' earlier experience with a specific set of Western institutions had created what Joireman (2001) describes as a "lock-in" in which a particular path was bound to prevail. Lawyers (more so, those trained in the British common law system) who were very active in the independence movement continued to occupy influential positions in government and civil service in the post-independence period. Also, since the modern African elites relied mostly on legal instruments in their independence struggle, they had become adept at negotiating the common laws and therefore had a vested interest in preserving them as dominant state institutions (Joireman 2001).

At the strategic governance level, it must be reiterated that colonial rule never satisfactorily resolved the native question and the state-society incongruence created by an externally imposed state system in Africa. Moreover, the first generation of African leaders were confronted with a dilemma: whereas the colonial legal order was less concerned with the rights of indigenous populations, the newly independent African states were expected to respect the civil and political rights of their citizens and uphold rule of law principles such as checks and balances, separation of powers, and independent judiciary (Prempeh 2013). "Alongside the new constitutional precept, the new African state had also received as part of its colonial bequest the authoritarian legal order—the full panoply of colonial legislations, orders, ordinances, by-laws, and judicial precedents—upon which colonial authority was based" (Prempeh 2013, 171). In addition to functioning as the default legal regime, "this inherited sub-constitutional legal order, not the new constitutions, offered African elites real power and the bureaucratic machinery with which to exercise it effectively" (Prempeh 2013, 171). Since it would be disinguous for nationalist leaders to simply use the same justification behind the inherited colonial regime, the new defense for retaining and enforcing the most authoritarian aspects of the colonial legal order was found in the ideology of nationalism and legality, which emphasizes state-enforced law and order.

For the civil law tradition, the notion of executive primacy (which constrains the judiciary from interfering in the conduct of state affairs) would become a powerful mechanism for keeping the judicial system at bay or coopting it into state-sponsored projects. Although the common law is more hospitable to judicial review and a system of checks and balances, these principles and practices were hardly institutionalized in British colonies. And even if new constitutional reforms attempted to engineer these practices in the system, the socialization of African judges meant that juristic ideas and doctrines such as literalness and analytical positivism, deference to the state, narrow legalistic reasoning, and the social class background and values of judges would all culminate in a conservative, rather than an activist, legal system. Forming a nation where a state already existed would be the greatest challenge African leaders were to confront. Ironically, it was because of this challenge that "the colonial legal infrastructure, with its unitary centralised executive bureaucracy, systems of revenue extraction, subordinate courts, and compliant chiefs, would answer almost perfectly the needs of Africa's founding elites" (Prempeh 2013, 167).

Under colonial tutelage, African elites have learned the duplicity of the rule of law: it could be presented as an emancipatory liberal project while serving primarily as a mechanism for asserting, enabling, and legitimating state power (Joireman 2006; Prempeh 2013). Rather than constraining power, the rule of law bequeathed to them was one in which the English law as well as institutions responsible for its enforcement (namely, the formal courts, police, and other law enforcement agencies) could be deployed as instrument of executive power. Although law was helpful during the last days of decolonization, colonial rule taught the founding African leaders the primacy of politics over law to the extent that they came to "view courts primarily as the institution through which government impose its policy behind a cloak of magisterial propriety" (Prempeh 2013, 170). But as Sierra Leone and Liberia amply demonstrate, inherently embedded in this rule of law are structural, social, and cost-related injustices, which, over a period, would create resentment and dissatisfaction so strong as to destabilize the very order being reconstructed.

NOTES

1. For instance, while South Africa had been colonized by Dutchmen, Flemings, French Huguenots, and Scotchmen operating under the Chartered Company of Dutch East India between 1652 and 1795, the British arrived in this region only at the close of the eighteenth century to counteract French efforts to seize the Cape of Good Hope from the company (Johnston 1924; Huxley 1949). British colonization of South Africa in 1815 was followed by the arrival of Anglo-Saxon missionaries and explorers including Livingstone whose activities inspired the British government to expand its empire to Rhodesia, British Central Africa, British East Africa, and British

West Africa. Perhaps out of the exhaustion of the Napoleonic times, France occupied Algeria in 1830 and then extended its frontiers first to Morocco and Tunis and later beyond the Sahara Desert to West Africa, Central Africa, Northern Congoland, Madagascar, and French Somaliland. "Livingstone and other British missionaries and travellers from South Africa or the British enterprise in Sierra Leone, forced Portugal to reassert herself as ruler in Portuguese Guinea, Angola, the Western Congo, Mozambique, Zambezia, and the Delagoa Bay" (Johnston 1924, 606). Belgium moved to establish Belgian rule over the Congo Free State, which stretched to the Northern French and Northwestern Portuguese frontiers only after King Leopold II had occupied a vast swathe of territory under the Association Internationalé Africainé in 1876 (Ryckmans 1955). Following a mission by Nachtigal and Baron Von der Decken across the Sahara, Germany captured the Cameroons, Southwest Africa, and the hinterland of Zanzibar only to be expelled from Africa after its World War I defeat (Johnston 1924). Spain sought the permission of France, Germany, and Britain to bring under her flag a large strip of the Western Sahara as well as the Island of Fernando Po off the Western Equatorial Africa that was acquired from Portugal. After failing to secure Tunis and Ethiopia, Italy compensated itself with the occupation of Tripoli and Cyrenaica but based on the acquiescence of France and Britain and threat posed by German ambition under the guise of an Austro-Hungarian Chartered Company (Johnston 1924). Less inclined to be involved in foreign entanglement, the United States seemed content with maintaining a paternal interest over Liberia as one of the destinations (in addition to Sierra Leone) for repatriating Africans whose ancestors were slaves forcefully torn from the continent during the transatlantic slave trade that prospered North America.

2. For example, following the creation of the Society for German Colonisation, a mission to Zanzibar returned with twelve treaties, giving the society rights over the territories of Useguha, Ngura, Usagara, and Ukami (Fortnightly Review, May 1865–June 1890). Among treaties to regulate colonial power relations in East Africa were the Anglo-French Declaration of 1862, Anglo-German Agreement of 1886, and the Joint Declaration by General Mathews (representing the Sultan of Zanzibar) and German Vice-Consul Hunholt (Fortnightly Review, May 1865–June 1890).

3. White- and black-settlers did not enjoy the same privileges, but the overall settler group was more represented under the English law than indigenous Africans.

4. African common law countries, all former colonies of Great Britain, include Botswana, Egypt, Gambia, Kenya, Malawi, Namibia, Nigeria, Sierra Leone, Tanzania, Uganda, Zambia, and Zimbabwe. African civil law countries, mostly former French colonies but also Lusophone countries, include Algeria, Angola, Burkina Faso, Democratic Republic of Congo, Cote D'Ivoire, Gabon, Guinea, Madagascar, Mali, Morocco, Mozambique, Niger, Senegal, Togo, Tunisia, and Congo Brazzaville (Joireman 2004). Some countries like Cameroon have mixed civil law and common law traditions.

5. Some accounts of the rule of law suggest that the idea has a longer intellectual pedigree going as far back as the writings of Plato and Aristotle. But Dicey is often seen as the leading proponent of the fundamental rule of law principles that underpin the operation of modern liberal democratic systems.

6. Most civil codes were adopted in the nineteenth and twentieth centuries: French Code Civil 1804, Austrian Bürerliches Gesetzbuch 1811, German Bürerliches Gesetzbuch 1896, Japanese Minpō 1896, Swiss Zivilgesetzbuch 1907, Italian Code 1942, etc. (Pejovic 2001).

7. According to Pejovic, the term "inquisitorial" has a negative connotation, referring to the notorious Spanish Inquisition known for its use of torture to obtain confessions and a more active judge in civil law proceedings does not justify the use of the term (Pejovic 2001).

8. Indirect rule is normally associated to British colonial system of administration as opposed to the policy of assimilation by the French. Obarrio (2011) argues that the British common law system was more accommodative of customary law unlike the civil Napoleonic codes that were impervious to African customs and traditional forms of justice. However, Joireman insists that "everywhere the colonial metropole established their own systems of law and dispute resolution, disregarding pre-existing mechanisms of conflict resolution as primitive or appropriate for native only" (2001, 571).

9. It is important to point out that most of the British officials who supervised native courts and presided over disputes were administrative officers (e.g., district commissioners and district officers) who had no legal training or practical judicial experience (Chanock 1985; Moore 1992). Hooker (1975) also draws attention to the mistaken tendency of equating law to the existence of written texts, which then relegates anything unwritten as not a law.

10. Gluckman (1969) noted that conflict resolution in precolonial Africa was based mainly on a common-sense approach and the informal proceedings in traditional courts often achieved similar forensic ends as those achieved in formal courts. It was usual to hear evidence from both litigants before requiring witnesses, to eliminate irrelevant information such as hearsays, and to derive judgment from an accumulating logic of arguments heard. Gluckman identifies three situations where reference to the supernatural was necessary: (1) where the contending parties before the judge are too powerful for the judge to give a decision against one of them; (2) where the offense complained of is itself related to occult practices; (3) where there is strong suspicion but no definite proof and one party requires witnesses to take an oath. In these situations, the effect of occult procedure is to shift some of the responsibility for determining the guilt off the judges (Max Gluckman 1969).

Part II

COLONIAL LEGACIES AND CONTEMPORARY LEGAL RECONSTRUCTIONS

Chapter 4

The Rule of Law and Political Power in Sierra Leone and Liberia

I have interwoven the abstract post/neocolonial rule of law critique with the broad historical evidence of legal development in Africa since the European scramble for colonies to the decolonization period. In the previous chapter I generated historical insights related to the role of modern law in Africa's relations with European powers and in dealing with the native question that colonialism inevitably precipitated. Consistent with the coloniality of law conceptualized in chapter 2, the previous chapter has confirmed that the rule of law as introduced by colonial rulers reproduced and reinforced social domination both outside and within newly established modern states. Externally, international law legitimized European colonization, denied the sovereignty and subjective personality of African nations, and integrated them unequally into the capitalist industrial economy. Internally, the European legal systems, whether based on the civil law or common law traditions, were an instrument of governmentality rather than freedom. Moreover, the transported European laws institutionalized hierarchical socioeconomic and political structures that benefited the minority settler and Westernized population at the expense of the indigenous majority. Backed by superior European power, the modern law simply overturned the social order of Africa, that is, legitimizing the fact that a tiny foreign minority could rule over the indigenous majority with far-reaching structural, social, and cost-related implications. From unequal dualistic structures, subordination of indigenous value systems to the increasing cost of access to the modern state system, legal development planted the seeds of social conflict and disorder that successive African leaders were ironically poised to uphold and consolidate.

But it is one thing to excavate legal development in the broader construction of African under European legal colonialism and quite another to capture the historical nuances of specific trajectories shaped by circumstances internal to each African state. The present chapter (and subsequent two) as comparative analysis of Sierra Leone and Liberia ensures that the continent's complex and multifaceted experiences are not substituted by a general portrait of legal development in Africa. Focused specifically on the relationship between the rule of law and political power, the chapter analyzes the politics of reform to indicate, contrary to conventional expectations, that transported legal norms and institutions consolidate, rather than weaken, the excessive power of the ruling class. Taking a deep historical approach that foregrounds the settler-colonial founding of both countries, the chapter attributes this inherent contradiction in the modern rule of law to the legacy and continued influence of Euro-American legal tutelage. Although structured to acknowledge major historical junctures such as the end of settler-colonial domination, postcolonial authoritarianism, period of civil war, and post-conflict reform, the chapter stresses continuities in terms of the logic and structures of domination. Transition from one historical epoch to another is presented as legal development while underscoring that such changes do very little to destabilize the modern state as the primary instrument for accessing and consolidating unaccountable power.

SETTLER-COLONIAL LEGAL DEVELOPMENT

Like many other African countries, precolonial societies in Sierra Leone had functional political systems with institutions capable of maintaining law and order as well as checking the potential excesses of rulers. Administratively, the historical evidence demonstrates the existence of various forms of authority ranging from inland personal hegemonies, traditional kingdoms to secular republics (Abraham 2003; Barrows 1976). In terms of the administration of justice, the usual practice was to constitute a panel of elders to resolve disputes according to customary norms of acceptable behavior (Abraham 1978; Alie 1999; Finnegan and Murray 1970). But in 1896, almost a century following the 1808 establishment of a Crown colony in Freetown (initially established as home for freed slaves following the end of the transatlantic slave trade), the hinterland of Sierra Leone was formerly declared a British protectorate, leading to external interference into what otherwise may have been an organic evolution of indigenous governance systems.

In terms of European international law and diplomacy, the changing geopolitics of the West African region precipitated the decision of the British to abandon their long-standing non-expansionist policy. Specifically, it was a geostrategic move in line with the 1885 Berlin principle of "effective occupation" to keep at bay Britain's imperial rivals, particularly the French, whose territorial dominion in West Africa extended to neighboring Guinea and Ivory

Coast. In the late 1800s, French troops were advancing into territories within British sphere of influence along the northeastern flank of Sierra Leone under the guise of pursuing Guinean Sofa warriors led by their recalcitrant traditional ruler, Samori Toure (Alie 1990). Initial attempts to halt French annexation of Sierra Leonean territory resulted in the first physical confrontation between colonial powers in the nineteenth-century European scramble for Africa—the December 22, 1893, Waima incident in which a small number of British and French soldiers were killed (Alie 1990). Realizing that some local rulers were unwilling to surrender their sovereignty through "friendship treaties" and considering the geostrategic and economic (see chapter 5) importance of the hinterland, the Colonial Office granted approval to Governor Frederick Cardew to officially annex the interior parts of Sierra Leone. While military deterrence was provided by the British West African Frontier Force (WAFF), the police became a paramilitary or civilian force for law and order (Turay 1987).

Based on the 1882 Anglo-Liberian and 1885 Anglo-Franco boundary agreements, the British protectorate was defined as territories that were bounded on the northeast by the line of frontier bordering Guinea, on the southeast by the line of frontier bordering Liberia, and on the southwest by the Atlantic Ocean, except portions of the colony comprising the peninsula of Sierra Leone and outlying Islands (The Protectorate Ordinance, Cap. 60(2), 1896). Formalized by an Order-in-Council under the Foreign Jurisdiction Act, the 1896 Protectorate declaration brought all territories adjacent to the colony under Her Majesty's protection through an indirect rule system that utilized traditional authority structures for extractive and regulatory purposes, including collection of taxes, preservation of law and order, and mobilization of labor for agriculture and public works. For administrative convenience, pre-existing boundaries were redrawn dividing the protectorate into five territorial districts, each under the supervision of a European District Commissioner. Districts were subdivided into chiefdoms headed by paramount chiefs, especially those who had signed "treaties of friendship" (later known as treaty chiefs) but who became answerable to the District Commissioner mandated to report to the governor any conducts deemed subversive to the interest of good government in his district (Cap. 60(25), 1896). To meet administrative cost, a minimum tax of five shillings was imposed on every dwelling house (excluding a house owned or occupied by a non-native) to be collected by chiefs, who would receive a rebate of 5 percent on amounts collected.

In legal affairs, the most noticeable demonstration of indirect rule was in the field of law and its attendant courts system. In the colony, "the English common law prevailed and the jurisdiction of the courts was completely patterned after the British system with statutes passed in Britain applicable to British subjects" (Collier 1970, 54). But in the protectorate, a separate justice

system was constructed via a number of Court Ordinances that established a
hierarchy of three courts.[1] The lowest court in this hierarchy was the Court
of Native Chiefs, which was given jurisdiction according to native law in all
civil cases arising exclusively between natives other than cases involving a
question of title to land.[2] In criminal cases, "their jurisdiction was limited to
matters arising exclusively between natives but excluding cases of murder,
culpable homicide, pretended witchcraft, slave dealing, and certain other
serious crimes such as cannibalism, or offences relating to certain secret
societies" (Brooke 1953, 5). Next was the combined Court of the District
Commissioner and Native Chief that had jurisdiction over practically all
cases between natives and offenses committed by natives against non-natives,
including the power to inflict death sentences. Although two or more chiefs
were nominated to sit with the Commissioner in this court, the power to make
decisions was the prerogative of the District Commissioner. Above the combined court was the separate Court of the District Commissioner authorized to
settle any matter, particularly those involving commercial disputes, breach of
contracts with expatriates, and allegation of slave dealings (Abraham 2003;
Smart-Joko 1986; Kilson 1966; Kup 1975).

Major restructuring of Native Administration by the colonial government
took place in the 1930s. In addition to the Native Courts Ordinance, which
came into force on January 1, 1933, the Chiefdom Treasuries and Tribal
Authorities Ordinances of 1937 introduced to the Protectorate a system of
chiefdom governance in force in Nigeria and Tanganyika. The 1932 Forced
Labor Ordinance was passed to set limits to the amount of free labor chiefs
could extract from their subjects. A Tribal Authority (TA), comprising men
of note elected by the people according to native custom and approved by the
governor in a published *Gazette*, was established primarily to pass by-laws
necessary for maintaining order and regulating crime in the protectorate.
As long as such laws were "not repugnant to morality" or in conflict with
colonial ordinances, the Tribal Authority could issue orders prohibiting acts
that might cause a breach of the peace as well as requiring the registration of
birth and death of natives (Tribal Authorities Ordinance, Cap 60(8), 1938).
To assist Tribal Authorities and Native Courts to enforce law and order, a
Chiefdom Police Force to be supervised by a District Watch Committee was
established (Chiefdom Police Act, Cap. 128). In the area of revenue collection, a local tax of four shillings per adult male was introduced in addition to
other fees and licenses. In return of the requirement to deposit revenues in the
Chiefdom Treasury, Paramount Chiefs were to receive a fixed monthly salary
from the government. Tribal authorities, expected to represent twenty taxpay-
ers, were later to constitute the electoral college to elect paramount chiefs
among aspirants from contending ruling houses in a chiefdom. Efforts to
further modernize local governance and introduce distributive functions led

to the formation of modern District Councils in 1946 as a second tier of local government, according to Commissioner Hubert's Rural Development Plan.

Although the absence of formal colonial experience sets Liberia apart from the historical trajectory common to most African states, the evolution and contemporary manifestations of state-society relations in this country offer important parallels with neighboring Sierra Leone. Like Freetown, Monrovia, which has now become the capital of Liberia, was originally founded for freed slaves, the first batches from the United States and Barbados arriving in 1822.[3] For about half a century since the founding of a settler society by the American Colonization Society (ACS), the colony's territorial reach was limited to few coastal enclaves, administered separately by a system of laws and government patterned after the American model and common law tradition (Levitt 2005; Lowenkopf 1976). The 1847 national constitution, written by an American professor at Harvard, Simon Greenleaf, denied indigenous Liberians citizenship rights while embracing the American notion of liberty for the mulatto settlers (Chalmers 2018). However, imperial rivalries in the aftermath of the 1885 Berlin conference meant that Liberia could no longer rely on its 1847 declaration of independence to maintain territorial integrity—effective control of territories was necessary in the face of European imperial and commercial interests along the West African coast (Levitt 2005; Sawyer 1992).

In order to deter European encroachment and maintain formal authority over the hinterland of Liberia, the Liberian government opted for the indirect rule system implemented by Britain in neighboring Sierra Leone. Ruling over indigenous peoples through their chiefs was found useful as it "allowed Liberian settlers nominal political control over [the hinterland] and at the same time opened economic and political avenues for settler exploitation" (Harris 2012, 47).[4] Indirect rule was introduced in earnest by President Arthur Barclay (1904–1912), who simply replicated the Sierra Leone model in terms of establishing an administrative and judicial hierarchy and relegating the role of resource extraction and mobilization to chiefs who became government-commissioned officials (Sawyer 1992). Chiefs received a commission of 10 percent for taxes collected, including a hut tax levied on every inhabitable house in their chiefdom. An important mechanism for the enforcement of law and order was the Liberian Frontier Force (LFF) established with substantial British input. Based on the recommendation of Braithwaith Wallis, the British Consul to Liberia, President Barclay appointed British Captain Mackay Caldwell to organize the LFF, who in turn employed the assistance of two other British officers and ten sergeants from the Sierra Leone Frontier Force (Levitt 2005).

The Rules and Regulation Governing the Hinterland (hereafter Hinterland Rules) reorganized the administration of justice in the hinterland into courts of general jurisdiction and courts of limited jurisdiction. The courts of general jurisdiction consisted of the Provincial Circuit Court of Assize and administrative courts of provincial and districts commissioners while those of limited jurisdiction included the joint courts of district commissioners and paramount chiefs and courts of paramount chiefs. Article 38 (3) of the Hinterland Rules made a distinction between civilized people and natives in the application of Liberia's criminal code in the interior. Whereas all cases arising between civilized people shall be tried in the District Commissioner's Court, all suits between a civilized person and a native should be heard in the Joint Court of the District Commissioner and Paramount Chief. Similarly, Article 40 stated that all cases arising between strangers and members of a tribe, except when they are civilized people, should be tried by the paramount chiefs' courts. A complex system of appeal was put in place in which appeals from judgments of district commissioners were to be heard by provincial commissioners and those from judgments of county commissioners referred to the courts of county superintendents, which operated under the Ministry of Interior. Administratively, the hinterland was divided into three provinces (western, central, and eastern), each further subdivided into chiefdoms. This arrangement left the interior in a politically subordinate relationship with the coastal counties whose jurisdiction came directly under the authority of statute laws based on the 1847 constitution.

Like almost all eighteen presidents before him, President William V. S. Tubman (1944–1971) was an Americo-Liberian. Yet, by hailing from Harper in Cape Palmas, he was the first head of state to emerge from outside the original core settlements of Monteserrado and Grand Bassa Counties, and this outside background tremendously impacted his policies regarding internal affairs. Immediately after he assumed office in 1944, President Tubman launched his National Unification policy that was aimed at ending intercommunal conflict by removing barriers that prevented indigenous Liberians from being part of the national body politic. The declaration of the unification policy was complemented two years later in 1946 by legislation extending suffrage to property holders in the interior who became eligible to vote and hold elective offices (Sawyer 1992). Also, in order to allow the indigenous elite to participate in central legislative processes, Tubman allotted three seats in the House of Representatives to the interior (one seat for each province). Although limited to those who paid hut tax, this extension of suffrage was a fundamental step toward expanding citizenship rights as the previous practice was to consider indigenes as collective subjects of a clan or tribal group to be represented by a single delegate selected by the government.

But competition among ethnic groups for official recognition during the Tubman era exacerbated tribal consciousness of their separate identities (Nelson 1985). For example, while members of the Vai ethnic group were the most willing to take advantage of Tubman's policies, the Kru and Grebo ethnic groups, which had been in frequent wars with the Republic, were more circumspect in their response. Crucially, Tubman's indirect rule system was both highly circumscribed and deceptive in that gradual assimilation of indigenous people into the national community was permitted insofar as it did not unseat or challenge the privileged status of the settler ruling oligarchy. The president was willing to extend political opportunities to the hinterland but without altering the rules that favored the dominance of Americo-Liberians, particularly his ruling clique of family members, Masonic Lodge members, and close associates. His personal relations with indigenous elites were transformed into a patronage network in which those who relied on his personal influence to attain public office were in turn beholden to become "praise singers" popularizing his unification program. Indigenous political representation was to take place only within the framework of the ruling True Whig Party (TWP) dominated by Americo-Liberian leadership. When the Kru leader of the Reformation Party, Didhwo Twe, sought to challenge Tubman's third-term bid and to contest the 1951 elections, he was immediately charged with treason and forced into exile in Sierra Leone (Lowenkopf 1976).

Further attempts to rectify the inferior political status of the Hinterland came in the form of reorganizing provinces into four counties (Grand Gedeh, Lofa, Nimba, and Bong), each allocated two senators plus representatives proportional to their population size. Yet these reforms came too late and were inadequate to challenge the entrenched power base of Americo-Liberians of the coastal counties. Despite ground-breaking efforts to bring the indigenous population into the mainstream socioeconomic system, Tubman, like his predecessors, ardently believed in settler supremacist ideology, and he laid the foundation for a continuation of Americo-Liberian hegemony. Until his death in office in 1971, Tubman deliberately thwarted any attempt by the indigenous population to take advantage of their numerical strength and rights of origin to destabilize the old guard's privileged power position— a political system best described as oligarchic democracy.

A core member of the True Whig Party and Tubman's vice president for nineteen years (1952–1971), the succeeding President William Tolbert demonstrated contradictory tendencies of reform and continuation of settler oligarchic legacy. Attempting to restructure state administration, Tolbert initially sought to "dismantle Tubman's extensive patronage network and to replace it with a formal and rational civil service of Tolbert loyalists" (Levitt 2005, 192). In extending the rationalization of administration to internal affairs, the president attempted to abandon Tubman's informal ties with traditional rulers in favor of more impersonal rules of conduct such as regular elections to the position of chieftaincy, although retaining the powerful position of Supreme Zo. And to express his government's commitment to protecting civil rights and free speech, he disbanded the powerful PRO system and ordered the release of political prisoners incarcerated by Tubman, including former diplomat Henry Boima Fahnbullah. Tolbert's tolerance of civil society led to the emergence of numerous associations, the most influential being the Movement for Justice in Africa (MOJA) founded by Togba Nah Tipoteh and the Progressive Alliances of Liberians (PAL) organized in the United States by Gabriel Baccus Matthews. MOJA, in particular, was a left-wing Pan-Africanist movement based on the University of Liberia campus and with a leader of an ethnic Kru origin. But it soon became inevitable that these new social forces (the majority being indigenous and settler youth) were headed for a collision course with country's old guard and its robust oligarchic political culture.

As soon as criticisms of the political establishment began targeting government officials who were close to the presidency and family members with strategic political and economic holdings, Tolbert invoked emergency state powers to suppress the expression of critical opinions. Among the notorious examples of the president's interference with the judiciary were the $250,000 libel lawsuit against journalist Albert Porte won by his brother Stephen Tolbert and the Supreme Court's banning of a popular newspaper known as *Revelation*. Once it became increasingly clear that independent candidate Amos Sawyer was going to put up a formidable challenge to the establishment's candidate in the November 1979 mayoral election in Monrovia, the proposed election was indefinitely postponed and property requirements for voting rights enforced. However, the increasing political consciousness and activism were never reversed until the brutal overthrow of Tubman ended Americo-Liberian domination.

Contrary to the colonial domination paradigm, this early historical evidence suggests that protectorate administration under indirect rule in both countries was not without active participation, local resistance, and agency of interior people. There were important violent uprisings among some traditional rulers who mobilized their people to protest against what they perceived as the deceptiveness of friendship treaties, illegal punitive expeditions, brutality of Frontier Forces, and imposition of a hut tax without their consent. For instance, resistance to Americo-settler domination culminated in numerous deadly conflicts led by indigenous rulers in rural Liberia (Lewitt 2005). Starting with an embargo on trade with the colony, the Mende uprising in Sierra Leone equally turned out to be a brutal massacre of members of the Frontier Force, traders, missionaries, and Krios who were considered collaborators of colonial rule (Abraham 2003; Alie 1990). Growing disdain for chiefs and violations of local laws by European and Krio traders were precursors of what culminated in the famous 1898 Hut Tax War in the northern region of Sierra Leone (Wylie 1977). The violent Mende rebellion against protectorate rule was an outburst of accumulated discontent against the Frontier Police, who had become notorious for eroding traditional authority and abusing their powers to extort money from people and molest locals through arbitrary detention and public flogging (Abraham 2003).[5]

Although violent rebellions yielded to superior colonial authority, "Governor Cardew was taken by surprise because he never thought that the natives he so despised as savages had any institutions capable of this kind of organization" (Abraham 2003, 194). It also became clear that beyond formal declarations, the extension of state authority into interior areas would be fraught by ongoing contestation, resistance, and negotiation with traditional authorities and their people. The subversive spaces to plan local insurrections (such as secret society bushes), which were beyond the reach of a limited colonial state, would evolve into an unofficial realm of social order today from which traditional authorities bargain with, constrain, and challenge those at the center (Boone 2003).

These initial attempts to extend formal authority also raised profound legitimacy questions with far-reaching implications both for the modern statebuilding project and for rural governance in both countries. Initially, the impetus for declaring a protectorate over the hinterland was externally driven to meet the geostrategic and economic concerns of the colonial metropole instead of an effort to administer public service in local areas. By focusing on regulative and extractive functions, the few bureaucratic institutions that interior residents encountered were known only in terms of their coercive roles and centralized authority structures. While indirect rule conferred formal recognition to amenable traditional institutions, they were taken out of the precolonial norm of downward accountability and adopted the same imperial regulative agenda associated with the modern political economy (Mamdani 1996).

Furthermore, and perhaps more importantly, indirect rule introduced major structural changes that were to shape questions of citizenship, property rights, and access to justice in the post-colony. Based on this settler-colonial history, the local legal systems were bifurcated not only between formal English and customary law systems but also in terms of customary mechanisms within and outside the state-constituted system (Mamdani 1996). Apart from practices that were considered inconsistent with Anglo-Saxon law, limited settler-colonial state capacity left by default a vast swathe of territories under precolonial governance authority. Those in this marginalized realm were regarded as subjects of their local chiefdoms rather than citizens of a national state even after the declaration of a protectorate nationwide (Fanthorpe 2001, 2005). Reinforcing this dual notion of citizenship was the introduction of a segregated legal system defined in terms of the tensions between "native" and "non-native" and "indigene" and "stranger" identities. In terms of governance, settler-colonial legal development and indirect rule produced parallel structures of authority and the relationship between them would constitute a central dimension of the postcolonial/settler political order. The modernization agenda in both countries would be presided over by the "new" educated elites who have been exposed to Western law and interested in retaining hegemonic bureaucratic and political institutions left behind by their white or mulatto counterparts. At the same time, there are unsettled questions of how to deal with traditional legal systems and authorities that remained relevant to a majority population outside the modern state system.

POSTCOLONIAL RULE OF STATE LAW

In April 1980, a group of non-commissioned officers of the Liberian army capitalized on social grievances and assassinated President Tolbert in his living quarters of the Executive Mansion. Led by Master Sergeant Samuel K. Doe, the majority of the seventeen coup makers hailed from hinterland ethnic groups such as the Krahn, Dan, and Kru of southern and northcentral Liberia. In what seemed the purging of old guards, thirteen key officials of Tolbert's government were later publicly executed on a beach in Monrovia by a firing squad. At first sight, this coup appeared to signal the end of more than 150 years of settler domination of Liberian politics—the dawn of real Liberian independence for the majority indigenous population. But while the People's Redemption Council (PRC) was composed mainly of indigenous elites, it operated solely on military decrees and Doe himself was "a product of corrupt military culture steeped deep in the crooked fabric of the Liberian oligarchy" (Levitt 2005, 199). As a military junta, his government did not need popular legitimacy to consolidate power as liberal use of the gun could produce the same outcome (Sawyer 1992). Even when pressure from the Americans forced President Doe to call elections in October 1985, he turned to brute force to manipulate the polls under his National Democratic Party of Liberia (NDPL). In fact, Doe debarred from contesting the 1985 elections four presidential candidates from the hinterland, thereby effectively shutting down any possibility for the emergence of a formidable indigenous political movement (Harris 2012).

Doe's regime lacked any clear political ideology or agenda. Since its onset, development efforts were muted by a strong "impulse to satisfied personal greed by raids on the public treasury and use of the gun on people" (Sawyer 1992, 294). Doe fomented ethnic hatred against the Gio and Mano ethnic groups in the wake of an aborted coup plotted by a Gio descendant—Thomas Quiwonkpa. The killing of Quiwonkpa was accompanied by a systematic purge of members of the Gios and Manos (suspected sympathizers) from the military and other state institutions, using brutal extrajudicial means. Members of these two groups were subject to virulent and vicious attacks by the Krahn-dominated Armed Forces of Liberia (AFL), particularly in their homeland of Nimba and Grand Gedeh counties (Waugh 2011). In the meantime, some members of the Mandigo ethnic group were granted privileged access to commercial opportunities protected by the government. As Doe continued to incite ethnic antagonism, the majority of indigenous Liberians became enraged that political power had been appropriated and abused yet again in the name of ethnic differences (TRC 2010). Whereas ethnic identity had been used by the Americo-Liberian elite to exclude the majority indigenous population from enjoying equal citizenship rights in Liberia, the same ethno-political marker now served as the basis to eliminate Doe's perceived political opponents (Foster et al. 2009). Yet these disassociations from Doe's perverse ethnic politics did little to prevent Liberia's civil war from assuming a crucial ethnic dimension when it broke out in 1989. The 1989 Christmas Eve outbreak of war in Liberia, just as the one that followed in Sierra Leone two years later, could best be described as the cumulative effect of deep-seated political and socioeconomic grievances, notwithstanding the role of diamonds and other natural resources in their prolongation.

The struggle for independence in Sierra Leone was initially overshadowed by a colony-protectorate divide based on narrow ethno-regional interests that stymied the mobilization of collective nationalist opposition against colonial rule (Barrows 1976). Worried that democratic elections would tilt the balance of power in favor of the protectorate and leery of the ability of interior elites to take over from colonial rule, the Krios, who are descendants of freed slaves resident in the Freetown colony, wanted a separatist policy rather than independence for the entire country (Collier 1970). Other grievances raised by the Krios included the unequal land tenure system that prevented them from acquiring provincial land and the illegality of allowing British protected persons representation in the national Legislative Council meant only for British subjects (Collier 1970; Kup 1975; Wyse 1989).

Meanwhile, deteriorating Anglo-Krio relations meant that the colonial government was now willing to constitutionally rectify the colony-protectorate power imbalance by allowing traditional rulers ascendancy in national politics (Cartwright 1970). Starting with Governor Ransford Slater (1922–1927), the colonial administration began to recognize the need for protectorate representation in the colony-dominated legislature in proportion to its geographic size and contribution to the economy. The Protectorate Assembly was formed in 1946 as a deliberative body comprising mostly paramount chiefs and designed to advise the government on matters affecting the interior. Indirectly elected by an electoral college of traditional authorities, most of the protectorate seats were filled by paramount chiefs and this strategy of including traditional rulers in national politics formed the basis of fourteen seats reserved for paramount chiefs (one per district) in the current parliament.

The Western-educated protectorate elites wanted to challenge the growing national influence of traditional authorities, but they needed an alliance with chiefs to confront the hegemony of the colony. The Protectorate Educational Progressive Union (PEPU), which was originally a pressure group formed by the emerging interior educated class to press for greater representation, later became the Sierra Leone People's Party (SLPP), the first political party of Sierra Leone with a support base underwritten by chiefs in Mendeland. Moreover, the first cadre of educated protectorate elites were inextricably connected to the institution of chieftaincy by personal and kinship relations that have continued to reinforce itself. The origin of this connection relates to the fact that when Christian missionaries and the colonial government started extending formal education to the protectorate, enrolment in schools was limited to the sons and nominees of paramount chiefs.[6] For instance, Sir Milton Margai, the Durham-trained medical doctor who negotiated Sierra Leone's independence in 1961 and became the country's first prime minister, hailed from a ruling house in the southern district of Moyamba (Kilson 1966).[7] The second prime minister, Albert Margai, was an Inner Temple–trained lawyer and took over from his brother in 1964.

The Margais (particularly Albert Margai) introduced a certain brand of exclusionary tribal politics that blended patronage rule with coercive legal instruments in ways that put executive authority beyond judicial and legislative oversight. Albert Margai's 1965 Public Order Act, for example, made provisions for charges against seditious libel and guaranteed arbitrary powers of government during a state of emergency. His 1963 Local Court Act was intended "to amend the law related to local courts and to make certain consequential changes for the administration of justice in the provinces" (Local Court Act, No. 20, 1963). Yet he retained certain colonial provisions, such as supervision by the Ministry of Internal Affairs and the role of paramount chiefs in appointing court chairmen, in order to maintain executive control over law and order in chiefdoms and to politicize the local court system for partisan political benefits.

Notwithstanding his opposition to Albert Margai's earlier proposal for a one-party system, President Siaka Stevens (1978–1985) declared Sierra Leone a one-party state in 1978. This declaration of one-party rule was simply a formalization of what had existed in practice since the attainment of Republican status in 1971, which conferred on Stevens the title of presidency with enormous executive powers. He used the death penalty to eliminate opposition leaders, while the 1965 Public Order Act legalized arbitrary detentions, disappearances, and torture. The execution of Ibrahim Bash-Taqi,

Mohamed S. Fornah, and fourteen others in July 1975 on allegation of treason is a classic example of politically motivated trials stage-managed by Stevens. As heinous as these state-sponsored brutalities were, they must be interpreted as a continuation of colonial authoritarianism, Stevens's revisionist strategy to achieve regime security after three successive coups between 1967 and 1968 alone and considering the hollow foundation of constitutional governance and state authority laid by the departing British colonial government (Cox 1976). "From that weak start, Stevens was necessarily concerned with consolidation of power, which led to the development of a patrimonial system and one-party state" (Hanlon 2005, 1). As with the Tolbert and Doe regimes in Liberia that enjoyed American support for ideological reasons, it must also be noted that Stevens was in power during the Cold War period and his leftist-leaning policies and Soviet backing enabled him to continue colonial-style authoritarianism.

Although Stevens was notorious for consolidating ethnic politics based on a patronage system of material rewards in exchange for loyalty (like the colonial and postcolonial Margai regimes), he did effectively use coercive legal instruments to retard local development and grassroot opposition movements, all in a bid to keep maintaining tight state control over the social lives of people. Close supervision of the patronage system and accumulation of resources needed to keep the system operational also meant centralization of the extractive, regulative, and distributive instruments of the state. In 1972, the government abolished District Councils and instead set up an interim committee to make recommendations on how their functions and assets should be distributed among government departments against the recommendation of a Local Government Review Committee. Dubbed as the "era of chieftaincy petition," a large number of petitions full of trumped-up charges against chiefs known to have been supporters of the SLPP were filed with the Ministry of Internal Affairs, which in turn would call for commissions of inquiry into allegations (Tangri 1976, 1980). Ruling houses that gained power through government support opened the door for Stevens's APC (All People's Congress) party infiltration into SLPP strongholds, leading to bloody incidents, including the infamous Ndorgboryosoi rebellion of 1982.

Increasing reliance on state coercion rather than consent to rule and the quest for personal protection after retirement translated into Stevens's 1985 decision to handpick the head of the Armed Forces, Major-General J. S. Momoh, to succeed him. A northerner from the Limba ethnic group, Momoh's inept administration, before he was toppled by the military in 1992, was simply a continuation of Stevens's patronage politics centered on a small ruling ethnic coalition from his hometown, Binkolo. Unlike his predecessor, though, the IMF structural adjustment program coupled with dwindling rent from the mining sector meant patronage resources for

Momoh and his *Ekutay* ruling cronies were rapidly drying up. Shortage of patronage largesse to sustain patron-client networks and buy off dissatisfied elements contributed to the outbreak of the March 1991 insurgency and April 1992 coup, both capitalizing on chronic grievances against the ruling patrimonial elite (Reno 1997, 1998). Sierra Leone's civil war (1991–2002) was considered linked to Liberia because Charles Taylor made available a group of NPFL fighters to Foday Sankoh of the Revolutionary United Front (RUF) to launch a similar anti-government war in Sierra Leone beginning from the border districts of Pujehun and Kailahun in March 1991. In addition to the magnitude of wanton destruction (Hanlon 2005; HRW 2005), the Sierra Leone war, just as in Liberia, became an attack on authority structures of both formal and traditional leaders who were "perceived as part of the corrupt and decadent system that insurgents wanted" to eradicate (Alie 2004, 140).

POST-CONFLICT RULE OF LAW REFORM

On July 7, 1999, the Government of Sierra and RUF signed the final Peace Accord in the Togolese capital Lomé, but it was not until 2002 that President Kabbah declared the war officially over. At the core of the country's reconstruction agenda was rebuilding the rule of law, with support from donor partners, the UN, and other members of the international community (Gbla 2008). Donor assistance for establishing a broad justice sector reform strategy in Sierra Leone was spearheaded by its long-standing bilateral partner, the United Kingdom.[8] British intervention coincided with the formulation of the United Kingdom's new Africa Conflict Prevention Pool, announced by Her Majesty's Government in April 2001, as a coordinated approach for managing British overseas contribution toward prevention and reduction of violent conflict. While the International Military Advisory and Training Team (IMATT) was in charge of the military reforms, the Commonwealth Community Safety and Security Project (CCSSP) was to enhance the professional capacity of the Sierra Leone Police with British-born Keith Biddle as the country's first postwar Inspector-General. Aimed at restoring and strengthening the rule of law, the CCSSP resulted in the training of about 9,000 police officers, cadet courses at the Bramshill Police Training College in England, (re)building of police stations, and provision of logistics, including 155 Land Rovers, 158 motor bikes, 71 large and medium carriers, 10 ambulances, and 10 cars (Kargbo 2012). Institutions set up to improve on the performance and transparency of the criminal justice system included the Police Local Partnership Boards, Complaint, Discipline, and Internal Investigation Department (CDIID) as well as the Police Disciplinary Regulation Code.

Moving from postwar emergency to a coherent and integrated justice sector-wide strategy, DFID launched a Justice Sector Development Program (JSDP) that incorporated elements of both the CCSSP and an earlier Law Development Program in Sierra Leone. With a duration lasting from July 2005 to December 2011, JSDP was a £28 million project to "support the development of an effective and accountable justice sector that is capable of meeting the needs and interest of poor, marginalized, and vulnerable people" (DFID 2004). In pursuance of this goal, the Justice Sector Coordination Office (JSCO) was established within the Ministry of Justice to coordinate the implementation of the country's three integrated Justice Sector Reform Strategic and Investment Plans (JSRS&IP) 2008–2018. Launched in 2007, the first plan was intended to refocus justice sector priorities from the formal system to the delivery of primary justice, that is, semi-formal and informal justice systems at the community level. Acknowledging that the formal legal system remains inaccessible to 70 percent of the population, the strategy aimed to provide justice at the community level by ensuring that alternative systems of delivering justice were properly functional, in accordance with international standards, and under effective formal oversight (Government of Sierra Leone 2007). Succeeding JSDP was the Access of Security and Justice Program (ASJP), a five-year program (2011–2016) designed to align with the Government's JSRS&IP. ASJP aimed "to consolidate peace and stability by increasing access to responsive, accountable, and effective security and justice services, especially for the poor, vulnerable, and those living in remote and marginalized areas."[9]

These programs were managed by the British Council and a total of seventeen different projects were implemented to develop legislative and policy frameworks as well as enhance the human resource and management capacity of the justice sector to improve access to justice for vulnerable groups (DFID 2011). In addition to producing a sector-wide integrated justice reform strategy, infrastructural development included construction of two new prisons, ninety-four accommodation units for prison staff, three new court buildings in Freetown, fifteen new Police Family Support Units, and two juvenile facilities (DFID 2011). Among the new courts in Freetown is the Fast-Track Commercial Court, fully automated to ensure speed, efficiency, and transparency in dealing with commercial disputes. A Judicial and Legal Training Institute has also been established to provide continuous judicial education to judges and magistrates (Awareness Times 2009). In allocating JSDP funds for sector groups, 60 percent of the total program budget was for legal and judicial development, 30 percent for public sector and administrative management, and 10 percent for public finance management. In collaboration with other agencies such as the UNDP and United Nations Mission in Sierra Leone (UNAMSIL), new courts and residences for judges have been built and existing ones refurbished in regional headquarter towns outside Freetown.

In addition to justice sector reform, Sierra Leone also underwent a transitional justice (TJ) process, commonly associated with two internationalized formal institutions—the Truth and Reconciliation Commission (TRC) and Special Court for Sierra Leone (SCSL). While the TRC was established to foster restorative justice and reconciliation, the SCSL was mandated to hold criminally accountable those bearing greatest responsibility for the country's brutal civil war (1991–2002).[10] The Special Court was empowered to prosecute persons responsible for crimes against humanity, war crimes, intentional attacks on civilians and peacekeepers, and the conscription of children (SCSL Statute 2002). Although the court was to prosecute offenses relating to the abuse of girls and wanton destruction of private and public property under Sierra Leonean law (Article 5), it referred to international treaties and conventions for serious violations of humanitarian law, including the Geneva Conventions and the Additional Protocol II. Attracting more international attention than the TRC, the Special Court's initial budget of $75 million was quadrupled to $300 million in December 2013 when it formerly closed (Gberie 2014). The court had a permanent staff of 422 (mostly foreign nationals) and 11 judges were paid $240,000 tax free per annum along with huge allowances (Gberie 2014). After the trial of former President Charles Taylor of Liberia was transferred to The Hague, it took approximately nine years and $250 million to be concluded (Keating 2012).

As in neighboring Sierra Leone, Liberia's justice reform is supported by donor funding and technical assistance, more so from the United Nations Mission in Liberia (UNMIL) and the United States. Reflecting America's long-standing relations with Liberia, parties to the comprehensive peace agreement (CPA) had requested that the United States play a lead role in restructuring the post-conflict state of Liberia. This request coincided with growing American interest under the Bush administration to deal with failed states in Africa to prevent the spread of terrorism and other transnational organized crimes (US Department of States 2010). Following the 2005 election victory of Ellen Johnson-Sirleaf, the US government launched a broad-based, multifaceted rule of law program designated to help plant the foundation for rebuilding Liberia's devastated justice and economic systems (USAID 2009, 2010). In general, overall funding in the Liberian rule of law sector was estimated to cost about $13 million annually and the US government unilaterally contributed approximately half of this amount (USAID 2009). In a 2009 review commissioned by the USAID, it is noted that in a three-year period the United States spent $25,545,505 on rule of law programming in areas of advocacy and public awareness, capacity and institution building, and enhancing access to justice (USAID 2009).

Justice sector development constituted part of Liberia's postwar Governance and Economic Management Assistance Program (GEMAP) rather than the separate sector-focused strategy implemented in Sierra Leone. Unlike Sierra Leone, where an internationalized tribunal was established to prosecute warlords, the international community was less interested in criminal accountability in Liberia, even though comparable mass atrocities were committed during its civil war. Instead of commitment to accountability measures, donor-supported reconstruction efforts of particularly the United States were intended to restore political stability in the West African subregion and strengthen national institutions to maintain domestic law and order. US funding was channeled through the Department of Justice (which had a Resident Legal Advisor placed within the US Embassy in Liberia), the Pacific Architects and Engineers (PAE, for a team of on-the-ground legal advisors assisting various government institutions), the American Bar Association (ABA, working with the Judicial Institute of Liberia), the Carter Centre (focused on traditional justice and mediation systems), and Dyncorp International (contracted by the State Department to train Liberia's military and security forces). Technical guidance to most American rule of law programs came from the Bureau of International Narcotics and Law Enforcement Affairs (INL), whose primary objectives are "to improve judicial and law enforcement effectiveness, bolster accountability and transparency of criminal justice agencies, and institutionalize respect for human rights and the rule of law" (US Department of States 2010). Other US-based institutions attracted to Liberia include the Millennium Challenge Corporation, which is "promoting" the rule of law through its governance scorecard that has six so-called "ruling justly" and eight "economic freedom" indicators.

Substantially, more programmatic activity was aimed at capacity-building of various justice sector institutions and awareness raising on issues related particularly to gender equality and women's rights (USAID 2009). The Justice Sector Support Project (JSSL), implemented by PAE, created a wide range of training materials that American law fellows utilized in a series of training activities for judicial officers and court administrators. ABA assisted the Supreme Court and Judicial Institute of Liberia to train a new group of judges, lawyers, and court staff on the operation of proper justice systems (US Department of States 2010). Emphasis on protecting women within the criminal justice system culminated in the creation of the Sexual and Gender Based Violent Crime Unit in the police force (Pewee and Reeves 2010). For its part, the Resident Legal Advisor (noted above) was hired to work on anti-corruption matters, leading to the development of legal and ethical infrastructure for creating a unit to investigate, prosecute, or prevent public corruption. Unlike transitional justice processes in Sierra Leone, which was more comprehensively designed to foster both criminal accountability and forgiveness, Liberia's formal TJ agenda focused only on establishing a truth commission—the Liberian Truth and Reconciliation Commission.

Despite these reform interventions, the overwhelming majority of those who participated in this study (as all the evaluation studies conducted since the beginning of post-conflict reform almost two decades ago) indicate that state institutions remain largely unaccountable to Sierra Leoneans and Liberians. While formal justice actors have been involved in these donor-funded capacity-building programs, none of the thirty interviewed in this study seemed to believe such programs have meaningfully impacted the effective administration of justice. A senior judge who worked closely with DFID-funded Law Development Project and JSDP in Sierra Leone said that "they have poured a lot of resources into the formal system under the English law," and yet "the vehicles are not there, salaries still very low, and poor case file and time management."[11] Sitting in a poorly ventilated and paper-congested law court office that "still lacks water supply," he admits that "we still don't know how best to ensure that cases are heard speedily and in a timely manner."[12] A lawyer in Freetown cited "a couple of small innovations, including a fast-track commercial court which is trying to give the impression that we are able to resolve commercial cases speedily so that investors would feel confident to come into the country," adding that "they put in some real money into it."[13] Another senior judge in Liberia remembered only the "conduct of training, workshops, and seminars for law school graduates, magistrates, city solicitors, and public defenders."[14] Cynically describing rule of law reform programs as "library funding" provided to international and local professionals, a private legal practitioner, whose experience is similar to the majority of lawyers interviewed, summarized the standard practice as such:

> First of all, those who give the funds are not patient and they come with a particular mindset. They set their terms and conditions either in London or Washington, come with a package, and they want to roll it out on their own terms and timelines. This is library funding: you bring the money, seminars are conducted, reports are written, and salaries are paid to those who bring these monies because they have to pay mortgages abroad. I have received funds from donors but I have always told them not to come and prescribe.[15]

Those who use a problem-solving approach have extensively documented the reasons why rule of law reform in Sierra Leone and Liberia has failed to significantly improve governance in both countries and their findings are often consistent with the broader neoliberal institutionalist literature. Issues related to withdrawal of donor funding, uncoordinated and duplicated efforts, unsustainable interventions, hubris and arrogance of interveners, cost of expatriates, lack of political will and commitment to reform, deep-seated corruption and incompetence, lack of local ownership, and so on were also confirmed by participants in this study. After stating that the language of "country leadership, country ownership, and sustainability" in the Paris Declaration has become a cliché in donor lexicon, one local consultant noted that donors "sometimes have fallen prey of the nuances of primitive political processes, the partisanship, politicization, etc."[16] But despite these failures in international efforts to rebuild the rule of law as a principle of good governance, legal and judicial reforms have largely succeeded in restoring and strengthening the postcolonial state as I discuss below, looking at both the international and domestic dimensions of restoration.

RESTORATION OF RELATIONS WITH THE INTERNATIONAL COMMUNITY

Although the international community's renewed attention to peacekeeping and peacebuilding in these "West African tragic twins" in the late 1990s was desperately needed (Adebajo 2004), the postwar efforts to rebuild the rule of law restored and consolidated each country's relationship with Western powers without questioning their historical origins. Both the United States and the United Kingdom reemerged as leading external actors with an image of a peacekeeper, peacebuilder, and reformer that had nothing to do with the structural and political violence that culminated in civil war in both countries. The dominant narrative framed America's new foreign policy as part of the Bush administration's effort to prevent failed states from becoming a breeding ground for terrorism and other transnational organized crimes that may threaten international peace and security. It was also seen as a moment for the Americans to demonstrate moral leadership in Africa with the appointment of Rev. Jesse Jackson as US Special Envoy for the Promotion of Democracy in Africa. The United States played an influential role in funding the Special Court of Sierra Leone as well as shaping its mandate and operations with the court's first prosecutor being the American-born David Crane. At the time, the limited jurisdiction of the Special Court was used by American foreign policy experts and politicians in their opposition to the nascent ICC, whose broader and permanent jurisdiction was considered as a threat to US sovereignty to act as a global hegemonic power. Likewise, the UK Prime Minister Tony Blair and his Labour Government's assistance to Sierra Leone coincided with Blair's new "ethical foreign policy" in Africa, which included initiatives such as the African Conflict Prevention Pool, Commission for Africa, and the New African Initiative. Britain's objectives in Sierra Leone were regarded as purely humanitarian: promotion of peace in a former colony in line with the UN peacebuilding agenda and promotion of prosperity based on the neoliberal assumption that economic growth may induce peace (Kargbo 2012).

These dominant moralized discourses about Western intervention were rooted in specific causal explanations of civil wars in West Africa, including who was perceived as most responsible and what form of justice should be pursued to address the legacies of atrocity crimes. Both countries were often cited as examples of failed states in Africa; that is, they once had functional governance systems that collapsed due to breakdowns of central and local administrative structures (International Crisis Group 2004). The literature on contemporary agrarian or peasant rebellion, which links political violence to a crisis in rural patrimony, is based on research conducted in the Manor River basin where these countries are located (Richards 1996, 2005; Mokuwa et al. 2011). Sierra Leone's TRC report attributes the country's civil war to demolition of the rule of law, a process initiated by Prime Minister Albert Margai and pursued to violent levels by subsequent authoritarian rulers, particularly President Stevens (Vol. 3A, Cap 2). Liberia's TRC report notes that the country's "conflict has its origin in the history and founding of the Liberian modern state," but only as an additional finding just as its counterpart in Sierra Leone says very little about the link between British colonialism and political violence in the post-colony (TRC 2009, 17). The Special Court was required to produce a narrative of atrocity crimes that was solely internal to Sierra Leone and Liberia as if their warlords and autocrats emerged only in postcolonial/settler times. As in Sierra Leone, the dominant narrative is post-settler, insisting that the modern state of Liberia collapsed in the 1980s, followed by a civil war that ravaged the country until 2005.

In both countries, this characterization of political conflict not only fails to significantly historicize problems intrinsic to the modern state (including its colonial and settler origins) but is also unable to challenge its legal and normative frameworks in which reforms are implemented (Kurz 2010). By minimizing or ignoring the settler-colonial history of state formation in each country, the TJ narrative not only prevented their historical relations with Western powers from being scrutinized but, in presenting themselves as proponent of post-atrocity justice, these powers also became the liberal-democratic models Sierra Leone and Liberia must again aspire to become. Although his research focuses on security sector reform, Dyck equally finds biases in "policy-oriented and problem-solving" narratives that fail to "problematise both countries' historical experiences with Western countries and question the sociohistorical structures" created during settler-colonial domination (2013, 81). He notes that postcolonial states have been maintained as the primary means of economic accumulation and power with little modifications to the preexisting colonial structures and without any interrogation of the political and ideological motivations of external patrons who collaborated with a narrow group of local elites. Yet how could TJ interventions, which were predominantly funded by the United States and the United Kingdom, advance narratives that foreground the role of these powers in establishing unjust state structures and producing a ruling class that perpetuated heinous violations in the name of accessing or preserving political power? In addition to undercutting the new ethical foreign policies of the Blair and Bush administrations, such TJ discourses that require dismantling the postcolonial state itself would be inconceivable to the international community's statebuilding as peacebuilding strategy in both countries.

Restoring a relationship with the international community, which does not question the colonial past or modern state system, also meant that new war-to-peace transitional leaders in both countries would buy into the dominant rule of law promotion agenda. Most of the early postwar statebuilding efforts in Sierra Leone took place during the eleven-year SLPP rule (1996–2007) under President Tejan Kabbah, who was an example of contemporary African leaders' ability to combine donor expectation about institution building and the interests of a dominant ruling class. On assuming power, Kabbah represented one of those senior African international bureaucrats whose return to the continent after professional experience abroad in the late 1990s was central to the international community's response to the political leadership crisis that was evident in some countries just after the Cold War. Considering the reputational problems of home-based autocratic leaders, Kabbah, who had worked for the UNDP as a senior administrator for over twenty years, was by default the favorite candidate for the international community working in war-torn Sierra Leone.

Likewise, the first postwar presidential election of Liberia (October 2005) was won by Madam Ellen Johnson-Sirleaf, a Harvard-trained economist and former official of the UN and World Bank. It was under the leadership of Johnson-Sirleaf, who returned to the country with enormous international backing, that Liberia's immediate postwar recovery agenda would be implemented. While in power, Madam Sirleaf gained a reputation as one of the West's most favorite African leaders for embracing neoliberal governance reforms, particularly those promoted by the United States as this respondent in Monrovia admitted.

And the international community endorses this as seen by the Nobel Peace Prize. The fundamental reason why this country is in a mess is that its educational system trains people to be more American than Americans themselves. In a statement to the US Congress the president ended by saying I would make you Americans proud of me. How about Nimba county or people in Monteserado county?[17]

Focused on access to justice for ordinary Liberians (see chapter 6), this respondent is asking questions related to an assumption that is hardly questioned in the literature: the idea that rule of law interventions are designed purely in the interest of those appressed by power. In Sierra Leone and Liberia, the politics of reform meant that interveners were not merely benevolent peacebuilders, concerned only about justice and peace abroad without any ideological and political interests to preserve. When Madam Sirleaf told the US Congress that she would make America proud, it did not mean that she was less interested in seeking justice and peace for Liberians. Rather, it meant that her administration's postwar recovery agenda would remain consistent with America's conception of peace and liberal values, even if this meant silencing its complicity in Americo-Liberian domination and oppression that lasted for more than a century. As with Sierra Leone's relationship with the United Kingdom, the government of Liberia not only removed America's past from TJ processes but also wanted to make the United States proud as post-conflict legal reconstruction was being carried out under American tutelage.

Of course, Western foreign policies in West Africa did not always align with the priorities of national governments that had dual commitment to accepting international rule of law standards at the same time protecting the interest of a ruling class whose survival often rests on close patrimonial connection with traditional authorities. As the British, more than the Americans, were particularly poised to promote liberal-democratic values, this tension was more evident in the Kabbah–Blair relations. For instance, the DFID initially supported President Kabbah's proposal to restore and reinforce the institution of chieftaincy through the Paramount Chief Restoration Programme (PCRP) but then rescinded the program when public concern about supporting a traditional mode of dominance appeared to conflict with Blair's ethical foreign policy image in Africa. As this example shows, whenever such tensions emerged, reform becomes a compromise between donor concerns and those of national governments, depending on the latter's degree of dependence on the former, which was extremely high for both Sierra Leone and Liberia in the postwar period.

RESTORING THE POSTCOLONIAL STATE

Meanwhile, post-conflict rule of law reforms in Sierra Leone and Liberia succeeded in restoring some of "the same old men who were responsible for the war, both in government and a reinstated chieftaincy system" (Hanlon 2005, 1). In general, reform interventions, which stressed restoration and strengthening of national justice systems, turned out to have increased the capacity and functionality of the state as the primary means to access and consolidate power, often through coercive and exclusionary practices. Whereas reformers view legal and judicial reforms as placing institutional limits on the exercise of power, leaders in both countries see the rule of state law as an instrument to redistribute power, reconfigure a local ruling coalition, legitimate ruling party policies, enforce law and order, and delegitimize organized or individual opposition. As in the periods of colonial-settler and postcolonial/settler rule, the determination of who wins and who loses in the reform process is largely based on the political calculus of the ruling class, at the central and local levels.

In the context of central-local power relations, the legal and judicial reforms are an effective regulatory mechanism used by central authorities to gain control over local population and resources, although its use is often based on the political cost that local leaders can impose. One civil society leader in Sierra Leone, who was implementing a Christian Aid–funded Chiefdom Governance Reform project, did not hesitate to mention that "the whole aspect of human rights reform is about power balancing."[18] New laws such as the 2011 Local Court Act have criminalized the judicial functions of local chiefs, transfer supervision of local courts from the Ministry of Internal Affairs to the Ministry of Justice, and prohibited the application of customary law in Freetown. Traditional authorities (local chiefs and tribal heads) perceive such efforts to extend the rule of law into chiefdom administration as the most significant legal development in the history of chieftaincy in Sierra Leone. A total of sixty out of sixty-five traditional authorities interviewed in this research (across the three provinces of Sierra Leone and Freetown) disagree with the decision to concentrate judicial authority for applying customary law into the formal justice department. Be they ceremonial or modern chiefs and from paramount to town chiefs, these authorities expressed strong disapproval of the move described as an attempt by the central state to undermine the institution of chieftaincy that is distrusted by some members of the international community.

The leadership of the National Council of Paramount Chiefs expressed serious concern about the creation of parallel authority structures when local court chairmen become autonomous agents answerable to regional committees instead of local paramount chiefs.[19] This concern about the creation of competing authority structures resonates with all senior chiefs in all chiefdoms who perceived an independent court chairman as a threat to their monopoly over the use of coercive power in their chiefdom as this comment illustrates.

This has been the trend throughout history to move the courts from the control of the chiefs. It started in 1938 when Native Administration was introduced with this court system as one of its features. From that point, we had gradual changes all tending to move chiefs away from these courts. Under the 1963 Act, the paramount chiefs had some influence because they nominate those who became court chairmen. But today, even before the 2011 Act, that responsibility was shared between the MP and chiefdom councils. The long and short of this is that the court is being moved from being owned by the people.[20]

Unlike the UK-supported legal reform in Sierra Leone, Liberia has maintained its prewar institutional arrangement including a dual justice system whereby the rules of customary laws are applied separately by traditional chiefs and local government officials alongside the formal justice system that interprets the formal English law. However, by placing a premium on statist reforms, postwar reconstruction has left almost intact the 1905 Rules and Regulations Governing the Hinterland, which placed traditional justice systems under the Ministry of Internal Affairs. Maintaining the application of customary law under the supervision of an executive ministry has been an attempt by peacebuilders to relegate traditional justice practices as an abnormal or inferior form of "administrative justice" in the same way that Americo-Liberian colonialism regarded them as inferior "native court practices" to be civilized by the superior state system. If the matter requires judicial action, the Minister of Legal Affairs would make a request to the police or law courts to act accordingly, which means subordinating customary law to the rule of state law. Consequently, the majority of fifty Liberians who participated in this study (particularly those of indigenous and rural origin) perceived the restoration of post-conflict state structures reminiscent of the colonial statebuilding project that protected Americo-Liberian elite interest as this comment indicates.

> We still going around begging for donations when the resources are here. So what is this bankruptcy of thoughts? Public funds are being diverted for private use. We have not learned from the war as expected and one of the reasons is that this president has brought mostly Liberians in America who are keen to grab without any love for the country, nation and people. They are just interested in grabbing and to live abroad.[21]

To be sure, Sierra Leone and Liberia have implemented many legal reform programs in the name of protecting and advancing the civil and political rights of the citizenry. The problem though is that the elitist, centralized, hierarchical, and formalized nature of those reforms ends up reconstructing a legal system that is more suited for protecting state officials than preserving the rights of citizens, even when state authorities do not blatantly violate the law. What makes this strategy particularly pernicious is that, absent any dismantling of postcolonial state structures, rebuilding the state capacity equals consolidation of the ruling class (often aligned to a dominant ethnic group or region) to acquire more resources and power against the opposition. As Kandeh (2012) argues, this result is inevitable because in both countries the state and ruling class have not been decoupled and state officials make no distinction between public power and private wealth. It explains why, as the Sierra Leone Police was being equipped and trained by the British to become "a force for good," it overzealously enforced the 1965 Public Order Act against opposition parties, labor unions, student associations, and the general public, killing about nine people and injuring over eighty through the use of excessive (sometimes lethal) force in the first postwar decade (Amnesty International 2019). Similarly, a study in Liberia notes that "while rule of law training programmes enhanced security of property rights and reduced the incidence of some types of crimes," such programs "did not improve trust in the police, courts, or governments more generally" (Blair et al. 2019, 641). As this respondent stressed, no one should be surprised at these outcomes, when rule of law reform prioritizes capacity-building over access to justice.

> Donor projects have been more about providing training, providing computers, and giving police officers new uniforms, batons, and boots. It is to bureaucratise the system. There is more consistency and predictability because the laws are codified and precedence should be followed. But the trust issue is still a problem. Because of the nature of the state architecture, it is such that the Vice-President is the head of the Police Council, which creates room for the institution to be politicised. What is needed is that critical shift from training and materials to behaviour change.[22]

In terms of the modern state architecture, which has been reinstated by rule of law reform, the legal system in both countries draws from a deliberate combination of US presidential constitutionalism and the British common law tradition to ensure special protection of the ruling class. In addition to the concentration of power, these institutional structures have always been carefully (re)configured to ensure that the executive is positioned to influence judicial and law enforcement agencies. Reminiscent of British colonial administrative structures, such fusion of executive and judicial powers is embodied in the Office of the Attorney General and Minister of Justice, headed by an official who is both a cabinet minister and principal legal adviser to the government, qualified to be a justice of the Supreme Court. Even though it is part of the cabinet, this office oversees all offenses prosecuted in the name of the Republic of Sierra Leone while supervising the administration of the courts and other judicial mechanisms responsible for carrying out those prosecutions. Similarly, the Ministry of Internal Affairs (which is traditionally headed by the head of state himself) performs a supervisory role over the Sierra Leone Police and prison agencies that conduct criminal investigations, prosecute criminal matters, and enforce judicial verdicts. At the regional level, the regional customary law officer who supervises the local court system is also the official legal counsel, that is, the attorney representing state interests outside Freetown.

Unlike Sierra Leone, where fusion of power is common, Liberia's constitution enshrines principles for separation of powers and checks and balances, forbidding any public official in one branch of government from holding office or exercising any of the powers assigned to other branches. A double legislative oversight of executive authority, the Liberian Parliament is a bicameral structure with a Senate and House of Representatives, both coequally involved in the legislative process. Yet, as in Sierra Leone, the structures of power in Liberia remain highly centralized and elitist, with Monrovia as the center of legal, judicial, and executive power. Legal reform efforts reaffirm the authority of an executive president who is the head of state, Head of Government, and Commander-in-Chief of the Armed Forces. While there are local administrative units responsible for implementing state policies at the subnational level, these functionaries and agents usually serve at the pleasure of the central government. For example, each superintendent of Liberia's fifteen counties (i.e., administrative divisions that are subdivided into districts and clans) is appointed by the president. Although the Constitution calls for the election of majors and paramount chiefs, these positions have been filled by presidential appointments from 1985 to date. In both countries, this hierarchical organization of legal and bureaucratic structures allows for what is commonly known as "orders from above," that is, executive control through institutional power.

Considering the common law's deference to precedent, conservatism, and formal-legalism, the ruling class in both countries have found the judiciary as convenient arena to make otherwise politically controversial decisions, silence critical opinions, and attack the opposition. For example, in a very controversial move, President Ernest Bai Koroma welcomed a lawsuit by his former VP Sam Sumana whom he had sacked in September 2015. Ignoring efforts by the West African Network for Peacebuilding to mediate the conflict, the matter was brought before the Supreme Court to decide whether the president had the constitutional authority to relieve the VP of his duties without recourse to a parliamentary impeachment procedure laid out in Sections 50 and 51 of the 1991 Constitution. Apart from relying on ten of the country's most renown lawyers for his defense, the president may have counted on the conservatism of the judiciary, which lacks any precedent of challenging executive authority. Also, in a last desperate attempt to maintain power, the APC party (through one of its members, also a lawyer) requested the High Court for an interim injunction, resulting in a postponement of the runoff presidential election scheduled for March 27, 2018, although they lost the election. Adopting the same judicial maneuver and relying on the judicial precedent, the newly elected SLPP government petitioned the election result of fourteen opposition parliamentarians and, in their absence, hastily elected an SLPP Speaker of Parliament, despite lacking the majority of legislative seats according to the 2018 polls.

Another characteristic of the system is to provide ordinary citizens legal recourse in theory while including a series of legal and administrative bottlenecks which favor the state—and, by extension, the ruling elite. For example, the notion of *locus standi*, which bestows the right to bring an action or be heard in court, is among the prominent procedural norms used to declare a case against state authorities as inadmissible. While the burden is on the complainant to prove valid reason to appear before the court, the judge has discretion to dismiss the matter without considering the merit of the case. This was the fate of the Sierra Leone Association of Journalists' (SLAJ) lawsuit against the Attorney General and Minister of Justice to challenge the constitutionality of the criminal libel provision of the 1965 Public Order Act, which was repealed only recently (OSIWA and Suma 2014). Without adjudicating the merit of journalists' concerns, the Supreme Court ruled that SLAJ did not have the *locus standi* to initiate an action because the organization itself was not under threat by the law in question. When the Minister of Information at the time, Ibrahim Ben Kargbo, was questioned about the government's failure to repeal the Public Order Act as promised, he stated that the matter was out of government's hands as soon as SLAJ filed a lawsuit (VOA, 28 December 2009). To transfer all controversial questions to the judiciary, he said, "we are running a system of separation of powers and once a journalist took the government to court, it became *sub judicé* and we could not discuss it anymore" (VOA, 28 December 2009). To further restrict legal proceedings against government officials, the State Proceeding Act, which requires a complainant to serve a three-month written notification to the Attorney General, was passed in 2000. Section 18 of the Act stipulates that no court may compel the government or its officials to undergo restitution, even if they lose a suit brought against them.

Despite an international reputation as a human rights defender (including a Nobel Peace Prize), the administration of Johnson-Sirleaf in Liberia adopted legal and judicial strategies to protect the ruling elites in ways reminiscent of practices in Sierra Leone. Throughout her two terms in office, "impunity for individuals who committed atrocities during the civil wars as well as for those responsible for current and continuing crimes" remained a serious problem (US State Department 2017, 20). For example, Liberia's TRC found that high-profile politicians were responsible for war crimes, crimes against humanity, and economic crimes during the period of civil war. To promote accountability, the Commission recommended the establishment of an Extraordinary Criminal Tribunal to prosecute those responsible for such egregious crimes, including the leaders of all warring factions. For lesser crimes, the Commission requested the Ministry of Justice to empower existing domestic courts and called for public sanctions "intended to redress impunity, ensure accountability, and maintain integrity in public service" (TRC 2009, 360). When the president and other politicians realized that their names were among the forty-nine recommended for public sanction—including a ban from public office for thirty years—the report was immediately discredited as unconstitutional (Human Rights Watch 2011).

On corruption and crony capitalism, one human rights report noted that whereas the government dismissed or suspended some officials implicated in corruption cases, "it tended to recommend prosecution only against low-level civil servants" (US Department of States 2017, 20). Among high-ranking officials suspected of corruption were family members and close associates of the president, including her three sons: Charles Sirleaf, Deputy Governor of the Central Bank; Robert Sirleaf, Senior Adviser and Chairman of the National Oil Company of Liberia (NOCAL); and Fombah Sirleaf, Head of the National Security Agency (NSA). In October 2014, the Justice Minister Christiana Tah resigned, claiming that the president impeded her investigation into an allegation of fraud against the NSA (US Department of State 2017). This comment by a High Court Justice in Monrovia deserves to be quoted lengthily because it eloquently summarizes how the modern law operates in Liberia in contrast to pre-settler traditional systems of accountability and why legal reform cannot be a substitute for significant structural change.

Here in Liberia, they pass laws for the governed not for the governors. You hear people say that they are above the law. Justice here has been about the extent to which one is in a position to influence the judiciary. But this is not the traditional way of resolving conflict. According to the traditional system, your punishment tends to be more severe when you broke the law, if you are the son of chief, high priest, or chief zoe as we call some of them here because it is assumed that you ought to know better. You should set an example. That was our strong traditional system. But in the modern system, the president's son is above the law and the closer you are to the center of power the more likely you would get justice as against one who is far away from the center of power. So justice operates in the reverse order in the current system. As simple as it may sound, this is one of the greatest problems facing the judiciary. It calls for a change of attitude and this change cannot take place within the context of the same old system that has perpetuated the order of corruption. It calls for a change of attitude, a new concept of justice, a new way of seeing life itself.[23]

Also, while reforming the justice system is aimed at enhancing its judicial independence (which remains highly questionable), there is relatively little attention to issues of judicial accountability. Judges wield enormous discretionary powers in administering bail policies and handing down judgments, even though there is limited room for decentralized public oversight of decisions such as who qualifies to sit on the bench and how they are promoted.[24] Operating a justice system that is protected from public scrutiny and bereft of a decentralized accountability machinery positions judicial officials to taking "orders from above," particularly in a political system where the executive equally wields enormous power. As discussed in the next chapter, such politics of legal and judicial reforms, which is rooted in the coloniality of English law and reestablishment of dominant state structures, also serves the dominant political economy.

NOTES

1. The initial ordinances included Protectorate Courts Ordinances No. 20 of 1896 and No. 11 of 1897; Protectorate Court Ordinance No. 33 of 1901, which repealed the two Ordinances of 1896 and 1897; and the Protectorate Courts Jurisdiction Ordinance No. 6 of 1903 (Cap. 169 in the 1925 Edition of the Laws, which was repealed by the Native Courts Ordinance No. 40 of 1932).

2. A definition of "native" was inserted in the Protectorate Ordinance (Cap. 185) by the amending Ordinance No. 15 of 1949. The term means any member of the aboriginal races or tribes of Africa ordinarily resident within the Protectorate or within the territories adjacent thereto outside Sierra Leone. Non-natives include Europeans, Syrians, and Krios or Sierra Leoneans at the time. Non-natives later became known as strangers in the interior (Brooke 1953).

3. The first settlers were later joined by other emigrants, including free-born African Americans from Virginia, North Carolina, New York, Philadelphia, and Rhode Island as well as "recaptured" Africans liberated on the high seas by American naval vessels. Members of the second group (recaptives) were mainly from the Congo Basin (hence, the Congoes), where slave ships bound for America were intercepted following the abolition of slave trade in the United States.

4. Starting here, the term "Americo-Liberian" will be used to refer essentially to the ruling political and economic elites of the broader settler group whom, Nelson (1985) notes, constituted no more than 10 percent—about 1,500 to 2,000 people—of the entire Americo-Liberian population during the Tubman and Tolbert eras. It is important to note that, despite their common heritage, majority of Americo-Liberians belong to the non-elite class during the heydays of settler domination.

5. The British Frontier Police Force was established in January 1890 with the sole objective of ensuring peace and stability and protecting trade routes in the hinterland. The initial authorized strength of the force was 1 Inspector-General, 3 Inspectors, 4 Sub-Inspectors, and 280 other rank-and-file members drawn mostly from indigenous

young men. The officers were prohibited from interfering with local politics and dis-respecting traditional rulers. But taking advantage of the lack of effective command and control, officers constituted themselves into judges and petty despots wreaking havoc in the interior (Alie 1990).

6. For example, when the colonial government founded the Bo School for boys in 1906 as the first secondary school in the protectorate, an official notice announcing its opening stated that the school's main objective was to educate sons and nominees of paramount chiefs who were expected to take over chiefdom administration from their fathers as literate personnel (Kilson 1966).

7. It must be noted that the Margai ruling house is an example of modern external invention of chieftaincy as this family is one of the ruling houses that gained political ascendancy at the behest of the central colonial authorities. This controversy over the legitimacy of ruling houses was a central issue even in the recently concluded 2010 chieftaincy election that pitted the Russell ruling house against the Margais who have occupied chieftaincy in the Moyamba Chiefdom of Lower Banta for more than a century.

8. Other donors included the United Nations Development Program (UNDP), the World Bank, and the United Nations Mission in Sierra Leone (UNAMSIL), USAID and US Embassy, and the International Committee for the Red Cross.

9. See https://www.dai.com/our-work/projects/sierra-leone-access-security-and-justice-programme-asjp (accessed on 4 March 2017).

10. The Special Court was established by UN Security Council Resolution 1315 and an agreement signed between the Government of Sierra Leone (which requested the court) and the UN in 2002. The TRC was based on Article XXVI of the Lomé Peace Accord and the TRC Act of 2002.

11. Author's interview, Senior High Court judge, Freetown, June 13, 2014.

12. Author's interview, Senior High Court judge, Freetown, June 13, 2014.

13. Author's interview, human right lawyer, Freetown, February 25, 2014.

14. Author's interview, High Court Judge, Monrovia, July 20, 2014.

15. Author's interview, human rights lawyer, Northern Region, May 26, 2014.

16. Author's interview, local consultant, Freetown, June 12, 2014.

17. Author's interview, professional economist and political activist, Monrovia, July 26, 2014.

18. Author's interview, civil society leader, Freetown, June 6, 2014.

19. Author's interviews, Chairman, National Council of Paramount Chiefs, Freetown, June 26, 2014; Deputy Chairman, National Council of Paramount Chiefs, Eastern Province, May 26, 2014.

20. Author's interview, Chairman, National Council of Paramount Chiefs, Freetown (June 26, 2014).

21. Author's interview, High Court Judge, Monrovia, July 20, 2014.

22. Author's interview, civil society leader and local consultant, Freetown, March 4, 2014.

23. Author's interview, High Court Justice, Monrovia, July 20, 2014.

24. Author's interview, lawyer and civil society leader, Freetown, March 4, 2014.

Chapter 5

The Rule of Law and the Economy of Sierra Leone and Liberia

Rebuilding the rule of law was the central focus of post-conflict reconstruction efforts in Sierra Leone and Liberia but, as I underscored in the previous chapter, legal development under international tutelage is nothing new to both countries. Since their settler-colonial founding, Euro-American powers have been supportive of the idea of rebuilding legal-rational institutions as the preeminent way of organizing political life in Sierra Leone and Liberia. The problem I have argued is that the English law, used as the primary tool for legal reconstruction, has historically favored the establishment of state structures that protect the dominant ruling class—from Americo-Liberians and Krios to educated protectorate elites. As their dominant legal system is based on the Anglo-Saxon common law tradition, both countries have historically accommodated indigenous/customary law, with some variations in terms of institutional authority and practices. Indirect rule also meant that subnational localities have been governed via traditional authority structures. But governance of the administration of customary law has predominantly been about the extension of state control into the hinterland and the establishment of a local ruling coalition.

In both countries, the previous chapter notes that state authority is synonymous to the ruling class, with dominant elites wielding unfettered access to public resources and the coercive apparatuses of the state often for personal political gain. Following the end of settler-colonial domination, the indigenous ruling class made effective use of a panoply of state legal and coercive instruments to consolidate power and maintain law and order where their legitimacy was in question. This abuse of political authority—at both the central and local levels—was embedded in the very settler-colonial founding of each state and largely responsible for persistent political conflict, including the recent civil wars. Ironically, international efforts to rebuild the rule of law post-conflict have largely ended up restoring and reinforcing such domination both within each country and in their relations with the international system. Relations with Euro-American powers, including the United Kingdom in Sierra Leone and the United States in Liberia, were simply restored and strengthened without any interrogation of the settler-colonial history even in TJ processes that claim to be retrospective. As long-term reforms focus on re-establishing and strengthening the modern state, institutional structures that historically benefited the governing elites were simply restored. National government welcomed capacity-building and training from the international community only to utilize the "professional" personnel and technologies to protect the state—shorthand for the ruling class.

But since the politics of legal reconstruction is inextricably linked to the broader political economy, the present chapter continues this empirical analysis by examining the relationship between the rule of law and the economy. This chapter begins with an examination of the political economy of settler-colonial rule to draw out the basic legal structures and practices that continued to determine distribution of economic profits in the postcolonial/settler era. Then the chapter proceeds to post-conflict neoliberal reforms with the objective of identifying new laws and institutions designed to facilitate economic growth, who stands to benefit from the post-conflict economic boom, who pays the social cost of capitalist growth, and what does the rule of law have to do with distribution. It goes on to argue that, in addition to uneven distribution of profit, rule of law reform reinforces barriers that make it difficult for low-income people to thrive and access justice, paying close attention to the relationship between law and the informal economy that represents a vital source of livelihood for majority Sierra Leoneans and Liberians.

THE SETTLER-COLONIAL ECONOMY AND LAW

In establishing the settler-colonial economy, land and law became the two most important factors (Galli and Ronnback 2020). What is today Freetown emerged from the "Province of Freedom," a new settlement founded in 1787 for slaves repatriated back to Africa following the abolition of the transatlantic slave trade. Although disagreement around whether the land was ceded entirely to the settlers led one indigenous group to attack and burn down the settlement in 1789, the area continued to be administered by a Chartered Sierra Leone Company (a subsidiary of the St. George's Bay Company), which changed its name from Granville Town (named after a British abolitionist) to Freetown in 1791 (Fyle and Foray 2006). Then Freetown was brought directly under British rule as a Crown colony in 1808. After almost a decade of colonial administration, British Governor Charles McCarthy negotiated with Temne rulers to bring the entire western peninsula under Crown rule with new British-named villages established around Freetown (Fyle and Foray 2006). Crown lands were subsequently expanded through the Public Lands Ordinance (CAP 116, April 1896), Crown Land Conservatory Ordinance (CAP 118, January 1903), Unoccupied Land Ordinance (CAP 117, April 1911), Forestry Ordinance (CAP 189, August 1912), and Concession Ordinance (CAP 121, December 1931). Among these ordinances, the most consequential included CAP 189, which made it lawful for the governor to constitute a forest reserve, CAP 117, which permitted Crown authority over land whose title could not be ascertained, and CAP 116, which authorized the state to expropriate land for the service of the colony.

Since the early settlers (later joined by former slaves from Nova Scotia and Jamaica) had been promised free land for fighting on British side during the American War of Independence, it was the practice of colonial administrations to dole out to the settler population land wrested from indigenous rulers. Under English law, the land would first be vested in the Crown and then distributed to residents of the colony as town or farm plots (Clifford 2006). Among those benefiting from these plots were mostly Krios (i.e., former slaves and their descendants), Europeans, and other foreign businessmen who were permitted as British subjects to make a variety of land claims, including individual leasehold and freehold.[1] "In the legal and bureaucratic terminology of the period, [Krios] were British subjects" directly influenced by European administrators and missionaries "while the natives were British protected persons" (Kandeh 1992, 83).

However, when it became necessary to raise revenue for the administrative cost of running the colony, residents were required to register their land through a central registration system (Renner-Thomas 2010). To ensure that all grantees of Crown land register their titles, a General Registration Ordinance was passed in 1905, followed by the establishment of the Office of General Registrar in 1906. Realizing that residents were avoiding registration to evade property tax, the ordinance stipulated that every deed, contract, or conveyance must be registered within a certain period or risk nullification, a requirement that institutionalized a system of mandatory registration of landholdings in Freetown. These legal developments also led to the founding of formal departments for surveys and lands and required residents to obtain licenses for cutting wood, removing trees, or using Crown lands for any other purposes (CAP 118, 3). To date, these kinds of English laws and the formal justice system that applies them remain the basis of tenure security in the western area, even though most of the population is now of indigenous-rural origin.

Meanwhile, prior to establishing formal control over the hinterland, European merchants and British subjects in the colony, who were engaged in trade with the indigenous population, had drawn the colonial government's attention to the commercial opportunities available outside the colony of Freetown. Growth in this unofficial trade not only supported the economy of Freetown but also coincided with the advent of the so-called legitimate trade, which was geared toward export of raw commodities to European industries in lieu of the abolished transatlantic slave trade. But numerous wars among local chiefs, competing for control of trading centers and routes as well as for expansion of their territories to acquire slaves for labor, were creating considerable hindrance to peaceful trade between the colony and interior areas. Whereas Europeans often described these pre-protectorate wars as primitive tribal wars or slave raids, Abraham (2003) argues that they were initiated by warrior leaders with the serious economic objective of controlling trade. The acquisition of slaves and captives was in part deemed necessary to ensure adequate supply of labor needed to produce legitimate crops for European and colony markets. In other words, the legitimate trade, which replaced the transatlantic slave trade, only diverted the demand for labor within Sierra Leone itself and was a major cause of hinterland wars.

Formal recognition of a separate communal tenure system dates to August 31, 1896, when Britain declared a protectorate (i.e., protected land) over the hinterland of Sierra Leone (Protectorate Ordinance, CAP 60, 1896). Formalized by an Order-in-Council under the Foreign Jurisdiction Act, the 1896 Protectorate declaration brought all territories adjacent to the colony under Her Majesty's protection through an indirect system of rule. Significantly, the colonial administration introduced ordinances designed to administer land and natural resources in the protectorate separately from the colony. For example, the Protectorate Lands Ordinance stated that "all land in the protectorate is vested in the tribal authorities (including the paramount chiefs, sub-chiefs, their councillors, and men of note) who hold such land on behalf of the native community" (CAP 122, Preamble, 1927). As part of the authority vested in these traditional rulers, they became responsible for allocating communal land to users, resolving land disputes, regulating the use of forest resources, and making bylaws deemed expedient for promoting social order in their chiefdom. Stipulated in the Tribal Authorities Ordinance, one of such bylaws was to "set aside land in or near a town for development of the town and general benefit of inhabitants of that town and its villages" (CAP 61, 1938, 8). Another provision, which became relevant for dealing with land disputes particularly in the northern savannah region where Fulani nomads had settled, was traditional authorities' ability "to prohibit, restrict, or regulate the movement of livestock of any description in their chiefdom" (CAP 61, 16).

Moreover, CAP 122 codified an ethno-regional segregation between natives and non-natives (or between indigenes and strangers) for the sole purpose of differentiating property rights in the protectorate from those of the colony. While natives could hold an indefinite interest in land, non-natives who were mainly Krios and foreigners from the colony could only lease land in the protectorate for a term of fifty years, renewable for a period not exceeding twenty-five years (CAP 122, 4). In addition, non-natives required the consent of traditional authorities to occupy any protectorate land for a limited period and payment of a "settler" or "tenancy" fee of £1 per annum for residing in the provinces (CAP 122, 13). A similar ethno-regional differentiation for taxation purposes was incorporated into the Protectorate Ordinance to exempt non-natives in the service of Her Majesty from paying the annual House Tax of 3 Shillings (CAP 60, 1933, 9). Each of these codes formally empowered traditional authorities as custodians of land and collectors of taxes in exchange for colonial protection, a patron-client relationship that began to undermine the legitimacy of chiefs in the eyes of their constituents. Most of these laws, originally designed in the name of protecting indigenous people and land, turned out to be discriminatory based on place of origin and ethnicity.

Considering the separate communal land tenure system that governed interior land and native-stranger dichotomy, utilization of the vast agrarian provincial land was highly constrained. Krios and other foreigners preferred to invest in trade and mining instead of agriculture because lease agreements did not ensure permanent alienable rights to communal land that could be recovered by chiefs when tenancy agreements expired or their terms were breached. These restrictions also meant that banks and other financial institutions were reticent to accept provincial land as collateral for loans, leaving chiefs and the central governments as the only potential investors in large-scale plantation farming outside family lands. Strangers who ventured to invest in provincial land had to depend on traditional authorities to ensure protection of their property and to resolve disputes emerging from contested and undocumented land entitlements. But these laws were created to ensure that the colonial administration could maintain control over the economy (a form of circumscribed economic liberalization) and to provide a lucrative source of wealth and power for local chiefs who supported colonial indirect rule (Berry 1992; Sierra Leone TRC Report 2004).

The restructuring of interior administration under indirect rule (narrated in the previous chapter) coincided with efforts to further open up some areas of the hinterland to the modern money economy, particularly the exportation of mineral resources and cash crop production in palm kernel, cocoa, coffee, and piassava.[2] Between the late 1920s and early 1930s, deposits of iron ore were discovered in the northern districts of Port Loko and Tonkolili. Following the discovery of rich deposits of alluvial diamond deposits in 1933, the Sierra Leone Selection Trust (SLST) Company—a subsidiary of De Beers—was

granted an exclusive prospecting and mining lease covering the whole of
Sierra Leone for ninety-nine years, although the company's operations were
concentrated in the eastern district of Kono. Not long after, three massive diamonds were discovered along the Woyie River, two in 1943 (weighing 249
and 532 carats, respectively) and a third in 1945 that was the largest alluvial
diamond known to the world at the time (weighing 770 carats).[3] Coopting
chiefs in the district and paying over £3 million in taxes to the colonial government, SLST's mining operations reached a peak of two million carats in
1960 (NMJD 2010). Later, the agreement was renegotiated so that the SLST
could surrender some of its concession to be managed under the Alluvial
Diamond Mining Scheme, a government-established scheme to break the
monopolistic position of highly capitalized foreign firms and to issue mining
licenses to Sierra Leoneans, provided chiefdom authorities and landowners
granted permission.[4] The construction of a single-track railway linking other
parts of the interior with the colony was an added impetus to cash crop production as produce could now be transported to Freetown for both colony
consumption and export to European markets.

Among those who disproportionately benefited from this early modern trade
and commercial laws were Krios, Europeans, Indians, and Middle Easterners
(mostly Lebanese who were called Syrians during the Ottoman Empire and
registered as aliens, naturalized British, and Afro-Lebanese) (Kaplan et al.
1976). Starting as trading partners of European firms and encouraged by the
colonial governments, the Lebanese in particular quickly emerged as the most
formidable group in commerce and trade, having almost total monopoly over
most business sectors after World War I. While the Krios enjoyed a superior
status of over "natives," the rise of Lebanese economic fortunes resulted
in non-Africans taking over as principal merchants, "buying goods in bulk
from Europeans and selling them in small amounts to cultivators and vice
versa" (Kaplan et al. 1976, 77). As Indians in East Africa, the Lebanese were
to remain the main competitors against indigenous businesses who aspired
to the middle class after being outcompeted by large-scale European firms.
Following the July 1919 anti-Lebanese riots in Freetown and some parts of
the interior, the Colonial Office in London awarded the Lebanese community
monetary compensation for damages sustained and promised to safeguard
their interest in Sierra Leone, a decision that disappointed many Krios as Van
Der Laan, a professor at the University of Sierra Leone, noted.

> The Government assurance of 1919 meant in effect that the right of long-term
> residence was granted to the Lebanese . . . The intervention from London was a
> bitter disappointment for many Africans, and in particular, for the Creoles . . . ,
> [who] were further disheartened by the knowledge that many British officials
> suspect them of having instigated the riots. They were worried that the Lebanese

would make further inroads into their long-established economic positions. Thus, bitterness and frustration marked Creole attitudes towards the Lebanese in the years that followed. (cited in Sillah 2016, 10)

In terms of access to land in Liberia, the Hinterland Rules stipulated that title to all lands in Liberia was vested in the sovereign state under Americo-Liberian rule. According to Article 66, land title could be translated into communal holdings upon application to the government by a tribe that would bear the cost of demarcating the land for such purpose. Where an application was processed, tribal authorities were to be considered as trustees of the demarcated communal land that could only be rented to outsiders with permission from the community. Transforming communal holdings into family titles conferred freehold claim to individual families, but this procedure also required petition to the government for division of tribal land and only tribes that had sufficiently advanced in the arts of (Western) civilization could submit a petition.

Perhaps owning to what Sawyer described as "persistent deterioration of government finances and growing demand for labor," the implementation of indirect rule by successive governments after Barclay's was geared toward greater centralization and supervision of local authorities (1992, 199). Vesting ownership of communal land and labor in sovereign state authority was in line with Liberia's integration into the global economic order. Known as the Fernando Po affair, a 1914 formal agreement between Liberia and Spain had committed the Liberian government to supply contracted labor to the Spanish island of Fernando Po. A thriving cacao plantation region, the island was in dire need of a dependable flow of workers that could not be obtained legally or cheaply from adjacent British and French colonies (Nelson 1985). Ironically reflecting the experience of slavery of Americo-Liberians, the government of Liberia exported indigenous workers, mostly from the Kru ethnic group, to the island under dubious and appalling conditions (Levitt 2005; Sawyer 1992).[5] Under the agreement terms, Liberian contractors were paid a fee for each worker and wages that accrued over the period of workers' contract were deposited in gold in Monrovia to be paid in local currency when they returned to Liberia (Nelson 1985). In 1930, a Commission of Inquiry set up by the League of Nations implicated notable government officials, including Vice President Allen B. Yancey, in a syndicate that procured involuntary labor by impressment, pawnage, and other practices that violated international law.

The League of Nations' report put Liberia under international censorship over its appalling relations with indigenous peoples, although the imperial powers had ulterior motives for being critical. As fallout from the report, President Charles D. B. King and Vice President Yancey were forced to resign and the succeeding Edwin Barclay administration (1930–1944) was under pressure to adopt reforms in native African affairs. In 1931, Britain and Germany, in conjunction with the United States, proposed an ultimatum that required President Barclay to implement radical reforms or risked the imposition of a League of Nations trusteeship. Considering British influence over the Liberian Frontier Force and Liberia's Receivership status that placed receipt of the country's customs revenues under foreign control, Britain in particular called for an Anglo-American Commission that would take over the running of key Liberian governance institutions. Britain intended to use this move to offset France's growing imperial influence in the West Africa region. But as the pre–World War II politics began to necessitate realignment of great power interests and in view of Barclay's decision to break diplomatic relations with Germany, the Liberian government was able to maintain its territorial sovereignty without making substantial commitment to implementing recommendations contained in the League of Nations' report until the end of Barclay's tenure in office.

The other situation marked the beginning of Liberia's concessionary lease system, which made vast communal lands available to foreigners for plantation estates, iron ore mining, and timber extraction. Signed between the Government of Liberia and Firestone Tire & Rubber Company of America in 1926, the Firestone agreement granted the company a lease of one million acres of land for ninety-nine years at a rent of six cents per acre. Article 2 of the Act establishing Firestone Plantations required the Liberian government to encourage, support, and assist efforts to secure adequate labor supply for the company. Through the Ministry of Interior's Bureau of Labor, district commissioners and chiefs were responsible for the continuous conscription and deployment of workers for Firestone in return for a commission on each day's work (Sawyer 1992). The role of chiefs in supplying involuntary paid labor for private enterprises was enshrined in the Hinterland Rules as part of their mandate to conscript laborers for public works and porterage, provided the tribal economy was taken into consideration. Firestone is credited as the first foreign investment to introduce modern cash economy into the hinterland. But the fact that the economic interest of Americo-Liberians, who mediated these concessions and contracts, took precedence over the welfare of indigenes (suppliers of land and labor) was indicative of an asymmetric economic relation bound to continue in subtle manipulative ways.

In order to stimulate economic growth and improve social services without imposing austerities and heavy taxation upon the prosperous economic class, Tubman implemented an open-door policy concurrently with his unification program (Nelson 1985). The open-door policy encouraged foreign firms to invest in Liberia by removing restrictions on repatriation of their profits and guaranteeing unimpeded access to land and natural resources in the interior.

The Liberian legislature passed laws that were lax on corporate responsibilities and regulations regarding labor rules and practices (Levitt 2005). With these concessions, there were, by early 1960s, twenty-five major companies operating in Liberia. Adding to the continued investment in rubber plantation by Firestone, the new policy opened up other investment areas, including Liberia's untapped iron ore reserves that turned out to be the largest deposits in the world at that time (Nelson 1985). For the first time in 100 years, Liberia was able to service its external debts and the country's economy was no longer controlled by foreign receivership. Concessions led to the construction of roads, rail lines, port facilities, and other modern infrastructure that connected some parts of the interior (e.g., plantation and mining enclaves) with the modern state and economy in Monrovia. However, merchant proprietorship, "organized around a small group of leading citizens and network of trading agents" (Sawyer 1991, 264), remained the natural source of leadership, even with the influx of foreign investors such as Lebanese businessmen who dominated middle-level commercial activities (Nelson 2985). The 1962 national census revealed that sharp disparity still existed in income and representation between coastal counties and hinterland districts, where the majority population with indigenous background continued to reside.

Thus, the impetus for declaring a protectorate over the hinterland was externally driven to meet the geostrategic and economic concerns of the settler-colonial metropole instead of an effort to administer public service in local areas. Clearly, the integration of local economies into the global political economy, which was facilitated by the English and modernized traditional laws, provided very little benefit to the indigenous productive population as the process occurred through concession agreements to profit only local elites and industries in the United States and Europe. The same extractive motives underpinned expansion of the cash economy as modern infrastructures were sporadically extended just for the purpose of exploiting cheap labor, mineral resources, and raw agricultural materials to benefit the metropole. While indirect rule conferred formal recognition to amenable traditional institutions, they were taken out of precolonial norms of downward accountability and adopted the same imperial regulative agenda associated with the modern political economy. Growing discontent against these excesses of chiefs and traditional authorities, coupled with the colonial government laissez-fair attitude toward supervising internal affairs, led to rural social conflicts including the 1955–1956 anti-chief riots in the northern region of Sierra Leone.

As the money economy permeated the interior, several traditional practices were refashioned to increase their commercial value for the benefit of chiefs, colonial officials, notable community members, and the market economy generally. For instance, the hitherto voluntary tribute system, through which indigenous people showed occasional appreciation to their chiefs, was transformed into regular free labor needed to cultivate chiefs' farms (Cartwright 1970; Keen 2005; Kilson 1966; Richards 2005). In some instances, produce acquired by chiefs from fines imposed in courts or customary gifts (handshakes) provided by subjects became worth their commercial, rather than symbolic, value and expected to be made in cash payments. The role of chiefs in supplying involuntary paid labor for private enterprises (such as Firestone) was enshrined in Liberia's Hinterland Rules as part of their mandate to conscript laborers for public works and porterage. The long-standing "pawning" and "indentured servant" system was transformed into a source of cheap labor transported to plantation enclaves like Fernando Po. Similarly, economic compensation demanded after winning a case led to the origin of "betting systems" and increasing emphasis on litigation instead of arbitration that usually resulted in compromise settlements. Also, "as court fines and fees became an important mechanism for generating revenue for local administration," adjudication of cases was viewed as a lucrative source of revenue (Alie 2008, 139).

PREWAR NEOLIBERAL REFORMS

It is also worth underscoring that, although the settler-colonial laws laid the structural foundations for a political economy that disproportionately benefited global capitalists and local elites at the expense of the majority population, the post–World War II macroeconomic policies by national governments and international financial institutions only exacerbated the problem. During this period, many indigenous African leaders wanted to eschew traditional neoclassical development approaches, which insisted on a universal linear path to development, in favor of economic models supported by neo-Marxist dependency theorists and experimented mostly in Latin American and Asian countries. With African socialism, state capitalism, developmental state, and import-substitution industrialization models gaining momentum, state-owned industries like the Sierra Leone Produce Marketing Board, National Diamond Mining Company, and the Wellington Industrial Estate in Sierra Leone became the mainstays of the economy after settler-colonial rule (Sesay et al. 2009). But in the 1970s, postcolonial economies were plunged into a global economic crisis, including the recession of 1973–1980, the OPEC oil price crisis, and mounting debts. Many faced a combination of severe balance of payments problems, high and variable inflation, slow growth, and high unemployment (Corbo and Fischer 1980). Additionally, the hosting of the OAU, which cost an estimated $200 million for Liberia in 1979 and Sierra Leone in 1980, plunged both countries into massive debt (Pham 2004).

These problems emerged from the cumulative effects of weak national policies and institutions combined with a drastic and unfavorable change in external conditions (terms of trade shocks, interest rate shocks, a worldwide recession, and a severe reduction in commercial bank lending) (Corbo and Fischer 1980). In Sierra Leone, the economy faced a steep decline. The ensuing inflationary pressure reduced growth rate to around 3 percent a year from its 7 percent and by the second half of the decade, the gross domestic product (GDP) had sunk to under 2 percent a year (Sesay et al. 2009). National parastatals became bankrupt, leading to a fall in government revenue. The net result of this recurrent revenue crisis was to increase the money supply and consequently hyperinflation. By the late 1980s inflation was running at 171 percent (Sesay et al. 2009). In Liberia, foreign debt grew from $158 million to over $600 million between 1970 and 1979 (Pham 2004). The fragility of the Tolbert administration was not helped by an economic stagnation during the global recession (1970s) when the world price of iron ore and rubber plummeted drastically and a massive demonstration to protest a proposed increase in the price of rice, the country's staple food. Known as the rice riots, Tolbert's decision to call in security forces, including the military, left about 200 people dead, hundreds injured, and looting of shops and commercial houses by the same security personnel.[6]

Against this backdrop, the World Bank and the IMF introduced structural adjustment and economic stabilization programs in the developing world to address the decline in national economies and regain access to foreign loans. Stabilization policies were the preserve of the IMF and included measures to improve macroeconomic balance and stability. Structural adjustment programs (SAPs), on the other hand, were controlled by the World Bank and aimed at rolling back the state and creating an enabling environment to bring the market "back on track" (Ezeonu 2003). These policies were overlapping and rooted in neoliberal economic principles, which became known as the Washington Consensus: fiscal discipline and an end to deficit, reduced public expenditure and reordering of government priorities, tax reform, flexible interest rates, competitive exchange rates, trade liberalization, a favorable environment for foreign direct investment (FDI), privatization, deregulation, and the promotion of property rights.[7] In 1986, Sierra Leone signed a loan with the IMF for US$40.5 million, just two years after IMF loans to Liberia increased its foreign debt to approximately $398 million, all on condition that SAP and stabilization policies be implemented (Mills-Jones 1988; Sesay et al. 2009). No doubt, the deeper financial cuts in education, health, and social care eventually worsened the plight of an already deprived population in both countries. As some researchers argue, the implementation of the SAP and stabilization measures became the "final straw that broke the camel's back" (Reno 2010; Sesay et al. 2009).

POST-CONFLICT NEOLIBERAL ECONOMIC RECOVERY

As if lessons were not learned, one of the ultimate objectives of legal reforms in post-conflict Sierra Leone and Liberia was economic recovery based on a neoliberal development model that prioritizes, inter alia, the private sector and deregulation of the market. In both countries, rebuilding the rule of law (particularly legal reform and justice sector development) has been central to attracting international capitalist investment. At the core of the JSDP in Sierra Leone was the "assumption that states with poorly functioning legal systems and poor crime control are unattractive to investors, so economic growth also suffers."[8] As far back as the 1980s when structural adjustment programs were introduced in the country, the World Bank had warned that "the lack of a transparent legal and regulatory framework and operationally functional legal and judicial services would constrain the growth of private commercial transactions" (World Bank 2004, 60). In making the link between justice sector reform and economic progress, DFID's director general, Mark Lowcock, underscored that

> Investors and businesses need to be confident that there is a stable and predictable regime for the maintenance of property rights and the implementation of contracts, and that where things go wrong there will be effective and fair redress through the courts. (*Awareness Times*, September 16, 2005)

Efforts to revamp Sierra Leone's economy began under the eleven-year administration of President Tejan Kabbah (1996–2007), who, as a former international bureaucrat, was committed to neoliberal economic principles that would entrust economic development in the private sector. Throughout his two terms in office, Kabbah's SLPP administration was also committed to the international community's newfound concept of good governance that stresses effective state institutions and principles of transparency. But if Kabbah laid the foundational governance principles, economic advancement was to be under the APC administration of President Ernest Bai Koroma (2007–2018), an experienced insurance broker and businessman who vowed to run the country as a business enterprise. The Justice Sector Coordination Office (JSCO) was established within the Ministry of Justice to coordinate the implementation of the country's Justice Sector Reform Strategic and Investment Plan (JSRS&IP) 2008–2018. The JSRS&IP was designed to deliver government's commitment to justice in its Poverty Reduction Strategy Paper (PRSP) and was linked to government's resource allocation processes through the Medium-Term Expenditure Framework. Pillar 1 of the PRSP notes that the UK-funded Law Reform project will "improve the environment for private sector development, including a review of the Companies

Act, Business Registration Act and Rules, Law on Bankruptcies, and laws to secure transactions" (PRSP 2005).

The APC government's 2008 Agenda for Change aimed at achieving an annual growth rate of 10 percent through substantial investments in supportive infrastructure, improved delivery of social services, and private sector development. The Agenda focused on four key priorities: provision of reliable power supply, raising quality and value-added productivity in agriculture, development of a national transportation network, and provision of improved social services. Principles of good governance and rule of law were to underpin the achievement of these goals insofar as they promoted macroeconomic stability and strengthened the legal and regulatory framework necessary for investment. Succeeding the Agenda for Change was a long-term roadmap for transforming Sierra Leone into a middle-income country by 2035—the Agenda for Prosperity (A4P). The first five years of this prosperity agenda (2013–2018) was "to build a stable economy, founded on private sector-led growth, and diversified across several competitive sectors to achieve [the country's] economic and human development vision" (Agenda for Prosperity 2013, 3).

With support from international financial institutions and bilateral donors, the Koroma administration aggressively pursued this Agenda for Prosperity by attracting massive foreign direct investments from multilateral corporations interested in the country's mineral resources and fertile land (Human Right Watch 2014). The government adopted an open-door policy that offered wide-ranging generous fiscal incentives to potential investors, including a ten-year corporate tax holiday, zero-import duty for agricultural investment, exclusive foreign ownership in all sectors, no limits on expatriate employees, as well as full repatriation of profits, dividends, and royalties (NMJD and Cord Aid 2013). Through technical support from the International Finance Corporation (IFC)—the World Bank's private sector arm—the Sierra Leone Investment & Export Promotion Agency (SLIEPA) advertised Sierra Leone as a prime location for agribusiness, highlighting the country's tropical climate and rich soil, relatively low rural labor rates compared to other developing countries, and a communal land tenure system that could be mediated by government to make land easily available for long-term lease. SLIEPA also stresses the role of legal and judicial reforms in neoliberal economic development, citing the refurbished national law court building and a newly established commercial court to enhance investor confidence. Its website includes the laws of Sierra Leone page with a link to a comprehensive list of laws; among them are fifty-four legislations passed in the last fifteen years to liberalize and modernize the local economy.[9] Furthermore, the agency touts duty-free access to large markets under treaties such as African Growth and Opportunity Act (AGOA) with the United States and the Cotonou Agreement with the European Union. Additionally, the Corporate Affairs Commission, which was receiving help from the British High Commission, standardized and simplified the registration of business enterprises including a one-stop shop plus an online registration system.

In March 2017, the government officially launched a National Land Policy that articulates "a clearer, more effective and just land tenure system to stimulate responsible investment and form a basis for the nation's continued development" (Land Policy 2017, 1). Although the policy promises to empower local communities to negotiate land deals with investors, it is fundamentally designed to liberalize existing land administration and management systems to ensure effective land delivery mechanisms to further attract investors in line with the Agenda for Prosperity. An investor's guide for business in Sierra Leone promises investors that the government plans to harmonize the country's land tenure systems, "establish a system of land title registration, and the creation of an institution to set aside land for large-scale investment" (Herber Smith Freehills 2015, 23).

Other efforts to strengthen corporate governance and justice in Sierra Leone include accession to the Extractive Industries Transparency International (EITI), which the country has complied with since 2014 after a brief suspension for insufficient disclosure. The country acceded to the International Convention on the Simplification and Harmonization of Customs Procedures under the World Customs Organization (WCO) in June 2015 and then notified the World Trade Organization (WTO) of its acceptance of the organization's Agreement on Trade Facilitation in May 2017. As a member of the World Intellectual Property Organization (WIPO), Sierra Leone is bound by agreements on Trade-related Intellectual Property Rights (TRIPs), although the Copyright Treaty and Berne Convention for the Protection of Literary and Artistic Rights have not been ratified (US Bureau of Economic and Business Affairs 2018). In March 2017, a commercial law summit on the theme "facilitating responsible private sector development through improvement in commercial law justice" was convened in Freetown by corporate organizations such as Hebert Smith Freehill LLP and UK-Sierra Leone Pro-Bono Network.

Liberia has followed a similar neoliberal development path under the administration of Madam Johnson-Sirleaf. During her administration, justice sector development was part of the Governance and Economic Management Assistance Program (GEMAP), designed to enhance state capacity for revenue generation and reduction in public expenditure. Taking over from the National Transitional Government of Gyude Bryant, President Sirleaf wasted no time to inaugurate her 150-day rapid impact project aimed at making the post-conflict state quickly visible in four priority or pillar areas: security, economic revitalization, basic services and infrastructure, and good governance. These same pillars continued to define her administration's medium- to long-term development strategy under the supervision of the Liberian

Reconstruction and Development Committee. In March 2008, the IMF restored Liberia's membership to the EITI, paving the way for the Poverty Reduction Strategy (PRS), the roadmap for medium-term socioeconomic recovery. "Apart from providing the conducive infrastructural environment for business to thrive," the government introduced "regulatory policies that facilitated the expansion and functioning of markets" (PRSP 2008, 60).

Dubbed LIFT Liberia, the PRS "focused on rebuilding management and accountability systems within the security sector, including the Bureau of Corrections and Rehabilitation, and emphasized rehabilitation programs within the justice system" (Human Rights Committee 2016, 17). Pillar 2 of the recovery strategy focused on revitalizing the economy by reopening the forestry and mining sectors, which had literally halted production due to war and UN sanctions (UN Security Council Resolution 1521, 2003). Specifically, the goal was to "restore production in rubber, timber, mining, cash crops, and other key natural resources and ensure the benefits accrue to the nation as a whole and not just a few" (PRSP 2008, 38). President Sirleaf's decision to cancel and review all logging concessions signed under the transitional government and the creation of the Forestry Reform Monitoring Committee prompted the UN Security Council in June 2006 to lift the international ban on Liberian timber export.

In the absence of clearly defined land rights policy, the government established a national Land Commission mandated to coordinate reforms of land laws and programs in Liberia. Established by an Act of the Legislature in August 2009, the Commission was to promote equitable and productive access to the nation's land in addition to ensuring the rule of law with respect to landholding to promote investment. Concurrently, a Forestry Development Authority (FDA) was created to allocate and manage Liberia's 4.39 million hectares of forest as forest management contract areas, timber sales contract areas, community management areas, or protected areas to capture and develop the country's wide range of forest resource benefits (SIIB Report 2012). Private Use Permits (PUPs) were one of the licenses to be issued by FDA to allow private landowners to utilize commercially viable forest assets situated on their property. "A sudden explosion in the use of PUPs saw over 40 percent of Liberia's forest granted to logging companies in just two years, making the permits the main source of commercial timber in Liberia" (Global Witness 2013, 16). A particularly notorious practice was to use forged and irregular land deeds to apply for PUPs and as of 2012 FDA had issued sixty-three permits, totaling 2,532,501 hectares of the land area of Liberia.

Meanwhile, the National Investment Commission (NIC) of Liberia assures international investors of laws that remove restrictions on reparation of capital and profits, guarantee ease of starting a business, and open access to Liberia's low-cost labor, which is set at US $5–6 per day.[10] In collaboration with the IFC and the Developing Market Associates (DMA), the commission has pushed for policies, laws, and programs designed to improve Liberia's investment climate and attract foreign investors into various sectors of the local economy.[11] NIC links Liberia's integration into the international market to the EU's Everything but Arms (EBA) initiative, AGOA, the country's Trade and Investment Framework Agreement with the United States, plus a supportive tax and concession regime. Like SLIEPA, the NIC advertises the country as "an investor's paradise," showcasing Liberia's "huge potential" for horticulture, agribusiness, aquatic, and real estate development. NIC presents to the world ten reasons for investing in Liberia, including its untapped natural resource base "endowed with several rich bodies of minerals and other raw materials such as gold, diamonds, iron ore, bauxite, rubber, timber and much more."[12] The commission relates these investment opportunities to the Agenda for Transformation, a five-year development plan (2012–2017) to position Liberia for becoming a middle-income country by 2030.

Following more than ten years of negotiating its terms of accession, Liberia joined the WTO as the organization's 163rd member on July 14, 2016.[13] In addition to ratifying WTO's protocol of accession, the government has expressed commitment to Liberia's treaty obligations, including arrangements on Technical Barriers to Trade (US Bureau of Economics and Business Affairs 2017). In April 2007, Liberia joined the World Bank Group's Multilateral Investment Guarantee Agency (MIGA), which protects "investments going into the country against risks of transfer restriction, expropriation, breach of contract, and war and civil disturbance (including terrorism)."[14] Concession agreements between investors and the government often contain clauses protecting companies against expropriation or nationalization and allowing for dispute resolution outside Liberia. The Investment Act of 2010 also protects the rights of investors to settle commercial disputes through either the country's judicial system or alternative dispute resolution mechanisms (US Bureau of Economics and Business 2017).

In terms of commercial justice, one of four civil divisions of Sierra Leone's High Court is the Commercial and Admiralty Division (in addition to Family and Probate, Land and Property, and General Civil) established by the High Court Rules of 2007. An extension of this Division is the Fast Track Commercial Court (FTCC), created in 2010 "to reduce the time and cost of dispute resolution while facilitating the process of contract enforcement to boost private investment and economic activity generally, and of course improve the confidence people have in the judicial system."[15] Receiving operational supports from DFID's Justice Recovery Programme up to October 2017, the FTCC follows the same procedural rules of the High Courts and has jurisdiction over commercial matters worth five million Leones ($600) or more. Sierra Leone is also a member of the Standing International Forum on

Commercial Court (SIFoCC), established in May 2017 to bring together representatives from twenty-five jurisdictions that are interested in global efforts to share knowledge and expertise, tackle shared problems, and prepare for future change development.[16]

Although Liberia is not a member of the SIFoCC, it has taken similar steps to develop a legal and institutional framework for commercial justice since the early 2000s. Liberia's commercial code provides for property sales, leases, finance, mortgages, secured transactions, and commercial arbitration (US Bureau of Economics and Business Affairs 2017). Additionally, a commercial court was established in 2010 as a specialized fast-track mechanism to deal with a rising number of commercial disputes, ranging from property rights, to business transactions, to contractual relationships. It has an extensive jurisdiction, including creation and foreclosure of maritime property, sales and leases, registration and foreclosure of mortgages, agreements by corporations and similar business relationships, and enforcement of decisions made by arbitral panels and commercial claims.

POST-CONFLICT ECONOMIC BOOM FOR WHOM

Although very far from being efficient and effective, these efforts to deregulate and liberalize the postwar economies of Sierra Leone and Liberia coincided with what can best be described as an economic boom especially from the late 2000s to 2014. A recent study on land deals and investment under the Koroma administration reveals that close to 500,000 hectares of farmland was leased or under negotiation for lease in Sierra Leone (The Oakland Institute 2011). Most of the land deals were negotiated to make available communal lands for large-scale industrial cultivation of sugarcane, palm oil, and other cash crops. For example, the government's flagship large-scale land deal with Addax Bioenergy Sierra Leone Ltd. granted the company 20,000 hectares of land to grow sugarcane for ethanol export for a lease period of fifty years with a probable extension of twenty-five years. Apart from agribusiness, the mining and other extractive sectors continued to be exploited for diamonds, iron ore, rutile, bauxite, gold, and timber exports. In 2013, Sierra Leone's GDP economic growth was approximately 20 percent, among the fastest in sub-Saharan Africa at the time, according to the IMF. Between 2009 and 2012, the value of natural resource exports exceeded $1.2 billion, accounting for about 70 percent of the country's exports, while inward FDI flows amounted to $579.1 million in 2013 (Hebert Smith Freehills 2015). Although iron ore extraction, which commenced in 2011, accounted largely for the significant growth in GDP during this period, diamond mining continued to play a substantial role as over 600,000 carats' worth of diamonds were exported in 2013 alone. Looking East, China invested heavily in the country's physical infrastructure, including the construction of tarmac roads and a 124-mile railway track solely for the purpose of transporting iron ore from a northern mining enclave to the coast for export.

During the administration of Madam Sirleaf, major concessionary contracts that were renegotiated including those with the Netherlands-based Mittal Steel Company and Firestone whose original concession agreements dated back to 1926. As Liberia continued to attract other leading global firms into its forestry, mining, and rubber sectors, exports increased from $175 million in 2006 to $299.2 million in 2011 (Government of Liberia 2012). Outside the traditional resource sectors, a substantial proportion of the 2012 estimated $16 billion FDI went into tree crop plantations, particularly oil palm (Government of Liberia 2012).

As palm oil becomes a booming business with almost sixty million tons of world production in 2014, Liberia and Sierra Leone are among the African countries that have become the new frontier for large-scale palm oil plantations in the face of land shortages in Asian countries like Indonesia and Malaysia.[17] Global Witness (2015) estimates that a total 1,086,110 hectares of Liberian land has been contracted to multinational companies for plantation purposes (Global Witness 2013). For instance, in 2010, the government signed a contract with Golden Veroleum (GVL), a subsidiary of Golden Agric-Resources (GAR), the world's second-largest producer of palm oil. GVL's concession contract makes available an area of interest covering 350,000 hectares within which the company is allowed to convert 260,000 hectares into an oil palm estate. The agreement is valid for sixty-five years with an opportunity for a thirty-three-year extension period. Other prominent plantation companies include Sime Darby Plantation Inc. whose estate covers 260,000 hectares, Liberian Agricultural Company with an estate of 210,332 hectares, and Equatorial Palm Oil Plc operating on 185,669 hectares (Global Witness 2013). From such concessionaires signed between the Sirleaf administration and multinational companies, the total value of investment into Liberia is projected to be in the range of US$19 billion in the next ten years (US State Department 2011).

Considering the abysmal state of the economy in both countries before and during the civil wars, the focus on economic growth is commendable. For those who are interested in the nexus between neoliberal economic development and liberal peace, foreign direct investment must be encouraged by legal-rational reforms—particularly in poor countries where people are in desperate need of jobs. Deregulation of the economy and extensive tax exemptions would unleash wealth creation opportunities, expanding the revenue base of these countries and exploiting natural resources that would otherwise lie fallow, progressive reformers usually claim. As the examples of Golden Veroleum Liberia and OCTEA Mining in Sierra Leone (discussed below) indicate, war-torn local communities do derive some fringe economic and social benefits from the liberalization of their economy. However, these neoliberal legal reforms largely succeeded in restoring a capitalist logic of production that disproportionately rewards the owner of capital at the expense of labor and the natural environment. The economic boom has reinstated a highly unequal society in which the profit generated from mining and agro-business is concentrated in a small class of individuals (at home and abroad), while those who have been historically marginalized continue to fend at the fringes of the boom. Rather than the emergence of a middle class that may mobilize to demand good governance and accountability, what has emerged is an alliance between economic and political elites (with control over capital and state law, they formed a perfect union). As this comment suggests, the union between capital and law became mutually reinforcing as the political class depended on economic elites for accumulation of personal wealth while the economic class relied on the state to protect its investment by law and other coercive instruments.

> It was done by economic tycoons who were in league with the politicians. That has not changed much because we still have politicians who are in charge, who are the richest in charge of the economy and they are in league with economic tycoons and business people and they are reaping were they have not sown and they are exploiting the majority of citizens. So we haven't really exploited the natural resources to the greatest advantage of our country because we still do things as if we are in the eighteenth century. African countries were export-led economies; all our natural resources are going in the rough form to Europe and so we want to feed their industry.[18]

Despite these impressive macroeconomic numbers (Sierra Leone and Liberia were among the fastest-growing economies before 2014), the African Progress Panel report notes that "too many Africans remain caught in downward spiral of poverty, insecurity, and marginalization" (Africa Progress Panel 2012, 6). As evident in the 2014 Ebola outbreak, which killed 8,755 people in Sierra Leone and Liberia, this massive economic growth has not translated into socioeconomic development such as improved service delivery in the area of healthcare and a better standard of living for the majority population. In 2017, the UNDP Human Development Index ranked Sierra Leone 184th out of 189 countries assessed on multiple indicators of development. Life expectancy at birth stood at 45.6 years, which is below the sub-Saharan average of 56.8 years, and more than 50 percent of the population subsist below the poverty line of $1.25 per day.

Several studies show that the country's postwar natural resource boom has disproportionately benefited a small economic class in collusion with the ruling elite at the expense of the masses whose land and labor are being exploited. Some of these reports even note that the living conditions of people directly affected by large-scale agricultural and mining activities were better-off prior to the economic boom.[19] While the World Bank estimated that unemployment in Sierra Leone stood at 60 percent, the Comprehensive Food Security and Vulnerability Analysis found in 2011 that 45 percent of households are food insecure, especially during the lean season. Clearly, these figures show that while rebuilding the rule of law may have facilitated an economic boom, the dividends of such development have failed to "trickle down" to the ordinary people in whose name the international community often justifies their reform efforts. These reforms have put "too much of [these countries'] resource wealth in the hands of narrow elites and, increasingly, foreign investors without being turned into tangible benefits for [their] people" (Africa Progress Panel 2012, 6).

But the rule of law has not only failed to deliver its emancipatory and empowerment promises. Its reforms have, as an instrument of neoliberal domination, also helped to recreate the same economic and social injustices that precipitated political violence since the settler-colonial founding of Sierra Leone and Liberia. For example, Hanlon (2005) cites the IMF Poverty Reduction and Growth Strategy for Sierra Leone to argue that its quantitative performance criteria and benchmarks, particularly restrictions on the government wage bill for social spending, resulted in renewal of violence, including the 1997 military coup against the Kabbah administration. Even a report commissioned by the World Bank found that growth-promoting policies that emphasize macroeconomic stability over social action were linked to increasing post-conflict social grievances (Collier et al. 2003). As the case studies of oil palm plantation in Butaw and diamond mining in Kono illustrate, neoliberal economic development, which has been enabled by the rule of law, turns out to have adverse social consequences particularly on people of low socioeconomic status who also happen to lack access to the formal legal and justice system.

POST-CONFLICT RECONFIGURATION
OF LAW, STATE, AND CAPITAL

Located in Sinoe County of south-eastern Liberia, Butaw is one of the local communities hosting the operations of Golden Veroleum Liberia (GVL), which has taken over 16,758 hectares of farmland for oil palm and supporting infrastructure. Among the company's eight core values is a pledge to respect community self-determination, land rights, sovereignty, culture and local traditions, and sacred sites through free, prior, and informed consent of communities.[20] Yet, in a letter written on October 1, 2012 and addressed to the Roundtable on Sustainable Palm Oil (RSPO) based in Malaysia, residents of Butaw complained about the operations of GVL, describing the company as a multinational palm oil company that has taken over their farmland. Among the grievances raised in the letter were the legality of the concession agreement; lack of free, prior, and informed community consent; damage to farmlands; inadequate compensation and community development fund; disrespect of sacred lands and the old town; inadequate job opportunities; and harassment and intimidation by the police funded by the company.[21]

Perhaps frustrated by the slow response to the complaint and government's complicity, Butaw organized a protest against GVL on May 26, 2015, after another letter by the Butaw Youth Association warning the company's Chief Executive Officer of "consequences" if he failed to hold a meeting with them (Al Jazeera America 2015). Ignited by about forty young men who blocked workers from entering the plantation, the riot attracted hundreds of young people who ransacked GVL's compound and attacked its management. As the Sinoe local police force was unable to control the situation, United Nations Mission in Liberia (UNMIL) peacekeepers were called in to disperse the protesters and evacuate foreign staff (Stokes 2015). Following an order issued by the Greenville City Magistrate Court, a search and seizure warrant was carried out by Liberia's elite Police Support Unit (PSU) in full body armor and with semi-automatic rifles. Among the crimes listed in the warrant were economic sabotage, terroristic threat, criminal mischief, and rioting.[22] Following the arrests, seventeen young men who had physical injuries were incarcerated in a crowded cell at Greenville. Among them was Fred Thompson, who died of unknown causes and was quickly buried without an autopsy, after forty-nine days of incarceration (Stokes 2015). When asked what GVL is doing to end the incarceration, the Head of Corporate Communication said the company "would expect people who are detained to be treated by the law" (Stokes 2015).

In responding to the violence, the Minister of Justice, Benedict Sannoh, issued a statement in February 2015 warning local communities to "stay away from concessionaries as the government will not countenance any action that will obstruct or otherwise disrupt the smooth operations of concessionaries operating therein."[23] Earlier in June 2011, President Sirleaf had warned the people of Sinoe County against "unpatriotic and non-nationalistic behavior" that would undermine GVL operations and discourage potential investors.[24] Another warning from the president was announced in December in reaction to local protest against another concessionaire as indicated in this statement.

When your government and the representatives sign any paper with a foreign country, the communities can't change it. . . . You are trying to undermine your

own government. You can't do that. If you do so all the foreign investors coming to Liberia will close their businesses and leave, then Liberia will go back
to the old days.[25]

Although Kono district was completely decimated during the Sierra Leone
civil war, resurgence of diamond mining activities in the 2000s led to an
increase in the number of mining chiefdoms from six to 10, accommodating eighteen mining companies, mostly foreign-owned (NMJD 2010). One
of these companies is OCTEA Mining (formerly Koidu Holdings Ltd.),
operating a Koidu Kimberley Project within Tankoro Chiefdom, measuring
approximately 4.9 km^2 with two kimberlite pipes.[26] An initial 25-year lease
agreement inherited by the company was renegotiated by the administration
of President Koroma, leading to a new contract signed in September 2010,
which extended the concession to July 2030, renewable for another period
of fifteen years. The initial lease is linked to the South African mercenary
firm Executive Outcome, which was promised a concession by the previous
administration of President Kabbah for their role in taking over the diamond
district of Kono and ending the civil war. Other global corporate actors connected to OCTEA are Tiffany & Co. and Benny Steinmetz, an Israeli billion-
aire. Injecting up to $1 billion into the mining sector, OCTEA Mining was the
biggest diamond mining company in postwar Sierra Leone, with 983 workers
and an additional 468 short-term contractors.[27] One of the board members of
the company during the mining boom was the Paramount Chief of Tankoro
Chiefdom.

However, Kono remains one of the most socially deprived districts in
Sierra Leone, with the Koidu headquarters town lacking basic public infrastructures such as paved roads, electricity, water supply, and good schools.
The district has only one barely functioning hospital, fifty-seven ill-equipped
peripheral health centers, two doctors, and eight community health officers
to serve a population of about 400,000 people (NMJD 2010). Apart from an
increase in crimes (including robbery, murder, and rape), Koidu has become
a flashpoint for violent riots against corporate development, often leading to a
state of emergency with central authorities invoking the Military Aid to Civil
Power (MACP) for long periods. In December 2007, police officers deployed
at Koidu Holdings shot dead two protesters, an incident that was followed
by a suspension of the company's operation and the establishment of the
Jenkins-Johnston Commission of Inquiry, which released a damning report
against the company. Five years later, in December 2012, two people were
again killed by police when miners embarked on a strike for better pay and
working conditions. In addition to demands for a Christmas bonus promised
by OCTEA Mining, "the workers were calling for an improvement in what
they described as appalling working conditions and an end to alleged racism"

The Rule of Law and the Economy 139

in the mines (BBC 2012). In this interview, one paralegal in Koidu provided more details about these social conditions.

> You know, people are really suffering in this chiefdom. There is a village in the chiefdom called Yamandu which used to have open access but now that village is inaccessible because of the operation of OCTEA. The bikes stop at Resettlement and you have to walk your way up there. And now the people do not have communication network because of this mountain of rocks piled by OCTEA, something they use to enjoy. You already have cracks on the buildings because they are still very close to the blasting sites. There has been a lot of road accident in the resettlement site because the trucks are plying the same roads people use. Before now people pay Le 1000 to hire a bike but because of the current distance they pay up to Le 3000 to get to their homes. Bikes don't go to area at night. There is also the problem of reclaiming land after artisanal mining. For this year alone, we had about 7 children who drowned in mining pits.[28]

These relations between local communities, the state, and corporate actors bear a remarkable resemblance to the settler-colonial economy that existed about half-a-century ago. Although law is often contested, it "is at the epicentre of a colonising power that makes subjects into living dead through acts of sovereign expression" as Chalmers notes in her study of Liberia's Central Prison system (2018, 6). What these communities are witnessing is capitalist law "with a repertoire of language, of legal forms, institutional practices" that prioritize the concept of market and contract, just as Chanock describes the apartheid legal culture of South Africa (2001, 23). One study in Liberia noted that concession negotiations often "prioritise the government's claim to land ownership over the customary land tenure of indigenous communities" (Centre of International Conflict Resolution 2012, 7). These concession agreements are virtually inaccessible to community members not only because copies are unavailable to them but also because they are drafted in highly legalistic and technical language, incomprehensible to a largely illiterate rural population. Based on the advice of corporate attorneys, these agreements often include escape clauses that companies use to sidestep corporate social responsibilities and avoid liability for funding community projects. NAMATI Liberia's Rachael Knight writes about contracts that contain vague phrases such as "to the best of the company's abilities," "in the manner the company deems fit," and "the company will reasonably endeavour to" that ensure corporate agents are under no obligation to fulfil community expectations (NAMATI 2018). Another respondent claimed that "the paramount chief often instructs illiterate people to sign documents for compensation without knowing what was written and even though they did not receive what they have signed for."[29]

But this law is also the customary law that settler-colonial rule reinvented. While Sierra Leone and Liberia still maintain a dual land tenure system, modern elites are pleased to defend paramount chiefs who serve as custodians of communal land, particularly in chiefdoms where they represent what Mamdani calls "decentralised despots" (Mamdani 1996). As in Tankoro Chiefdom where the paramount chief was a board member of the largest mining company, it makes strategic sense for the state and global capital to negotiate with powerful custodians of land rather than with an entire community. The British who pioneered indirect colonial rule in Africa know too well how rewarding this alliance with the protectorate elite can be that the DFID supported President Kabbah's proposal to restore and reinforce the institution of chieftaincy through the Paramount Chief Restoration Programme (PCRP). Spending about $2,277,442 over two years, the United Kingdom was even willing to build houses for returning paramount chiefs, rescinding the program only when public concern about supporting a traditional mode of dominance appeared to conflict with Blair's ethical foreign policy image (International Crisis Group 2004). As in settler-colonial times, this elite alliance suffices until central governments can harmonize the dual land tenure system into a single neoliberal framework as Sierra Leone's 2017 Land Policy signals. It must also be noted that settler-colonial laws in both countries historically recognize customary land title only in terms of the surface area, often granting the state exclusive rights over resources located 6 feet beneath the land, the origin of the concept of "surface rent" paid by corporate actors. The surface rent had been a source of dissatisfaction in communities where local elites mismanage and embezzle funds meant for landowners and the community.[30] Moreover, the idea that ownership in the hinterland is limited to just the land surface is suggestive of the continued legacies of settler-colonial rule.

The post-conflict reconfiguration of this alliance surely indicates that "when large corporate actors dominate states or become knitted with them, law becomes a product of the economy and what was once 'Western' dominance is now multinational corporate capitalism" (Mattei and Nader 2008, 6). Also, startling is the fact that law "regulates the most important parts of the daily life of people" and "constitutes a moral conquest more striking, more durable, and far more solid than the physical conquest" as political philosopher Fitzjames Stephen once noted (In Hussain 2003, 4). There is some faith in the power of law, even among people being oppressed by the law. For instance, the High Court of Sierra Leone ruled in March 2016 that a Chinese company, Orient Agriculture Ltd., must pay $52,300 as compensation to families uprooted from their farmland in Nimiyama Chiefdom, one of those rare cases perhaps meant to indicate that the system is not entirely unjust. Following the ruling, one of the affected residents gave credit to the law, saying that "previously we were amputees but now we are having our two full hands because the law is with us now" (Courtright 2016). Sonkita Conteh, who is NAMATI Sierra Leone's director and legal practitioner, viewed the judgement as an indication that "there is a way to squeeze justice out of a broken system" (Courtright 2016). While the good works of NAMATI must be commended, the study of law and colonization is relevant to remind lawyers and reformers that the legal system may be working as designed and such wins may only serve to validate the system that is not meant for social justice or the needs of the poor. The English law cannot mask social injustice, which is at the core of problems wrought by the penetration of global capital, if it appears blatantly partial (Thompson 1975).

Crucially, celebrating the rule of law when the weak intermittently wins against the powerful detracts from the fundamental ideological and structural problems that reproduce social inequalities and injustices in the system. Ideologically, none of the neoliberal legal reforms, premised on market principles of performance and reward, is capable of redistributing the benefits of economic growth to ensure better conditions of living for all, including affordable housing, public health services, environmental protection, and education. As a matter of principle, the neoliberal logic of legal reform even prevents the state from performing social and redistributive functions, limiting its role only to creating the enabling environment for individual citizens to thrive. Considering the influential role of Western liberal democracies in the reconstruction process as well as the neoliberal professional background of reform leaders in Sierra Leone and Liberia, it was a foregone conclusion that such neoliberalism policies would take precedence over concerns about socioeconomic rights and distributive justice. Rule of law reforms led to more liberal commercial laws that attracted private investors inside and outside each country than socially oriented laws to protect communal rights and social development, even when the trampling of local values and cultures has historically undercut the legitimacy of dominant legal systems.

Additionally, while building legal institutions is important for reducing transaction costs within the formal economy, the majority population in Sierra Leone an derive their livelihood from the informal economy, which comprises unregistered establishments, household unincorporated enterprises, and unregistered employment with no social security (Statistics Sierra Leone 2014).[31] Liberia's Institute of Statistics and Geo-Information Services and Ministry of Labour reports that almost three-quarter of a million Liberians are engaged in informal employment, representing about 68 percent of all employment (Liberia Institute of Statistics and Geo-Information Services and Ministry of Labour 2011, 49). Rather than considering the informal economy as an integral part of efforts to strengthen commercial justice, reform measures usually stigmatize the sector as dangerous for the modern economy, the source of illicit economic activities, and an environmental blight for foreign investors and tourists who are needed to make Sierra Leone and Liberia middle-income countries by 2030.

Based on an undifferentiated characterization of informal activities, policymakers and development experts tend to associate them with retrogressive attitudes (such as lawlessness, criminality, corruption, and slothfulness) as opposed to global capitalist values of efficiency and profit.[32] In terms of macroeconomic management, national governments and the World Bank frown at informal businesses that undermine efforts to increase the tax revenue share of GDP in both countries (World Bank 2003). As well, the informal economy is regarded as a hindrance to modernization efforts such as urban planning, city beautification, business registration, security for production and exchange, and transparent market relations. Where some recognition is granted, policymakers insist on the registration and formalization of small-scale business. Yet, one study notes that "in every aspect of the investment process, most firms find it simpler and more cost-effective to remain in the informal sector than to comply with cumbersome licencing processes, taxation, and other requirements to operate a business" (Statistics Sierra Leone 2014, 2).

Sierra Leone's 1965 Public Order Act criminalizes people in the informal sector as "idle and disorderly persons," "rogues and vagabonds," without "any visible means of subsistence and not giving good account of himself" (Cap 222, 7). Included in this category are "any suspected person or reputed thief frequenting any quay, wharf, or landing place, or any street, highway or avenue leading thereto, or any place of public resort or any avenue leading thereto, or any street or highway or place adjacent" (Cap 222, 8). Passed when the laws of Sierra Leone were still assented by the Queen of England, the Act was an attempt to "control and segregate the local population," disproportionately targeting "the poor, the homeless, homosexuals, sex workers, hawkers, people with substance use problems, and people with disabilities" (Voices 2017). Enabling "law enforcement to target people purely based on their social or economic status," such laws target people who have been structurally marginalized by the modern neoliberal economy (Voices 2017). And as this quote clearly spells out, these efforts to criminalize petty offenses remain one of the last vestiges of legal authoritarianism bequeathed to African elites by their European counterparts.

Imposed decades ago by British, French, and Portuguese colonialists, and retained by current African governments long after being repealed in their countries of origin, they continue to make the lives of Africa's most marginalized more hazardous. Many of these laws against loitering, being "a rogue and a vagabond," having no "ostensible means of assistance," or being "idle and disorderly" carry prison terms, and are still in place in Mauritius, Nigeria, Gambia, Zambia, Uganda, Botswana, Seychelles, Ghana, Tanzania, and Sierra Leone. (Voices 2017)

This quote captures the fact that modern law, since its establishment in colonial-setter times to the contemporary period, has rarely been an instrument for the weak or poor. When the poor meets the English law, it is often in its coercive capacity to maintain law and other or to punish a criminalized behavior. In concluding this chapter, it is worth returning to *Nimiyama Chiefdom v Orient Agriculture Ltd.* case, which lawyers would normally use to reinforce their faith in the English law as an instrument of emancipation, to note that there will always be occasions for small counterhegemonic wins. The core issue is the very essence of the legal system—its logic of domination is difficult to overturn even when it tends to accommodate some reforms. Even a director of the Human Right Commission of Sierra Leone is skeptical about the prospect of overturning entrenched corporate interest in the local economy by law, cautioning that "if there is a legal action against a government interest, the judiciary is not that strong to resist" (Courtright 2016). He added that in such scenario "the government will have the interest of the company because they will have direct benefit from what the company is doing, leaving the people" (Courtright 2016). As discussed in chapter 6, the experiences of inequality in the dominant legal and judicial systems are also deeply embedded in unequal social structures that have emerged out of settler-colonial rule, postcolonial modernization, and post-conflict reconstruction.

NOTES

1. See *Sierra Leone Gazette* of 14 March 1810; *Royal Gazette* of December 27, 1817; *Sierra Leone Advertiser* of 27 April 1818; and Takehiko Achiai, "The Bifurcated Development of Land Policy in Sierra Leone," *Journal of Asian and African Studies*, 40 (August 2016).

2. Plantations in cocoa and coffee were relatively on a small scale compared to production enclaves in other West African countries such as Ghana and Ivory Coast.

3. See http://www.koiduholdings.com/diamonds-of-sierra-leone.php.

4. The 1956 Alluvial Diamond Mining Ordinance and Rules legalized diamond mining by native Sierra Leone. According to Saylor (1967), two factors necessitated the establishment of this scheme: (i) it was becoming increasingly costly for the SLST to employ armed guards to prevent encroachment on its diamond deposits; and (ii) the government was losing a large amount of custom revenues as illegally mined diamonds were being smuggled into neighboring countries. The ordinance was to divert illicit mining and export of diamonds into official government channels for revenue purposes. But the majority of those who later benefited from this middle-level mining scheme were Lebanese investors who emerged to dominate Sierra Leone's economy as European and Krio businessmen withdrew.

5. Re-echoing the findings of the League of Nations, the Liberia's TRC Report (2010) notes that contract labor was nothing short of slave raiding and slave trading

using organized shipment methods with central government endorsement. In addition to Fernando Po, other shipment locations included the Panama Canal.

6. Reflecting on the history of the Armed Forces of Liberia, the action against civilians should not be surprising. Originally the Liberian Frontier Force (LFF), the primary preoccupation of soldiers had been to suppress indigenous insurrections, enforce law and order in the hinterland, recruit labor, and collect taxes and goods from local. In many cases, LFF soldiers were paid from the goods they accumulated from locals. The country's TRC report (2010) has documented a number of humiliations and suffering of indigenous peoples in the hands of LFF soldiers.

7. "Washington Consensus" has come to refer to development strategies focusing around privatization, liberalization, and macro-stability (meaning mostly price stability); a set of policies predicated upon a strong faith—stronger than warranted—in unfettered markets and aimed at reducing, or even minimizing, the role of government (see J. E. Stiglitz 2004).The term was originally coined by John Williamson (1990). But it has been subject to diverse interpretations and the practical application most often turns out quite different from Williamson's version.

8. In 2002, DFID developed a broad policy on safety, security, and access to justice (SSAJ) that built on its December 2000 Issue paper on Justice and Poverty Reduction. Two other documents that formed the basis of the SSAJ policy included the Government White Paper on "Eliminating World Poverty: A Challenge for the 21st Century" and a Strategy Paper on "Making Government Work for Poor People."

9. Business-related legislations since 2002 include the National Commission for Privatization Act, 2002; Sierra Leone Rutile Agreement Act, 2002; Marchant Shipping Act, 2003; Public Procurement Act, 2004; Investment Promotion Act, 2004; Mines and Minerals Act, 2004; External Telecommunication Tax Act, 2004; Investment Code, 2005; Telecommunications Act, 2006; Registration of Business Act, 2007; Investment and Export Promotion Agency Act, 2007; General Law (Business Start-Up) (Amendment), 2007; Diamond Cutting and Polishing Act, 2007; Sierra Leone Maritime Administration (Amendment) Act, 2007; Environment Protection Agency Act, 2008; Anti-Corruption Act, 2008; Companies Act, 2009; Good and Services Tax Act, 2009; Payment Systems Act, 2009; Home Mortgage Finance Act, 2009; Mines and Minerals (Amendment) Act, 2009; Bankruptcy Act, 2009; Weights and Measures Act, 2010; Customs Act, 2011; Petroleum (Exploration and Production) Act, 2011; National Electricity Act, 2011; Electricity and Water Regulatory Commission Act, 2011; Copyright Act, 2011; Credit Reference Act, 2011; Bank of Sierra Leone Act, 2011; Sierra Leone National Carrier Agreement Ratification Act, 2012; National Minerals Agency Act, 2012; Postal Services Regulatory Agency Act, 2012; Patents and Industrial Designs Act, 2012; Anti-Money Laundering and Combatting of Financial Terrorism Act, 2012; Sierra Leone Produce Marketing Act (Repeal) Act, 2013; Right to Access Information Act, 2013; Companies (Amendment) Act, 2014; Public-Private Partnership Act, 2014; Petroleum (Exploration and Production) (Amendment) Act, 2014; Petroleum Regulatory Agency Act 2014; Road Transport Authority (Amendment) Act, 2014; Trade Marks Act, 2014; Borrowers and Lenders Act, 2014; The Minimum Wage Order, 2014; The Stamp Duty Amendment Order, 2014; The Telecommunications (Amendment) Act,

2015; Legal Practitioners Act, 2015; Finance Act, 2016; Local Content Agency Act, 2016; Sierra Leone Small and Medium Enterprises Development Agency Act, 2016; Extractive Industry Act, 2016; Insurance Act, 2016; and Public Procurement Act, 2016 (See Sierra Leone Web, "Laws of Sierra Leone," http://www.sierra-leone.org/laws.html (accessed on October 15, 2018).

10. See http://investliberia.gov.lr/new/index.php (accessed on October 15, 2018).

11. Liberia (unlike Sierra Leon) does not have a comprehensive NIC-created database of all its laws but the following are legislations relevant to the creation of an attractive business environment since the early 2000s: The Minerals and Mining Law, 2000; The Forestry Development Authority Regulation No24 on Utilisation of Minor Forest Products, 2000; The Forestry Development Authority Regulation No26 on the Ban on Pit Sawing/Power Chain Sawing, 2001; The Public Procurement and Concessions Commission Act, 2005; Adoption of the National Forestry Reform Law, 2006; Forestry Development Authority Ten Core Regulations, 2007; Guidelines for Forest Management Planning in Liberia, 2009; Establishment of the Community Rights Act, 2009; Liberia Extractive Industries and Transparency Initiative (LEITI) Act, 2009; Land Commission Act, 2009; National Bureau of Concessions Act, 2010; Freedom of Information Act, 2010; The Investment Act, 2010; Liberia Revenue Authority Act, 2013; Abolishment of the Payment of Annual Land Rental Bid Premium on Contract Area and Merging of Export Taxes into Stumpage Act, 2013; Land Rights Policy, 2013; and The Liberia Land Authority Act, 2016; The Agriculture Law, 2017; The Banking Law, 2017; Labour Practices Law, 2017; General Business Law, 2017; Investment Incentive Act, 2017 (see Liberia Law database https://www.clientearth.org/liberia-law-database/ (accessed on November 2, 2018)).

12. See http://investliberia.gov.lr/new/index.php (accessed on October 15, 2018).

13. See https://www.wto.org/english/news_e/news16_e/acc_lbr_20jun16_e.htm (accessed on November 4, 2018).

14. See https://www.miga.org/press-release/liberia-joins-world-bank-groups-miga (accessed on November 5, 2018).

15. SIFoCC, Sierra Leone Country Profile at https://www.sifocc.org/countries/sierra-leone/.

16. See https://www.sifocc.org/about-us/#workofsifocc (accessed on November 3, 2018).

17. Palm oil is used for biofuel and as an ingredient in many foods and cosmetics. Many popular products from Starbucks, McDonalds, Unilever, and L'Oreal contain palm oil. The largest consumers of palm oil are India and the EU followed by China and the United States (Global Witness 2015).

18. Author's interview, civil society leader, Freetown, July 3, 2014.

19. Examples of recent studies include: Human Rights Watch, Whose Development? Human Rights Abuses in Sierra Leone's Mining Boom (February 2014): Network Movement for Justice and Development (NMJD) and Cord Aid, Land Rights Project: The Social, Economic, Political, Environmental, and Cultural Impact of Large-scale Land Investment in Sierra Leone (July 2013); The Oakland Institute, Understanding Land Investment in Africa: Country Report of Sierra Leone (2011); NMJD, Cost-Benefit Review of the Iron Ore Mining Agreement between

the Government of Sierra Leone and African Minerals Limited (May 2011); NMJD, Dancing with the Chameleon: Mining Communities in Sierra Leone and the many Faces of Frank Timis, Focus on Mining Companies Series No. 2 (June 2010).

20. See http://goldenveroleumliberia.com/index.php/about-gvl/our-values.

21. Letter of Complaint addressed to RSPO, Kuala Lumpur, Malaysia.

22. Stokes, E. "Riot on the Plantation." Al Jazeera America.

23. Government of Liberia, Statement by the Minister of Justice and Attorney General.

24. Government of Liberia, Speech by the President.

25. Centre for International Conflict Resolution, "Smell-no-Taste," 1.

26. See http://www.koiduholdings.com/company-mineral-rights.php.

27. See http://www.koiduholdings.com/company-key-facts.php.

28. Author's interview, paralegal, Eastern Sierra Leone, May 5, 2014.

29. Author's interview, paralegal, Eastern Sierra Leone, May 5, 2014.

30. Author's interview, paralegal, Eastern Sierra Leone, May 7, 2014.

31. According to recent statistics for Sierra Leone, the informal economy's share of GDP ranges from 45 percent to 70 percent and, whereas formal employees (i.e., formal wage and salaried workers with written contracts) constitute only 9 percent of the total workforce, over 35 percent of wage jobs and 88 percent of non-agricultural self-employed are informal (Danish Trade Council for International Development & Cooperation 2017).

32. For example, *The Sierra Leone Telegraph*, "President Koroma's War on Illegal Street Trading Starts on 1 January 2013," (29 December 2012); Milton A. Weeks, "Collective Bargaining Negotiations Between Street Vendors and City Government in Monrovia, Liberia," Women in Informal Employment Globalizing & Organizing (November 2012).

Chapter 6

The Rule of Law and Societies
in Sierra Leone and Liberia

In the previous two chapters I have examined the political economy of legal development in Sierra Leone and Liberia from their establishment as settler-colonial states to the period of post-conflict reconstruction. Continuing to dispel the notion that rebuilding the rule of law is a non-ideological technocratic enterprise, chapter 5 interrogated the ideological underpinnings of the colonial and postcolonial neoliberal economy, focusing on how both the modern and invented customary law facilitated the cash economy in the hinterland. In both countries, access to land and natural resources partly necessitated the transformation of rural (and largely subsistent) economies into producers of cheap raw materials and labor needed in the commercial metropole. One of the greatest obstacles to liberalization of the rural economy, though, was a communal system of property rights that hindered market access to local resources, particularly land. To circumvent this problem, settler-colonial governments introduced a variety of modern legal instruments, including leasehold, concession, and surface rent, that provided almost permanent access to global capital. As customary law became subordinated to English law, statutory agreements took precedence over customary property rights and the modern state became a grand possessor of property hitherto owned communally. But as the state emerged as an institutional expression of the interest of dominant groups, what was converted into statutory property easily became available to members of those groups—a process that privileged Americo-Liberians, Krios, foreigners, politicians, and economic elites I have argued.

To date, this political economy has ignited tensions between commercial (mostly outside) and communal (mostly local) interests, often resolved in favor of those with relatively greater access to statutory law and law enforcement agencies of the state. The modern law, I have noted, has also facilitated an unjust distribution of profit generated from the local economy, particularly as liberal rules allow owners of capital to reward themselves at the expense of workers and communities. But while statutory law grants access to the local economy, the very liberal nature of the modern law meant that it could not compel the ready availability of the labor force required to exploit the resources so accessed. Resolving this problem in both countries has historically led to the reinvention of a perverted form of customary law and traditional authority useful for supplying rural labor; yet, such bifurcation of the local economy ensures that the rights of workers are governed by customary rules while their labor is made available cheaply on the market.

Compounding the problem is that reform interventions in both the postcolonial and post-conflict periods have promoted policies that view the issue as a market, rather than a social justice, concern, as I have stressed in chapter 5. Macroeconomic policies imposed by the World Bank and the IMF worsened the social conditions that contributed to the outbreak of civil war in both countries and, although post-conflict rule of law reforms attracted the largest contingent of foreign investments ever seen, the economic boom that followed left most Sierra Leoneans and Liberians in the same, if not worse, precarious economic situation. Additionally, whereas the rule of law regulates and restricts access to the formal economy, the informal sector, which provides alternative livelihood to most people, remains largely marginalized by the modern English law.

This political economy of reform is hosted by the societies which, despite being marginalized by the distribution of rewards, must be concerned about how legal development affects their social interactions and survival. Therefore, the present chapter analyzes to the relationship between rule of law reforms and local societies in Sierra Leone and Liberia, paying closer attention to their conception of justice and dispute resolution practices. Drawn largely from the experiences and perspectives of ordinary people, I analyze how the social relevance of law affects people's interpretation, appreciation, and application of new rules and institutions introduced during the processes of legal reconstruction. I argue that legal development disproportionately benefits those who historically possess the social status, wealth, education, and influence to take advantage of legal institutions to resolve social and interpersonal conflicts. I also note that dispute resolution mechanisms outside the state system appeal to people of low socioeconomic status not merely because of cultural values and beliefs but because those mechanisms produce processes and outcomes that better suit their socioeconomic conditions compared to the state system. These arguments are made in five sections: (i) political economy of colonial and postcolonial customary law, (ii) post-conflict reform and non-state justice systems, (iii) restoring the superiority of English law, (iv) adversarial adjudication and local dispute resolution, and (v) access to justice for whom.

SETTLER-COLONIAL CUSTOMARY LAW, MODERNIZATION, AND SOCIETY

It must be recalled from the previous chapters that Freetown, the capital, has been the center of Sierra Leone's modern statebuilding system. From its original establishment as a settler colony for liberated Africans following the abolition of the transatlantic slave trade to becoming a British Crown colony, the administration of state justice has been concentrated in this region, a trend that has continued in the country's postwar reconstruction agenda. Here, property rights and commercial transactions are based on the formal English law, which privileges people who have acquired Western education and embraced Judeo-Christian values. It is also worth recollecting that there were indigenous inhabitants in the western area of Freetown before the arrival of freed slaves and that people from upcountry have moved to this urban center for a variety of reasons (see below).[1] This category of people of indigenous/rural descent constitutes the majority population, but they are peripheral to the modern system because its legal institutions have historically given advantage to descendants of early settlers (Krios), the educated class, and the central governing elites.

The ethno-political history of Sierra Leone suggests that while the Krios were the minority descendants from liberated Africans, their close association with the colonial administration accorded them an opportunity to access formal education and adopt Western values. Kandeh notes that "education and Christianization, especially anglicization, were viewed by Krios as central to their identity and the creolization of protectorate Africans" (1972, 87). Due to their early access to education and location in the colony, the Krios were considered British subjects capable of using modern institutions under the English common law, unlike their counterparts in the interior who were regarded as "protected persons" under native law. English law protected commerce and state administration, areas dominated by the Krios who regarded themselves as rightful heirs of colonial rule (Kup 1975; Wyse 1989). Harrell-Bond et al. have argued that "the organization of the administration of the colony gave advantage, on a fairly consistent basis, to the settler population" (1987, 3). These advantages have historically been inaccessible to the original inhabitants of Freetown and the protectorate because the English legal system viewed them as "natives" even when they resided in the colony. Natives were assimilated into the colony and Krio community only after attaining the markers of Western civilization, including Christianity and formal education (Kandeh 1992).

But once the national balance of power tilted in favor of provincial elites during the decolonization period, Krio social dominance in Freetown started giving way to educated protectorate elites, both traditional and modern. In

terms of population size, people of indigenous/rural origin have outnum-
bered the Krios due to prewar migration in search of better socioeconomic
opportunities and internal displacement during the civil war (Statistics Sierra
Leone 2015). Earlier in colonial times, the growing "native" population in
the colony prompted the colonial administration to institute a tribal authority
in Freetown to advice the British governor about how to deal with matters
affecting people of indigenous descent. Tribal heads were also appointed
to assist the colonial government in deterring criminal behavior among the
indigenous population and tracking down suspected criminals who escaped
back into the interior (Harrell-Bond et al. 1978). Unlike paramount chiefs in
provincial areas who oversaw an entire chiefdom, a tribal head was supposed
to be responsible for a specific ethnic group in the western area and he was
appointed directly by the governor, now the president. The 2011 tribal authority policy states that "the primary role of tribal heads is to promote harmony
of tradition and customs among ethnic groups in the western area by acting
to prevent and resolve conflicts through mediation of customary matters"
(16). This policy and the 2011 Local Court Act are also in consonance with
the position of successive governments to eschew the application of customary law in Freetown, going as far back as the 1967 National Reformation
Council, which abolished tribal headmen courts and extended the jurisdiction
of magistrate courts to include customary law.

The provincial regions (protectorate, under colonial rule) continue to be
predominantly populated by non-Krio Sierra Leoneans, with a much more
diverse ethno-regional, religious, and cultural backgrounds. But as noted in
chapter 4, colonial indirect rule of the protectorate was designed to utilize
ethno-regional identities for the purposes of maintaining the social order
required for the extension of formal authority and extraction of resources in
the interior. With this colonial influence, two factors need to be underscored
when accounting for how traditional culture evolved and survived since settler-colonial rule: local class tensions and power politics. For instance, rural
disturbances prior to independence were a form of rural radicalism intended
to challenge traditional authorities and the institution of chieftaincy, which
were being officially legitimated by the central state. Those writing from a
modernization perspective at the time went as far as to predict a postcolonial
populist uprising against customary institutions that had become too exploitative and exclusionary of the people they were created to protect or represent.[2]
Kilson, who was a leading exponent of the modernization argument, noted,
"the peasantry's changing perception of its relationship to chiefly rulers were
attributable to modernization forces which brought the peasants into touch
with new ideas and mode of life" (1966, 20). According to this view, uprising in the south where missionary education was mostly concentrated was to
be spearheaded by a vanguard of educated youngsters who could no longer

withstand the illegal levies of corrupt and extortionist customary institutions. Describing the Kono Progressive Union in the eastern mining district as the first radical class-oriented movement, Cartwright linked this development to the fact that "mine workers were strangers in their place of work, thrown together with men from other places and tribes and thus largely freed from the restraints on behavior by traditional authority" (1970, 69). Most of these men who had migrated from the north, where chieftaincy was a more sacred institution, were expected to return later with a radical orientation to instigate an intergenerational conflict in their homeland, part of the public and scholarly reasoning at the time.

The other aspect, epitomized by Barrows's (1976) and later Tangri's (1978) work, was local politics as the source of intermittent rural violence in modern colonial rule itself instead of static feudalistic institutions. The colonial practice of limiting chieftaincy to descendants of chiefs who signed "friendship treaties" with the government had resulted in a "ruling house" system and each chiefdom had more than one ruling family contending for that position.[3] With the advent of the cash economy, which transformed chieftaincy into a rich source of power, prestige, and wealth—even priced among the new educated elite—"the dynamics of local politics [were] in large measure channelled by the rules which govern competition" for this institution (Barrows 1976, 15). Since only individuals from "ruling houses" were eligible to become paramount chiefs and the period of normal incumbency was for life, the stakes in chieftaincy elections became extremely high. Meanwhile, by making deposition, which remained the only way to unseat a living paramount chief, an exclusive prerogative of the central government, this mechanism of leadership change became an important lever of national influence over chiefdom politics. "Opposition ruling families seeking to remove the incumbent paramount chiefs [would] petition for central government intervention in chiefdom affairs" just as the incumbents would want to "forge alliances with powerful elements at the central level in order to secure their tenure in office" (Barrows 1976, 16). This interpretation of tradition was also not a refutation of the claim that young people had genuine grievances against forced labor, excessive fines, and arbitrary penalties imposed by elders as the intergenerational conflict thesis would claim. Rather, local dynastic ambition was to intersect with these popular grievances to mobilize commoners for anti–ruling elite protest.

Similarly, the legacy of Americo-Liberian domination is a dual legal system that differentiates between Americo-Liberians who are predominantly based in Montserrado County (which host the capital Monrovia) and indigenous Liberians who were regarded as "uncivilized" people to be governed under statutory laws. But as in Sierra Leone, rural-urban migration due to concentration of social opportunities in Monrovia and the armed conflict over the years resulted in an influx of indigenous Liberians to Montserrado County. Whereas Americo-Liberians see the formal legal and justice system as their main forum for dispute resolution, Liberians of indigenous origin often see the state system as only a complement to non-state customary law and practices (Isser et al. 2009). In fact, unlike Sierra Leone where the application of customary law is highly regulated by the state, the 2005 revised Rules and Regulations Governing the Hinterland of Liberia recognizes that paramount chiefs "shall adjudicate all domestic and cultural matters, including relevant matters from the chiefdom to the clan chief's office" (Ministry of Internal Affairs 2005).

But as in colonial Sierra Leone, Americo-Liberian elites instrumentalized culture to divide and rule indigenous Liberians. A common development in settler-indigenous relations during the Tubman era (1944–1971) was the building of extensive personal relations and informal networks between the president and traditional rulers. The linchpin of Tubman's close association with traditional societies was his regular National Executive Council meetings, which created avenues for him to personally oversee and resolve matters related to the administration of interior affairs. In these meetings, the president always seized the opportunity "to adjudicate criminal and civil claims from the native populations at the presidential mansion through executive decisions, dismiss corrupt district commissioners, and secure traditional land tenure rights" (Levitt 2005, 188). In a symbolic show of his induction into traditional society, Tubman was declared the Supreme Zo (ceremonial head) of the male Poro Secret society, a position he had to reconcile with his role as Grand Master of the Masonic Order in Monrovia.[4] Given the president's identification with traditional culture, it became acceptable—even fashionable—for indigenous Africans who had been assimilated into settler society through the ward system to restore their African names and for public officials to wear African attire to grace public occasions. It became common place for members of the settler elite to talk proudly of their African heritage and historical kinship ties to the continent.

Notwithstanding these reforms, it would be historically inaccurate to attribute changes in settler-indigenous relations solely to Tubman's policy initiatives or to conclude that Liberia was witnessing two equal cultures coalescing into a new society. Levitt reminds us that "native Liberian decision-makers influenced the nature of settler-indigenous relations just as much, if not more than, settler politicians and the success of Tubman's policies can be attributed in part to the willingness of native kings to accommodate change" (2005, 188). He also argues that the decision to embrace peaceful relations after more than a century of continuous settler-indigenous conflicts was partly a strategic move by indigenous leaders in realization of the enhanced capabilities of the LFF (Liberian Frontier Force).

Conversely, Nelson (1985) draws attention to the superficiality of Tubman's integration policies by arguing that competition between ethnic groups for official recognition during the Tubman era exacerbated tribal consciousness of their separate identities. For example, while members of the Vai ethnic group were the most willing to take advantage of Tubman's policies, the Kru and Grebo ethnic groups, which had been in frequent wars with the Republic, were more circumspect in their response. Moreover, with this politicization of ethnic identity and President's Doe's ethno-military rule (1980–1990), it was inevitable that the civil war in Liberia would be affected by ethno-regional identity just as the one in Sierra Leone was being instigated in part by resentment against the abuse of traditional authorities instituted by British indirect colonial rule. What needs to be reiterated though is that the decay of tradition institutions emanated from encounters with the modern state during settler-colonial rule and postcolonial authoritarianism. It was the central modern state, in its quest for top-down control of local politics, that corrupted and undermined African traditional governance systems and this elitism must be separated from broader customary practices that remain vital for survival in poor socioeconomic conditions as I argued in an article published by *African Affairs* (Sesay 2019).

ENGAGING NON-STATE JUSTICE
SYSTEMS POST-CONFLICT

The periods between indigenous rule and post-conflict reconstruction in both countries have witnessed a continuation, if not exacerbation, of the similar social conditions discussed above, including the confluence between ethno-regional identity, class, and social status. The growth of non-Krio population continues to dramatically change the social and demographic organization of Freetown. For instance, lacking access to the same economic opportunities that colonialism granted the Krios and later educated protectorate elites, the majority population in Freetown faces massive social inequities that have been compounded by elitist neoliberal policies particularly in the postwar years. Their social condition corresponds to what Tamanaha (2015) calls the "urban ring" settlements populated by poor and less educated people. The divide between the core and urban ring is not spatial as "the poor sometimes live in the cosmopolitan center while the wealthy may live in enclaves" (Tamanaha 2015, 12). Rather, the urban ring concerns people surviving at the fringes of those with power and privilege to take advantage of the modern system.

During fieldwork in Sierra Leone, this author observed that this phenomenon of "urban ring" is growing in the western area of Freetown not just because of displacement during the war but also, and perhaps more importantly, because of the postwar economic boom in the country. It was stated in chapter 5 that the country's pre-Ebola economy was among the fastest growing in sub-Saharan Africa. One way that this economic growth seemed to have manifested itself has been an increasing urbanization with business elites investing in private projects alongside the state modernization agenda. But in this mainstream economy, most residents in Freetown belong to the lower working class, which constituted about 76 percent of the workforce in the late 2000s as noted in the previous chapter (Sierra Leone Union of Population Studies 2004). In addition, urbanization has been accompanied by a vibrant informal sector that accommodates most people of indigenous/rural origin who cannot enter the formal economy. For example, while economic and political elites are investing in personal housing estates in the sprawling modern capital, many unemployed people are making subsistence income in an informal quarrying industry, a local stone-crushing activity to produce concrete needed for building construction. Another informal occupation associated with the economic boom is a caretaker, someone who is allowed to reside temporarily on a construction site or land as watchman over that property. Others have sought subcontracting opportunities to provide labor to a contractor who pays them a daily wage without any formal contract. Economic growth seems to be driving these types of employment because it is arguably cheaper for the capitalist class to hire labor in an informal sector free from industrial regulations and official workers' benefits.

Interacting with residents in Freetown, this author found that people in this informal economy live a highly interdependent lifestyle, almost synonymous to communal living in the interior. Most employment opportunities of this informal, and sometimes underground, economy are obtained through informal trust networks, and job security often depends on cultivation and maintenance of these personal relationships, both vertical and horizontal. These informal relations are based not only on kinship ties derived from indigenous backgrounds but also on a network of relationships with "big men" of connection and wealth. Like residents in provincial areas, people in the peripheral urban ring seem to define access to justice in terms of both its relevance to their conflict resolution needs and the cost involved in seeking redress.

These conditions are also common in Monrovia as most participants in this study confirmed. Moreover, since the administration of formal justice is highly centralized in Monrovia, these challenges become acute for people living farther away from the administrative center in rural counties, districts, and villages just as in Sierra Leone. For instance, Krahn-dominated Grand Gedeh of southeastern Liberia is the third-largest county in the country and historically one of the most neglected.[5] Just before this research, the county's population was about 140,934 inhabitants and its total landmass estimated at 10,276 square kilometers.[6] A typical rural Liberian county, the roads linking Grand Gedeh to other parts of the country are in deplorable condition, unpaved for the most part and almost impassable by vehicle during the rainy season.[7] The Liberian National Police had about eighty-six police officers deployed in the entire county, with thirty-nine of them stationed in the headquarter town of Zwedru, while the rest were distributed across the remaining seven districts that contain sixteen chiefdoms and 236 smaller towns. The local judiciary included one circuit court operating on a quarterly basis and courts for traffic, revenue, and debt offenses, all housed in the same building at the central town of Zwedru. In addition, there were eight magistrate courts and about twenty poorly resourced Justice of the Peace (JP) courts.[8]

Meanwhile, as illustrated in chapter 4, post-conflict reforms in both countries mostly concentrated on rebuilding the state system. There were only few engagements with the non-state traditional and informal dispute resolution systems and, where attention was devoted to those systems, they were subjected to the same biases associated with mainstream rule of law assistance, including a problem-solving approach based on narrow technocracy, emphasis on international norms and standards, and the Weberian idea of state monopoly over the legitimate use of force. The only US-funded program designed with a broader scope outside Montserrado and the state justice system was the Carter Centre's Access to Justice Program, which aimed at engaging indigenous conflict management in Liberia to foster their respect of rule of law and human rights standards. With initial funding from the Department of State's Democracy, Human Rights and Labor Bureau, the Carter Centre launched a pilot project to raise traditional justice reform issues to a higher level of national dialogue among key rule of law stakeholders in Liberia. Initiated in 2007, the project supported engagement with the National Traditional Council (NTC) on customary justice issues such as public participation and the need to harmonize formal and traditional justice systems. Succeeding the pilot was a $6.75 million USAID-funded project titled Strengthening Citizen Participation in Government: Access to Justice and Information. The activities under the access to justice component were intended to enable the NTC and county-level traditional authorities to implement best practices in conflict resolution so that they can legitimately intervene to resolve local disputes. In April 2010, the Carter Centre, in partnership with UNMIL and the United States Institute of Peace (USIP), convened a national conference on enhancing access to justice that called for a Legal Working Group (LWG) to study the current status of Liberia's dual legal system (Carter Centre 2010).

In 2011, the Carter Centre received an additional $4 million in funding support to continue the original activities in addition to training community legal advisors (CLAs) and providing civic education on legal rights and empowerment issues. Working in collaboration with the Liberian Catholic Justice and Peace Commission (JPC), CLAs have been deployed in several counties "to provide rural citizens with free information on their rights under the law, help people interact with government courts and traditional authorities, mediate small-scale conflicts, and engage in advocacy around justice issues" (Flomoku and Reeves 2010, 45). Usually, civic and legal educators focus on existing national laws and new legislations relating to inheritance rights, rape and domestic violence, trial by ordeal, land disputes, and court fines.

In Sierra Leone, DFID commissioned Peter Tucker as a consultant for the Sierra Leone Customary Law Reform Project. This consultancy followed two earlier projects sponsored by DFID and managed by the British Council—the Paramount Chief Restoration Project (PCRP) and the Law Development Project. Based on the TRC recommendations, the Government of Sierra Leone (GOSL) in 2005 also commissioned a leading customary law expert to develop a position paper on customary law courts in Sierra Leone (Fofanah 2005). But the most formidable step to reform customary law was the establishment of a Local Courts Reform Committee. Funded by the UK Justice Sector Development Project (JSDP), this committee, in partnership with the Law Reform Commission, was mandated to review the 1963 Local Court Act No. 20 and draft a revised bill for parliament. In August 2011, the Sierra Leone Parliament passed a new Local Court Act No. 10, which repealed and replaced the 1963 Act in its entirety. Among major changes wrought by the 2011 Local Court Act is, first, the establishment of provincial Local Courts Service Committees for the purpose of advising the Judicial and Legal Service Commission on appointment, transfer, promotion, and dismissal of local court personnel. Under the 1963 Act, appointment was based on recommendation from Chiefdom Council headed by the paramount chief to the Minister of Local Government. Other institutional restructuring includes removal of local courts from the ambit of the Ministry of Local Government to the mainstream judiciary, headed by the Chief Justice, salaries of court functionaries to be paid from a consolidated revenue fund, secure tenure of court chairmen, and criminalization of adjudication without legal authority.

The new Act also redefines the linkages between the local court and English law courts. In addition to applying customary law, the local courts are now the court of first instance for minor criminal offenses and all civil cases governed by general law where the matter in dispute does not exceed one million Leones ($150). Moreover, the resident magistrate of a judicial district, who is a trained lawyer, serves as chairman of the District Appeal Court, constituted to hear appeals from the local court. The magistrate sits with two assessors in customary law, but their advice on customary matters is not binding on him as he has exclusive legal authority to make decisions regarding cases on appeal. Although legal practitioners do not have the right of audience in a local court, they are allowed representation once a matter has been brought before the District Appeal Court as well as the Local Appeals Division of the High Court and Supreme Court. Also, dissatisfied parties in the local courts can take their cases for judicial review to the Customary Law Officer who is equally trained in English law, serving primarily as State Counsel for an entire region. In terms of code of conduct, the local courts are guided by the same Rules of Court Committee whose responsibility is to formulate formal rules to regulate the procedures of all courts in Sierra Leone, including rules that prevent malicious, frivolous, and vexatious proceedings (Section 145, 1991 Constitution).

Considering that some aspects of customary law and traditional dispute resolution emerged in the context of colonial-setter rule and postcolonial/ settler authoritarianism, they need to be reformed rather than simply reinstated. The problem though is the one-size-fits-all approach that places undue premium on state authority and international standards, often neglecting the dispute resolution needs, priorities, and preferences of the majority population, which subsists largely outside the state system. For example, reformers (both international and domestic) view transferring local courts to the judiciary of Sierra Leone as consistent with the principle of separation of powers and makes for an efficient system as court officials are now answerable to one ministry instead of two (Sesay 2003). One High Court justice in Freetown describes the 2011 Act as a triumph for the rule of law, arguing that "as formal judicial institutions, local courts must be restructured in a way to get them to respond to the rule of law and good governance."[9] Invariably promoted as twenty-first-century modernization of justice, no one questions why traditional conflict resolution mechanisms should be made to conform to international standards in the first place. Questions of how doing so subverts the effectiveness of institutions that are meant to be informal and accessible to local populations are completely out of the reform debate in both countries. Moreover, as discussed below, reformers do not seem to realize that those whose lives and livelihood are rooted in poor socioeconomic conditions and informal trust networks often experience rule of law reform as reinforcing existing inequities and unequal access to "public goods."

RESTORING THE SUPERIORITY OF ENGLISH LAW

As noted, the legal history of both Sierra Leone and Liberia has been based on the superimposition of the English common law upon indigenous customary law, even though their majority populations have limited contact with the state. English law has become the general law not because it is applicable to the majority population but because it provides the legal basis for a modern state system and economy dominated by the governing class. Although people of rural and indigenous origin continue to populate urban centers, the central legal and administrative institutions remained rooted in rules that are more familiar to the ruling and educated class, bequeathed by the settler-colonial administrations. In both countries, the irony is that what became codified as state law emerged from Anglo-Saxon customary law, which was itself based on informal legal norms and practices of European people.[10] Such subordination by legal reform is particularly evident in Sierra Leone, where new laws such as the 2011 Local Court Act have criminalized the judicial functions of local chiefs and reaffirmed the prohibition against the application of customary law in Freetown, even though the city's majority inhabitants are of indigenous-rural origin. As in this comment, seven tribal heads included in this research unanimously perceived the prohibition of customary law in Freetown as superimposition of English law (which historically favored the Krios and educated elites) on their people.

> And as we all know, adjudication is a matter of choice and I have always been telling them that we have one constitution of Sierra Leone but operating on a two-tier system when it comes to the area of justice. I see no reason why we have the local court system in the provinces but not in the western area. Is it because the Krios who were very influential in those days thought it fit that only their own kith and kin should have access to the formal justice system and that they should deny us the provincials that right? So, I have always been telling them that they are not doing justice to our people who have been coming from the provinces.[11]

The post-conflict reinforcement of the superiority of English law is also seen in asymmetric relations between the official and non-official justice systems. Initially, most legal professionals (whether members of the bar or bench) who participated in this study tended to treat unofficial dispute resolution mechanisms with utmost condescension and distrust, irrespective of the social functions performed by these mechanisms in the informal economy and communal settings. A typical example of this attitude is how lawyers, judicial officials, and human rights activists characterize unofficial palaver huts in Sierra Leone (commonly known as chief barray). They describe them as "kangaroo courts," a term that originates solely from a formal legal perspective of what a legitimate court ought to be and which institutional actors have prerogative over judicial adjudication. In addition to the derogatory connation, some legal practitioners consider "kangaroo courts" as a threat to the law and order functions of the state. One lawyer, who said, "I fear the Kangaroo courts that we have in Freetown more than the Kangaroo courts we have upcountry," claimed that the unofficial courts "are terrorizing people and using traditional means."[12] Another lawyer, who serves both as Customary Law Officer and Regional State Counsel, went further to use the Local Court Act to deride unofficial courts as follows.

When the 2011 reform came into effect, the Local Court Act of 1963 was amended. The clause to prevent chiefs from adjudicating was retained and in addition to it there is now a penalty clause. But they continue to have the kangaroo courts. We call them kangaroo courts because these are courts in which no statements of the parties are taken down. You talk freely and the other party comes and talks freely. At the end of the day they give judgment in favour of whosoever they think deserves it. And if you are dissatisfied you cannot appeal. And the worst thing is they are extorting so much money from people. The local courts in some chiefdoms are virtually not functioning because all the matters are diverted to the chiefs who more or less extort huge sums of money from people.[13]

From this characterization, kangaroo courts are equated with negative terms such as "extortion," "illegitimacy," "abnormality," "aberration," and "disorder." Nonetheless, from this author's community observations and interviews, chief barrays are not as disorderly as portrayed by some of these legal practitioners. There are stipulated rules and procedures (though unwritten) that must be followed and the level of order required in certain proceedings may be comparable to the serenity found in Supreme Court sittings as one paralegal stated in her interview.[14] This study also found no correlation between legality (meaning, officially authorized by law) and legitimacy (meaning, appreciated by the people). Chief barrays lack the legal authority vested in state-constituted local courts; yet, as one former Customary Law Officer puts it, "sometimes people use these so-called illegal courts more than the legally constituted courts."[15] Post-conflict efforts to delegitimize unofficial courts is more a product of a liberal conception of justice held by lawyers and reformers who perceive "kangaroo court" as fundamental barriers to justice than a reflection of public perception of their operation and social relevance. In fact, many studies have found unofficial courts to be relatively more effective and trustworthy than the formal law courts and police (Isser et al. 2009; Institute of Governance Reform 2019; Sawyer 2008; Sesay 2019).

Another source of legal subordination is an increasing propensity by rule of law promoters to drastically limit the jurisdiction of traditional justice systems (administered by local chiefs and other customary authorities), despite their indispensability to the dispute resolution needs of most Liberians and Sierra Leoneans. The main target of this jurisdictional restriction is traditional institutions of criminal justice, most notably Liberia's trial by ordeal (TBO) practices, which range from the ingestion of a poisonous concoction (commonly known as *sassywood*) to oath taking and swearing to determine a defendant's guilt or innocence.[16] In 2008, the Ministries of Internal Affairs and Justice announced that Liberia would no longer permit the use of any ordeal-like extrajudicial procedures, adding that those who permit or administer *sassywood* and other TBOs are doing so illegally. With a strong backing from the international community, the Solicitor-General of Liberia spearheaded a widely publicized campaign to end the practice, showcasing exemplary prosecutions of traditional chiefs who violated the blanket prohibition. For rule of law and human rights activists this announcement was a progressive development to remove discriminatory primitive practices that amount to torture from Liberia's criminal justice system whereas rural Liberians expressed serious concerns about the creation of a justice vacuum in the absence of accessible judicial and law enforcement institutions. In the remote Grand Geddeh County, residents who are still using non-lethal forms of TBO lamented the blanket ban for undermining vital dispute resolution mechanisms that have proven indispensable in investigating cases considered inadmissible by the formal state system.

In Sierra Leone, these cases include what is known as "threatening remarks by native means," a serious problem affecting local communities but which cannot be investigated by the police or litigated in a formal court.[17] Citing the rules of court, a local court chairman insisted that such charges must be dismissed as "malicious, vexatious, and frivolous," while those affected said such threats destabilize social and economic interaction.[18] Kelsall (2009) examines this challenge in arguing that the Special Court for Sierra Leone was ill-suited for a society in which the personal is an inextricable blend of human and supernatural forces that cannot be subject to positivist evidential verification, liberal conception of law, and Judeo-Christian values. At the same time, when the state maintains prerogative over the legitimate use of force while being incapable of substantively exercising that authority nationwide and over certain disputes, it induces illegality as people turn to unofficial parallel structures even though they lack state-sanctioned rights and protection.

This is not to preclude the fact that unofficial dispute resolution mechanisms are flawed. In chapter 4, I argued that traditional authorities are resisting rule of law reforms due in part to the threat posed to the local balance of power and their material well-being. The lack of legal status means that mechanisms established by chiefs are not a formal court of record, their decisions are not officially recognized and cannot be appealed against in a court of law, and their operators are not formerly trained to administer justice. That they do not have a warrant of legal authority also implies that their judgments could be set aside in a court of law and their very existence is against the law. Where charges are levied, the amount requested is not standardized and the absence of a formal receipt of payment often implies that monies collected could not be formally accounted for. Parties are not obliged by law to comply with an invitation to attend and abide by decisions made in chiefs' barrays. Human rights advocates have a reason to be concerned about the rights of women in these unofficial legal systems, particularly in highly patriarchal societies as northeastern Sierra Leone and Grand Geddeh County in Liberia, where male-dominated traditions and customs deny women equal access to local decision-making power. In these local jurisdictions, the patriarchal practices in governance institutions like chieftaincy are likely to be reflected in rules of customary law, the institutions responsible for their application, and the ability of women to access justice. There were legitimate concerns about customary and Islamic law (as related to marriage, divorce, inheritance), as stated in the Sierra Leone TRC report, that led to the three gender laws (Devolution of Estates Act of 2007, Domestic Violence Act of 2007, and Registration of Customary Marriage and Divorce Act of 2009). Indeed, by just "coopting and reinforcing existing legal cultures," which were established by settler-colonial indirect rule, rule of law reformers "may be merely reifying the colonial legacy" (Pimentel 2010, 6).

The issue here is the often-wholesale castigation of these local cultural systems as unfit for reform while the rebuilding of equally flawed modern state structures is never called into question. As DFID's flip-flop on the Paramount Chief Restoration Project (PCRP) indicates, reformers tend to place African cultural institutions in a separate category where the options are limited to either their restoration or abandonment, preferring the state system, which may be equally or even more deficient, as the only legitimate subject of reform. Where reformers attempt to engage unofficial institutions and practices, the idea is usually to bring them into conformity with the modern state or international standards (Isser 2011). Worse still, those who engage non-state security and justice systems have done very little to differentiate between structures that emerged top-down in the context of colonialism and state weaknesses and those which are more socially oriented toward the needs and priorities of ordinary people.[19] As Hamoudi reminds us, it takes "a mind colonized in the assumption of legal centralism" to presume that the only possible solution to abusive customary practices is to bring them under the control of state institutions that are equally abusive (2014, 143). This notion of "colonised mind" is echoed in this interview of another Customary Law Officer in Freetown who insisted that superimposition of English law has nothing to do with legality, but everything to do with the politics of reform.

So, it is not a matter of legality; it is matter of political superiority. That's the problem. The English common law has no legal basis but political superiority. They wanted to maintain us as subjects and they were calling us British subjects while they remain the bosses. And we now in our own lifetime are supporting them and reinforcing these ideas. That is the accident of our history and nation and that's why we would remain Third World or developing nations.[20]

The subordination of customary law has been reinforced by the fact the dominant legal system in Sierra Leone and Liberia emerges from an international legal tutelage. This is partly a product of an orthodox judicial training and culture that post-conflict justice reform has only sought to reinforce. It must be recalled that settler-colonial administrations denied the provision of training facilities for legal education in most of their colonies in Africa as a matter of policy.[21] Instead, few Africans were offered the opportunity to travel abroad to acquire legal education, the most famous destination for British colonies being the Inns of Court in London. At independence, when more lawyers were needed to run the courts and various government bureaucracies, African lawyers trained in English law were automatically put in charge of legal training to ensure a smooth transition to local legal education (as most of them had acquired their education in England of other British Commonwealth countries). Invariably, most African law faculties and schools adopted an English legal education curriculum almost wholescale with a two-tier system of academic training in a recognized university for a bachelor of law (LLB) degree followed by a professional training at a law school for a call to the bar (Barrister/Solicitor Certificate).

Yet the issue, as Manteaw (2008) argues, was that African lawyers called to the English Bar were trained exclusively as barristers, not solicitors, and their legal training paid no attention to the challenges of practicing law in countries with multiple systems of law. Since independence, local legal training in Sierra Leone and Liberia has been dominated by private practice approach to juridical relationships focusing more on British contract law and American principles of constitutionalism and human rights. Also, the legal curricula in both countries are still heavily reliant on lecture pedagogy complemented with ad hoc legal clinics and a pupillage experience in the chambers of senior lawyers. Particularly problematic is that legal training has not been tailored to produce lawyers who would be sensitive and responsive to current local realities, needs, and priorities of justice. As in many postcolonial countries, local legal training in both countries was never "designed to meet domestic development needs, stimulate vibrant interest in customary law as it relates to the global legal order, and to fix basic structural problems" (Manteaw 2008, 938). Apart from a few modules in legal history and African family law, there is no rigorous comprehensive training in customary law or African legal traditions at both the academic and professional levels, according to those officials interviewed in this study. Students are educated to uphold the superiority of the English law that they would be interpreting, and such a law is referred to as general law, even though its application is limited to urban cosmopolitan areas. As one lawyer attests, legal training is still highly conventional and elitist, a situation that many young legal practitioners interviewed in this research considered as a serious problem.

The lack of human resource is a result of the lack of decentralization of legal training. Legal training over the years, until recently when we started the law department at the University of Makeni, was centralized in Freetown in the hands of few elites. But legal training is also conventional in Sierra Leone; it is only based for people who want to become lawyers. There is not that kind of legal education that can trained other people; for instance, law and justice officers in the courts, bailiffs, court clerks, registrars, police prosecutors. There is no formal training for these people [even though] these are the frontline soldiers for justice in Sierra Leone.[22]

The current justice reform programs intended to build professional capacity have only reinforced this orthodoxy by bringing in foreign professionals, supporting preexisting educational institutions, and developing training programs for local lawyers. With international legal experts from the ABA, British law schools, and legal firms in Western Europe and North America, most training support provided by reformers was to enhance the capacity of lawyers and other legal professionals rather than transforming the educational structure through initiatives such as curriculum review and introduction of new methods of learning oriented toward local realities. Of course, expatriates would have limited interest to expand training curricula to incorporate local content as their education and professional experience have been abroad. However, expatriates often do not realize that the vast majority of those who can afford such education are either descendants of, or related to, the historically dominant elite class (Manteaw 2008). Without this understanding, the alliance between an elitist legal system and the ruling class only becomes strengthened by rule of law reforms that prioritize the English law and state authority over indigenous and customary systems of justice with damaging social consequences as I discuss below.

ADVERSARIAL ADJUDICATION AND
LOCAL DISPUTE RESOLUTION

The preference for traditional justice practices in Sierra Leone and Liberia is usually not grounded in abstract notions of "tradition" and "culture" but based on rational consideration of the socioeconomic conditions of most citizens (part of which is the informal economy examined in chapter 5). Liberians who participated in this study subscribed to the view that resolving dispute through the formal justice channel undermines interpersonal relationships and breeds enmity that may affect long-term coexistence, particularly in homogenous communities. From the interviews and observation of local dispute resolution mechanisms, this justice norm reflects the social organization of most rural communities in Liberia, where there is a strong sense of informal reciprocal obligation. In these communities, decisions about appropriate redress is shaped by past social interaction as well as the consideration of how to minimize harm to long-term kinship and neighborhood relations. In other words, and as the comment below suggests, consideration of what to do about a dispute takes into account social issues that may seem extraneous to the matter in question but which are affected by the way such dispute is eventually resolved.

> I remember an incident in which I reported someone to the police. It was about a false allegation made by one neighbor that I am in love with her husband. I took her to court but later I was prevailed upon to remove the matter from court for in-house settlement. I agreed to withdraw that case from the court because of the man's relationship with my husband. He was a nice man and helpful to my family. When they were looking for Gio people during the Doe era, he was protecting my husband. Also, they brought big people who are in a position to appeal to me and I accepted their plea.[23]

This respondent's decision to withdraw a case from the police was informed by memory of an assistance a neighbor offered her family during the civil war in Liberia that witnessed pro-government Krahn people attacking members of the Gio ethnic group. What further motivated this decision was the instrumentality of "big people" whose reputation in the community could be relied upon as moral guarantor for interpersonal and communal conflict resolution. These people were in a position not only to appeal to this lady but also to guarantee an end of enmity between both parties. Her experience is consistent with one of the findings of a USIP-funded study: "most Liberians would be unsatisfied with the justice meted out by the formal system, even if it were able to deliver on the basics" (Isser et al. 2009, 3) As confirmed by fifteen respondents who also withdrew cases from the police or court, most rural Liberians are concerned that punitive actions would undermine informal trust networks upon which the social fabric of their extended family and/or community rests. Characterizing this practice as a widely accepted local justice norm, a farmer in Grand Geddeh in fact asserted that

> We have what we call community settlement. If people are having a dispute in a household, the landlord would get involved. If the landlord is not around, they would take the matter to the town chief. If the town chief cannot resolve it, then it is forwarded to higher local authorities. People prefer to settle their cases out of court because Liberians have a way of thinking. If someone takes you to court for just a minor issue, then he becomes your everlasting enemy. So, you just don't take someone to court like that.[24]

For Sierra Leone, questions about the social relevance of justice norms emanated from the historical and structural forces discussed earlier coupled with external interest in using its postwar reconstruction agenda as a model for institutionalizing international criminal justice. But the social implications in terms of survival in the informal economy and rural communal settings resemble the experiences of Liberia. For instance, Sierra Leoneans describe matters which violate the national penal codes as "police cases" (e.g., land disputes, murder, rape, wounding with intent) and all sixty ordinary citizens regarded them as matters for the criminal justice system. However, disputants (about twenty participants had been to the police or formal courts) expressed concerns about the adversarial and punitive nature of the criminal justice system, a norm linked to the common law tradition and reinforced by transitional justice mechanisms like the Special Court, which stressed individual criminal accountability and punishment. The court was a hybrid mechanism based on the principle of individual moral culpability, which holds an individual personally accountable because each rational autonomous person is responsible for his or her action (McEvoy and McGregor 2008). This international standard of retributive justice tended to exclude residents in communal settings who wanted redress more oriented toward compensation, reconciliation, and restoration of broken relationships (Alie 2008).

Unlike urban centers where interaction is more impersonal, people in communal settings loathe the punitive penalty imposed by the criminal justice system not just because they are interested in preserving kinship relations but also to avoid the likelihood of retaliatory consequences in a locally shared space. In such settings, the act of taking someone to the police or formal court is itself an act of enmity, particularly if traditional conflict resolution processes have not been exhausted. One respondent in the northern region of Sierra Leone stated that when you take a neighbor to the police for a minor crime and he is detained for your sake, he "would have a deep grudge against you for subjecting him to humiliation."[25] A respected ceremonial chief in the southern region echoed this concern, saying, "if your brother takes you to the police or court, he intends to give you trouble and to tarnish your character for good."[26] For this woman, out-of-court resolution of dispute is a long-standing traditional practice, now relevant for maintaining social cohesion and group solidarity.

But I have never taken a case to the local court. I don't take someone to court because doing so brings enmity in the community. The problem with the court is that you have to undergo a lot of expenses and this is what creates lasting enmity between people. My dad never took people to court, so I am used to that way. In fact, we have a law in our group which is that you should not summon a fellow member in court or report her to the police. This is part of our Village Savings and Loans Association. You cannot take a member to court to subject her to losses. Instead you should report the matter to the group and we would come together to settle the matter.[27]

This respondent who grew up in the interior but migrated to Freetown noted that his rural community attached some stigma to "handcuffs and cells" to the extent that those released from prison had to be "washed" before reintegration back into society.[28] This stigmatization may not be unconnected to the deplorable condition of prison facilities in the country. However, it raises important questions about the legitimacy of the state coercive institutions that international institution-builders have sought to restore. As historians who study both countries have documented, the modern statebuilding project has been a coercive enterprise for many rural communities since its introduction in the nineteenth century (Alie 1990; Sawyer 1992). Also, the periods of autocratic rule and civil war were characterized by injustices perpetuated by the state apparatus itself, an insight provided by this respondent who was involved in most justice sector reform projects in Sierra Leone.

> Basically, there has been an attempt to strengthen the formal justice system with police reforms and judicial reforms generally. Be that as it may, you know that formal justice hardly passes beyond the tarmac road; it normally stops on the tarmac road. And because of the injustices we have suffered in the hand of security forces, a lot of people are not prepared to accept formal justice systems. For many of them, formal justice strengthening is just like extension of ruling party or ruling government imperatives into their lives. These are things they are not comfortable with; they do not like the sight of the police; they do not like the sight of a magistrate. It has been a challenge for the entire justice apparatus to rebrand or re-launch itself in a way that becomes believable.[29]

To be sure, Sierra Leoneans and Liberians are not entirely averse to punitive justice, nor is communal life free of social conflict. For instance, most residents and paralegals admit that some chiefs are popular because they deliver "hot justice" that not only is fast but also imposes heavy fines on litigants, more so on those who lose a case. Sometimes litigants request this kind of adjudication when their intention is to subject their opponents to huge financial losses and teach them what they regard as a lesson. Heavy fines can hinder access to justice for poor people while giving undue advantage to those who are financially strong (one of the problems associated with formal justice, as noted below). In northern Sierra Leone, chiefs-in-kantha are considered particularly "hot adjudicators" as fines levied in the Kantha bush are usually exorbitantly higher than normal rates in chief barrays. Yet still, as one female ceremonial chief disclosed, most residents who visit the Kantha bush are disputants looking for "hot settlement" of their disputes.

I am Christian and so too is the paramount chief. Eleven of us were in the Kantha bush including two Muslims. The first thing we did every morning was prayer meeting before we sat on any case. We had so many cases to handle, referring some of them to the local court. Many people took their matters to the Kantha bush because of the kombolo [trouble] they wanted to subject their opponent to. What is a Le 50,000 [$12] fine under normal circumstances, becomes Le 120,000 [$30] when heard in the Kantha bush. People are stubborn in this chiefdom; they like disputes and to advantage other people. They were in the bush for eight months, but I spent only three months with them.[30]

But unlike unofficial dispute resolution, which takes a variety of forms and allows disputants to choose their preferred method, the English common law is inherently adversarial and punitive. Both the process and outcome of the common law tradition leave little room for dispute resolution that is sensitive to the value of informal trust networks in poor socioeconomic conditions and communal settings. Moreover, the liberal conception of justice, which equates a just outcome with a due process, cannot allow for a commitment to collective concerns that are extraneous to the facts of a case or the interest of disputants. Even where effort is made to introduce alternative dispute resolution (ADR) into the system, the foundational principles of the common law system (such as individual human rights, procedural justice, precedent rule) are diametrically opposed to a pluralistic approach to justice administration and dispensation.

ACCESS TO THE FORMAL LEGAL SYSTEM FOR WHOM

Based on its common law origin and legal globalization, the "formal system in Sierra Leone and Liberia is too process-oriented," with over 50 percent of lawyers in the study admitting that they "spend so much time clinging on to a process not realizing that it is creating injustices and we are not willing to move away from it."[31] Formalization in this context refers to complex procedural rules of court, which are highly technical and legalistic, "known only to court insiders such as judges and lawyers" (Dale 2008, 9). Most progressive lawyers interviewed in this study admitted that such reform programs have reinforced structural barriers, which are inherent in judicial and law enforcement procedures (formality, language, views of justice) particularly for people of low socioeconomic status (Dale 2008). This commitment to formal processes relates to the colonial judicial culture that lawyers are socialized into during their training and practice, beginning with dress code. A strict dress code requires lawyers to robe in their full legal regalia (including traditional gown, collar, and wig) when appearing before a superior court judge.

And some lecturers instruct their students to dress up in formal suit when attending their lectures. These conventional etiquettes seem to be associated with the social clout and status of being a lawyer, yet they create a court atmosphere that is intimidating for illiterate litigants who are not familiar with such formal settings.[32] For some legal practitioners, adhering to rules of court ironically becomes equated to, or more important than, the substance of justice meted out by the system and the result of this attitude has been a formal system that is too process-oriented. By this formal orientation, a certain rigidity has been built into the system, which makes it unable to move away from a process even if that procedure is no longer working or creating injustice.[33] One way that inherited colonial conventions have been upheld is through the pupillage system, which requires junior lawyers to understudy senior practitioners before they are allowed to litigate in court.

While the elitist nature of the legal profession in Sierra Leone dates to its historical foundation, transitional justice mechanisms and UK-funded judicial reforms have further heightened this consciousness that law is a lucrative profession connected to influential actors (Manteaw 2008). A typical example is the employment of foreign lawyers and local experts who were paid salaries based on international standards by the Special Court and DFID, thereby exposing the poor conditions of service of most local judicial officials. As one Sierra Leonean lawyer emphasized in his interview, that exposure created tension between local and internationally contracted staff and reinforced private legal practice for those seeking higher remuneration.

> There has been the inclusion of foreign judges to prop up the number at the judiciary and deal with certain cases. Most of that reform was paid for or supported by international institutions like UNDP and DFID. As successful as that was, it created a lot of tensions as well. Foreign judges and some local practitioners who were contracted to serve as judges were receiving pay in a way that was commensurate to experience in other countries and yet Sierra Leonean judges not under contract were paid paltry sums.[34]

Just like the economic class who benefited disproportionately from the transplantation of the common law during the settler-colonial period, there are some segments of the population (e.g., the educated, Krios, Americo-Liberians, corporate actors, and well-to-do) who appreciate the elitist and formal disposition of the state justice system. This is why Park notes that "rule of law institutions enjoy greatest efficacy in Freetown which had historically been dominated by Europeanized elites while such institutions may be all but insignificant in the provinces" where the majority population resides (2008, 547). Those with a good lawyer and requisite education and resources can use (or manipulate) formal rules of court to obtain outcomes in their favor. In particular, "some unsuccessful litigants may decide to drag the case through the various appeal processes and other legal mechanisms simply to frustrate the other side, most often with the advice and support of their counsel" (OSIWA and Suma 2014, 124). This artificial alignment between Europeanized Africans and the modern law is a reminder of Nobles's claim that "the Euro-American tradition fundamentally denies the African his historical roots or the grounding of self into the collective and social definition of one's people" (1974, 23). Long periods of the transatlantic slave trade and colonialism presented Euro-American culture "as the only civilised culture and some Africans under pressure and prescribed conditions assimilate into it" (Nobles 1974, 23). The question, however, is who is excluded and marginalized by the dominant system. For people with low socioeconomic status, the impact of building a centralized and bureaucratic system of justice is real in their day-to-day survival. Among the sixty ordinary Sierra Leoneans who participated in this study, there is a perception among those of low socioeconomic status (about 70 percent) that professionalization of the administration of justice takes state institutions further away from their day-to-day survival in the informal economy.

Citing the 2007 High Court Rules of Sierra Leone that require a petitioner to file a writ of summons before a civil proceeding can commence, one report (cited above) states categorically that "extremely formal rules [of] procedure have invariably prevented a largely illiterate and uniformed citizenry from accessing justice" (OSIWA and Suma 2014, 123). As one civil society activist and lawyer put it, "the justice system is centralized in the hands of few elites and legal training is conventional, designed only for people who want to become lawyers."[35] In a country whose majority population is largely illiterate and ethnically heterogenous, this lawyer exposes how an elitist system inhibits access.

> The major issue first is about access. We have a very complicated legal system. I have seen in court cases where indigent litigants have had to represent themselves and you have lawyers basically talking down to them, shouting and screaming at them. So, it is such that people feel you must have a lawyer even though you don't have to if you can "competently" represent yourself. But the system is structured in such a way that lawyers have an unfair advantage over a layman who chooses to represent himself which makes people think that they must have a lawyer.[36]

The system requires a legal counsel to "competently" navigate its formal structures but to date both countries have very few lawyers, and those practicing are concentrated in the capital cities and mostly interested in private practice. Also, concentrating judicial authority in sparsely located and poorly equipped courts has obvious cost implications, including financial expenses for the majority of (poor) people living in remote areas away from urban headquarter towns. Added to these expenses, extremely formal rules of court present a barrier to largely illiterate and uninformed citizens, who are compelled to hire a lawyer to seek redress through the legal state system. Among the court fees imposed on litigants is the cost of legal services that "constitutes the principal financial barrier to accessing the formal court," as the country's population of seven million is served by about forty practicing lawyers and twenty legal firms, mostly based in Freetown and provincial headquarters (OSIWA and Suma 2014, 121; US Embassy in Sierra Leone 2016). Litigations characterized by excessive delays often result in so much financial expenses that unsuccessful litigants may end up with nothing to compensate the successful party (OSIWA and Suma 2014). As most participants of low economic status complained in their interviews, this woman explains why she is reluctant to take civil and criminal disputes to the formal justice system, stressing the complex nexus between gender, class, and social status (although the focus here is on socioeconomic status broadly).

> It is difficult for women. Only a few women can afford to hire a lawyer or give money to the police to afford justice. Others have family attachment through which people can access a lawyer. In most cases, women forgo their right by leaving things to God. People take their cases to the local court, but many prefer to go first to the town chief. If you don't have money you can't approach the courts. The town chief is doing very well because he is always ready to make peace among people. He seldom asks for money. People who wants a dispute and have money may want to go directly to the local or magistrate court. I hear people say that they would not go to the chief as they want to their opponents to undergo financial losses.[37]

In the case of Liberia, structure-related barriers originated from the construction of an Americo-Liberian state that historically preserved the interest of westernized elites while subordinating the customs and traditional practices of indigenous Liberians. Unlike the UK-supported legal reform in Sierra Leone, Liberia has maintained its prewar institutional arrangement, including a dual justice system whereby the rules of customary laws are applied separately by traditional chiefs and local government officials alongside the formal justice system that interprets the formal English law. Liberia has a public defender system that is supposed to provide free legal representation to people who cannot afford the service of a lawyer, but the few public defenders are concentrated in urban centers and they do not handle customary and civil law cases. Conducted by Oxford's Center for African Studies, one study on court accessibility for a sample of 176 Liberian villages estimated the average transportation cost for a villager to reach the nearest formal court to be 150 Liberian dollars, taking an average of 3.5 hours. Another found that Liberia's countryside suffers a "sheer lack of qualified judges and lawyers, and an absolute lack of any formal court structures or personnel" (Isser et al. 2009, 13). However, the majority of fifty Liberians who participated in this study (particularly those of indigenous and rural origin) perceived the restoration of post-conflict state structures as reminiscent of the colonial statebuilding project that protected Americo-Liberian elite interest as this respondent emphasized.

> The reality of what we have is an injustice system—a system that perpetuates injustice. But conventionally they call it a justice system because they have a statute in front of the court building that says let justice be done to all people. The reality is that there is no justice for the majority of the people because the system does not consider the legal needs of poor and illiterate rural Liberians as deserving serious attention.[38]

Furthermore, when people in poor socioeconomic conditions make calculation of the cost of justice, the tendency has been to prefer settlement outside the state justice system, mostly in unofficial traditional dispute resolution. Chief barrays are not always cheap, and there is a high risk of disputants not being able to recover their expenses because those courts are not legally recognized. But the majority of respondents in this study viewed them as relatively affordable compared to what it would cost them to deal with the police or hire a lawyer to represent them in a magistrate court. Apart from paying lower court fees (summons fee is about Le 35,000, or $10), affordability for many includes additional expenses saved by a timely and speedy resolution of disputes, which is one of the attributes of unofficial dispute resolution. As the comment below demonstrates, speedy dispute resolution does not only remove the attendant expenses of frequent adjournments in the formal justice system but also allows people to return to their daily livelihood activities as soon as possible. This is an important consideration in an informal economy that thrives on interpersonal relationships and where people's daily livelihood depends on what they earn every day.

> Well, we have our local chiefs who are responsible for settling minor matters so that they don't escalate into a problem. I am a *drag man* [unemployed] who depends on stone breaking to survive each day; I don't have a lawyer and don't have money to hire a lawyer. But I can approach the chief with a small amount and he would ask me to wait while he invites the person I reported. If he is available, the chief may hear and settle the matter on that day. Both of us would then go home and live in peace. When I go to court, it would take time for him to be served. After he is served, they would then adjourn the matter for several

months. Meanwhile, the relationship between both of us has been broken. He would not come my way neither would I because we are in court. But the chiefs can amend the problem in few days and then restore peace between us.[39]

Beyond the cost of accessing the state system is the question of whether the needs of everybody are equally admissible in the common law system, considering its strict rules of evidence and admissibility. From artisanal mine workers and small-scale farmers in rural areas to petty traders and quarry workers in sprawling urban centers, these respondents spoke about issues that concern their well-being yet are untenable before a formalized justice system. For instance, the commercial courts are designed to reduce the time and cost for commercial litigation through modernized regulatory and administrative procedures. But the operation of these courts favors commercial businesses that are duly registered with proper documentation. About half of the residents included in this research cited personal experiences of their cases being dismissed by the police for lacking proper documentary evidence or simply not admissible in a formal court.[40] Yet, these formal documents such as title deeds to land and employment contracts are obtainable only in the mainstream economy, mostly by those who have the required resources and connections.

In her interview, one petty businesswoman in Freetown was thankful for the intervention of her local chief who could retrieve Le 500,000 [$60] from another woman who failed to deliver the items she was asked to purchase on an unregulated business trip.[41] That amount was this petty trader's total savings for many years and she stated that it would have been difficult to seek formal redress through formal mechanisms like the new commercial court in Freetown because her transaction was based only on an interpersonal relationship with no receipt of payment. In his interview, a commercial bike rider similarly underscored the contradiction in reform efforts aimed at formalizing the primary justice system when the rural population is largely illiterate and depends on unwritten customary law. Specifically, he wondered how "bush cases" (local land disputes) can be handled by the English justice system when landowners "do not have documents" and rely on the memory of "their people who can recall the history of such disputes."[42] For him, this explains why "many cases brought to the magistrate court are referred back to the community, unresolved."[43]

These inequities in the common law system are a reminder of Marc Galanter's (1974) "resource inequality" thesis, which holds that a party with financial power (the "haves") is likely to obtain a favorable adjudication of disputes. Chief among the defects that give the stronger party an advantage, according to Galanter, is case overload, which in turn increases delays and trial cost. Although this "party capability" argument is not unique to Sierra

Leone and Liberia, the situation is not helped by a grossly inequitable political economy that gives undue advantage to the already dominant class in society that includes the rich, educated, and influential, as fifteen community-based paralegals interviewed unanimously disclosed.[44] It was Rousseau (1763) who noted that the ideal court adjudicates impartially while a real court often favors the rich and powerful. But whereas this might be a universal reality, justice sector reform programs should not be implemented to reinforce unequal structures of power in countries that consistently rank at the bottom of the UNDP Human Development Index. That rule of law promotion, even when supported by well-meaning reformers, continues to reinforce structural, social, and cost-related inequities in law suggests a fundamental problem that cannot be tackled by narrow problem-solving policy prescriptions.

Thus, as with power politics (chapter 4) and the economy (chapter 5), the social ramifications of legal development have historically produced winners and losers, depending on one's proximity to the settler-colonial state and/or Western civilization. Whether or not transplanted legal traditions and institutions have been socially grounded matters less in terms of their impact on existing social relations, status, and privileges. For those whose identity and interest have become indistinguishable from the modern state, the Anglo-Saxon common law accords the institutional tools to defend and protect their privileges just as formal justice system operates in accordance with their dispute resolution preferences. Beyond the founding identity, those who managed to acquire Western education, civilization, and economic wealth also found the common law system both relevant for their upward social mobility and to safeguard acquired social standing. Often, though, the attainment of social status within the common law tradition means alienation from one's indigenous African culture at the same time that one cannot be fully European (Nobles 1974).

It is not that African legal traditions evolved to benefit groups that emerged dominant during an endogenous sociopolitical process as in Europe; rather, it was a process of cultural imposition that marginalized and subordinated indigenous/customary systems. Due to colonial indirect rule as well as the resilience of these systems, they have survived and adapted to numerous external encounters, from colonialism and postcolonial modernization to post-conflict reconstruction. The majority population whose social needs cannot be accommodated in the formal state have found these socially oriented systems (not the colonially invented ones) relevant for their survival and livelihood. But for a variety of reasons—ranging from fear of forum shopping, human rights concerns, to ideological commitment to bureaucratic culture—these systems are either dismissed as undeserving of reform or disciplined to conform to international standards and the rule of state law. It is doubly unjust that those experiencing structural, social, and cost-related barriers to accessing the modern state are denied the right to practice their own socially relevant traditions.

NOTES

1. In this chapter, people whose ancestry is traceable to inhabitants of Sierra Leone before the arrival of freed slaves would be regarded as people of indigenous origin or descent as distinct from the descendants of settlers following the founding of Freetown in 1787.

2. This perspective, which was pitted against the dynastic rivalry thesis, has been repeated in contemporary interpretations of the civil wars that broke out in the Mano River subregion in the early 1990s. As I shall demonstrate in chapter 4, the authors that have featured prominently in this contemporary repeat of what was originally a Kilson versus Barrows debate include Paul Richards, Richard Fanthorpe, Paul Jackson, Edwards Sawyer, Ibrahim Abdullah, and others.

3. Ruling houses are not just part of Sierra Leone's colonial history. In a recent survey to reconstruct the history of chieftaincy in Sierra Leone by Reed and Robinson (2013), it is noted that each of the 149 chiefdoms in Sierra Leone has two or more competing ruling houses.

4. While indigenous Liberians had their own secret societies that usually restricted membership kinsmen, ritualistic and exclusive fraternal orders were not entirely new to Americo-Liberians who were capable of blending fundamentalist Christian beliefs from Deep South of America with practices of freemasonry and membership for men in a Masonic lodge. The only distinction between indigenous secret societies and the Masonic lodges was Masonry's close association with the True Whig Party (TWG), which gave lodge members exclusive access to unparalleled political and economic power in Liberia (Waugh 2011).

5. This background information about Grand Gedeh is derived from The Grand Gedeh County Development Agenda (2008–12), prepared by the County Development Committee in collaboration with the Ministries of Planning and Economic Affairs and Internal Affairs of Liberia.

6. Grand Gedeh County Development Agenda (2008–12), ibid, p. 2

7. County Development Agenda, ibid., p. 23. Also, most of those interviewed in the county lamented the county's deplorable road situation, especially from Ganta to the headquarter town of Zwedru. Some recalled periods of food shortage and price hikes when vehicles were unable to use the road to transport commercial goods from Monrovia.

8. County Development Agenda, ibid., p. 20.

9. Author's interview, High Court Justice, Freetown (June 13, 2014).

10. This is an important clarification. While customary English law originated in response to vagaries of the informal political economy of Britain, the legal rules transported to British colonies were codified into ordinances, which later became the

foundation of modern statebuilding in postcolonial Africa. This is also reflected in recognition of African customary law as all recognized customary rules were to be codified to be accorded official status.

11. Author's interview, tribal head, Freetown (March 28, 2014).

12. Author's interview, human rights lawyer, Freetown (March 28, 2014).

13. Author's interview, State Counsel and Customary Law Officer, Northern Province (March 13, 2014).

14. Author's interview, paralegals, Northern Province (June 2, 2014).

15. Author's interview, High Court Justice, Freetown (June 13, 2014).

16. It is expected that a defendant would throw up the concoction if he or she is innocent. The poisonous element of the concoction is made from the toxic bark of the sasswood tree (Peter T. Lesson and Christopher J. Coyne, "Sassywood," paper presented at the Comparative Economics Conference, University of Pittsburgh, September 9–10, 2011).

17. These threats are often linked to spiritual forces, including witchcraft. It is difficult to acquire information on these issues, but respondents attested that they are a crucial problem affecting the informal economy.

18. Author's interview, local court chairman, Southern Province, Sierra Leone (May 31, 2014).

19. I make this distinction between endogenous and exogenous African traditional justice systems in an article that examines informal institutional change in the context of post-conflict rule of law reform (Sesay 2019).

20. Author's interview with Customary Law Officer and Principal State Counsel (June 14, 2014).

21. It was more important to train historians, missionaries, and educators than lawyers because Africans who wished to read law were regarded as preparing for a career in politics that may be self-destructive of the colonial project.

22. Author's interview, Barrister and Solicitor, Northern Province (May 26, 2014).

23. Author's interview, resident, Monrovia (July 18, 2014).

24. Author's interview, rural businesswoman, Grand Geddeh County (August 19, 2015).

25. Author's interview, small-scale farmer, Northern Province (August 10, 2014).

26. Author's interview, section chief, Southern Province (June 19, 2014).

27. Author's interview, businesswoman, Southern Province (May 31, 2014).

28. Author's interview, resident, Freetown (August 14, 2014).

29. Author's interview, local consultant, Freetown (March 4, 2014).

30. Author's interview, Ceremonial Chief, Northern Province (April 15, 2014).

31. Author's interview, human rights lawyer, Freetown (February 25, 2014).

32. Author's interview, Human Rights Commissioner, Freetown (March 26, 2014).

33. Author's interview, human rights lawyer, Freetown (February 25, 2014).

34. Author's interview, lawyer, Freetown (March 5, 2014).

35. Author's interview, Barrister and Solicitor, Northern Province, Sierra Leone (May 26, 2014).

36. Author's interview, Barrister and Solicitor, Freetown (March 4, 2014).

37. Author's interview, businesswoman, Southern Province (June 26, 2014).

38. Author's interview, civil society leader, Monrovia (July 26, 2014).

39. Author's interview, resident, Freetown (August 14, 2014).

40. Author's interviews, residents, Freetown (August 10 & 14, 2014).

41. Author's interview, local businesswoman, Freetown (August 10, 2014).

42. Author's interview, bike rider, Northern Province (April 15, 2014).

43. Author's interview, bike rider, Northern Province (April 15, 2014).

44. Author's interviews, community-based paralegals, Northern, Eastern, and Southern regions (March 11 & 14, May 5–7, May 29–31, June 2, 2014).

Chapter 7

Conclusions and Reflections

The field of liberal development and security has been subjected to sustained post/neocolonial criticisms for some time now, with critical scholars focusing on international intervention, peacekeeping and peacebuilding, neoliberal economic policies, and security sector reform programs as avenues for the continuation of unequal relations in global governance. Meanwhile, international law has maintained an image of a benign and neutral mechanism for development and order, thereby diverting significant attention from the potential that it has been used as a tool for perpetuating structural injustices within and between nations. Ironically, while rule of law promotion has become a central plank of liberal intervention in the Global South (especially in peacebuilding and statebuilding), it has managed to transcend criticisms that have exposed the political and ideological underpinnings of these interventions. Against this backdrop, I have sought to mount a more principled and sustained post/neocolonial critique of international law as social domination within the context of post-conflict peacebuilding and reconstruction in Africa in order to reconstruct the interlinkages between legal colonization and legal globalization.

Perhaps the most comprehensive and holistic treatment of rule of law promotion in Africa to date, the book has argued that the project often produces adverse consequences that harm those it supposed to help because coloniality remains at its core (chapter 2). It historicizes this coloniality in the context of legal development in colonial Africa (chapter 3) and then empirically examines the structural, social, and cost-related inequities in law through a comparative analysis of two post-conflict African states: Sierra Leone and Liberia. The postcolonial rule of law critique advanced in this book combines a theoretical layer that interweaves the superimposition, Eurocentrism, and doctrinal legality of law as well as an empirical layer that excavates the harms associated with legal globalization in the economy, politics, and society. The empirical chapters 4–6 focus on international law both as it relates to the role of powerful Western actors (from settler-colonial rule to post-conflict legal reconstruction) and its real cost on the everyday lives of Africans. What follows is a series of reflections about multiple forms of domination by law, the sites of domination, and the ongoing coloniality of modern law.

MULTIPLE FORMS OF DOMINATION THROUGH LAW

The empirical chapters 4–6 are in-depth examination of externally driven reconstruction processes in war-torn Sierra Leone and Liberia, arguing that the local population often experiences rule of law reforms as reinforcing domination in multiple ways: structural, social, and cost-related. Firstly, rule of law institutions have legitimated structural inequities that were needed to subordinate customary and indigenous structures of governance. The main source of the tension between rule of law and legal pluralism, structural domination takes the form of primacy of state law over preexisting legal and normative traditions. The process requires an understanding of legality that concentrates sovereignty in the modern state as the primary source of authoritative law, even if the common law proves accommodating to indigenous and customary practices. Historically, the practice has been to tolerate preexisting traditions and customs only to the extent that they conform to international standards or the dominant state law, a hierarchical control that requires the state to take precedence whenever a conflict between statutory and non-statutory law emerges. Although the hierarchical organization of legal authority is neither unique to Africa nor necessarily undesirable, the issue is a lack of separation between the state and dominant group interests. In other words, rebuilding state law has ended up re-institutionalizing the elitism and exclusionary politics embedded in the modern state, just as legal colonization invented customary laws that transformed some local rulers into decentralized despots during the period of colonial rule.

Furthermore, the modern law created unequal internal structures within a single state to legitimate binary constructions such as native and non-native, citizen and subject, indigene and stranger, settler and non-settler, colony and protectorate, urban and rural, all to constitute differentiated legal subjects. Built into the colonial state are unequal structures for the construction of citizenship based on race, ethnicity, class, and other markers of social status that became institutionalized over time. Part of the reason for subsequent development disparities, legal binaries created structural inequities to be reinforced by highly formalized and elitist state-building processes that insisted on colonial languages, religions, education, and cultures as national in contrast to the local. The contrast usually came with specific connotations about superior-inferior relations: colonial customary law complemented the populations of indigenous descent who had limited and inferior status in the state while the statutory law reflected the interest and needs of people close to colonial rule and Western civilization who became a superior category.

The most enduring structure of inequity is the modern state itself because it denies the right of self-determination to hitherto disparate groups, which have been compelled under colonialism to coexist within a single legal entity. Based on the Westphalian or Weberian model, the modern state in Africa emerged to have juridical monopoly over the legitimate use of force. However, the state's inability to match its juridical authority with the required empirical capacity to govern has resulted in parallel governance structures, which, despite lacking official legality, remain socially relevant to the majority population whose interests were excluded from the colonial statebuilding project. Maintaining juridical authority without substantive capacity to control usually necessitates an emphasis on the law and order function of the state system and a selective co-optation of local elites. This strategy was adopted in the process of colonial indirect rule, resulting in codification of the special status of certain ethnic groups and traditional authorities who became known as "treaty chiefs" or modern ruling houses. Instead of exercising their authority through social mechanisms, traditional authorities became reliant on state law and its formal coercive apparatuses to control their local subjects. But within this very hierarchy of legal authority structures lies the ever-ubiquitous potential for resentment, injustice, subversion, and violence as state-sponsored actors attempt to assert power, while those marginalized by the system try to resist illegitimate control.

This is not to say that precolonial African societies were entirely egalitarian and harmonious. There were multiple polities in pre-colonial times, from African political kingdoms and empires, non-hegemonic states, to stateless societies (Herbst 2003). Many African kingdoms and empires were highly bureaucratized, and hierarchical organization of political authority privileged one group over another. The point, perhaps one of the lasting impacts of colonial legal violence, is that modern state formation was externally driven and a top-down imposition that ultimately robbed the continent of the endogenous political process that usually preceded the establishment of European nation-states. Once the modern state had been imposed, however ineffectual, successive African elites were more inclined to defend and use it to exercise and consolidate political power. And since this perverse colonial construction has rarely been dismantled (perhaps, except for post-apartheid South Africa), many African states remain imbued with a perpetual legitimacy crisis. In short, structural inequalities emerged from the construction of a colonial state that historically preserved the interest of Westernized elites—both central and local—while subordinating the customary and indigenous practices of the ordinary population.

Secondly, the globalization of legal norms and institutions has historically produced negative social consequences for many Africans because people's conception of law and justice reflects their socioeconomic circumstances and conditions. One of the social problems is rooted in the fact that initially the English law originated to cater for the dispute resolution needs of certain groups of people, including non-natives, Europeans and non-European settlers, Christians, European merchants, the educated and all those who had acquired sufficient European civilization to exercise their citizenship rights. In fact, for these groups that emerged out of the process of colonial rule, their identity was co-constituted with the English law for their existence never predated the transplantation of the Anglo-Saxon tradition. Consider, for example, the Krios and Americo-Liberians, whose legal culture and practices became more wedded to the common law than to indigenous customary law. As discussed above, indirect rule tolerated some accommodation for indigenous customary law as subordinate to or separate from the general English law. In subordinating or separating preexisting legal cultures, however, the English common law succeeded in devaluing the needs, priorities, and rights of the indigenous rural population. Those rights and values were to be realized within the confines of an inferior codified customary law, meaning they were unequal to general citizenship and those under the jurisdiction of invented customary law had only mediated access to the state. For people of indigenous/rural descent to claim rights enshrined in the common law, they need to acquire Western civilization, whether through migration to the metropole, obtaining formal education, or acquiring capital.

This subordination of the values and cultures of the majority population must be construed as part of legal violence wrought by common law. Before the English law became general law, Sierra Leone and Liberia were governed by multiple indigenous and customary laws, often reflective of the diversity of ethnic, linguistic, and cultural identities. It would have been inevitable that legal development in both countries would have naturally resulted in the dominance of one culture over the others in line with the evolution of society. But because the English law was superimposed, there has been a mismatch between the law and organization of social and economic life, even in metropolitan areas where the state legal system is concentrated. Examined extensively in chapters 5 and 6, the informal economy and communal settings have become mostly affected by this disjuncture because they are environments where informal trust networks and reciprocal obligations are considered vital for survival and livelihood. In these spaces, people of low socioeconomic status turn to kinship relations, informal association, personal friendship, and undocumented contracts for subsistence particularly when the formal system marginalizes them.

At the same time, the adversarial and punitive nature of the common law tradition undermines such vital sources of coexistence in these communities. Whereas impersonal contractual relations often characterize the European societies in which the common law tradition emerged (e.g., the individualization of property rights), the personalized nature of social life in communal Africa settings means that the individual and collective personhoods are often intertwined. Therefore, the common law system that is limited to the interest and preferences of disputants as autonomous agents tends to be associated with procedures and outcomes considered unsatisfactory to the majority population (Isser et al. 2009). What the common law may dismiss as extraneous factors (untenable in a court of law) is of interest to ordinary people because their survival depends on an informal social order absent an equitable formal state and economic system.

Social exclusion from the English law is also a consequence of a process-oriented legal system that stresses formal procedures, the English language, strict rules of admissibility, scientifically verifiable evidence, formal rules of court, all constituting a complicated modern structure. Those in the informal economy and communal settings usually encounter social conflicts and interpersonal disputes, which are unlikely to be admissible in the formal courts just as the emphasis on judicial precedent is inconsistent with innovative efforts to accommodate the needs of the informal sector. Another social cost of the English law is related to the criminalization of informal sources of livelihood or their regulation by coercive state agencies as illustrated by the 1965 Public Order Act in Sierra Leone. Moreover, the undue emphasis on elitist, standardized, and formalized processes disadvantages populations that are largely poor and formally uneducated. Apart from an inability to competently navigate the formal system, the operation of common law usually creates an intimidating environment that is experienced as inhospitable to people of low socioeconomic status. Conversely, those who historically share the same elitist culture have found such common law settings conducive for them to defend their privileges and protect their rights and property.

Thirdly, the common law tradition imposes severe cost particularly on ordinary people who need to access the formal state system. When considering the cost of access, it must be reiterated that the common law was extended to Africa originally to serve the economic class, which needed law to protect property rights and enforce contracts particularly when dealing with African communal traditions. For example, indirect rule of the protectorate ensured that commercial disputes between natives and non-natives were brought under the jurisdiction of the District Commissioner or Superintendent who applied common law in his court. That the elitist character of privileged groups came to be reflected in the English law itself is consistent with legal development in Western Europe or North America, where the rule of law was initially in favor of the wealthy and aristocracy. The law protected the aristocracy over the commoner in Europe just as white men with property in America enjoyed the rule of law long before it was extended to women, African Americans, and other racialized minorities. In both Western Europe and North America, rule of law protection was gradually extended to the commoners alongside processes of democratization, even though racialized people still do not enjoy full citizenship rights. In Africa, the misnomer in contemporary rule of law promotion is that the project continues to be implemented within the same undemocratic global and domestic structures that colonialism helped to bring about a century ago. In other words, legal norms and institutions are being transported on top of discriminatory political, economic, and social structures outside and within targeted states.

Historically, those who study and practice the English law often emerged from the same social classes they predominantly serve. For instance, the first generation of Africans to study law abroad were, by default of the elitist and expensive nature of the field, part of the elite society that was based on either wealth or connection with colonial rule. Apart from the Krios and Americo-Liberians, only sons and nominees of paramount chiefs could afford legal education, one of the reasons why the second prime minister of Sierra Leone was born to a ruling family, for example. Since its early emergence, the legal field was a lucrative profession especially for lawyers who choose private or international practice over public service. Considering that the common law encourages litigation and adversarial adjudication, the combination of the positions of barrister and solicitor is common in African common law jurisdictions. Meanwhile, since ordinary people cannot competently navigate the state system, they are compelled to pay legal fees to barristers and solicitors to represent them in transactions dealing with the state, especially in judicial and legal matters. In addition to legal fees, many Sierra Leoneans and Liberians are overburdened by other charges or forgone opportunities they incur during the period of navigating an overcentralized, overwhelmed, and formalized state system, often obtaining unsatisfactory results as discussed above. Those in the informal economy are particularly concerned about the processing time and other expenses that could have been invested in livelihood activities. While legal fees are expensive everywhere, it is ironic that rule of law reforms, which claim to emancipate marginalized populations in poorest nations of the world, often turn out to reinforce their marginalization.

MULTIPLE SPACES OF DOMINATION THROUGH LAW

Where is rule of law promotion experienced as reinforcing social domination? In agreement with the turn to "the local" in peacebuilding, this book has drawn from a subnational study of Sierra Leone and Liberia to examine three specific contexts in which the globalization of legal norms and institutions reinforce domination: politics, economics, and society. In terms of political history, I have acknowledged that Sierra Leone and Liberia diverge in significant ways in their history of legal and judicial development. The modern state of Sierra Leone is a product of British colonial rule, which introduced the English common law and separated the legal systems of "natives" who were British "protected persons" from the "non-natives" who were regarded as British subjects. Although Sierra Leone was not a white-settler colony, the relationship between the colonial and indigenous legal systems was underpinned by racial prejudice, with formal recognition granted only to local practices and values considered consistent with the white man's conception of morality, equity, and justice. Sierra Leoneans whose lifestyles, education, and belief systems approximated British civilization (mostly the Krios who were descendants of "freed" slaves) were allowed greater access to the sociolegal structures established in the colony, while those incapable of doing so (mostly protectorate residents) were confined to the colonial version of customary law. Indirect rule of the protectorate was under the supervision of white colonial masters who served as district commissioners, presiding over joint courts as well as those founded exclusively for matters affecting "non-natives." Whenever the two legal systems clashed, the superior "non-native" system, which applied the English law, always took precedence.

At the onset of independence, this ethno-racial hierarchy became ethno-elitist, with educated protectorate elites (who had been exposed to Western education) taking over state administration from colonial masters. Despite coming from indigenous-rural origins, the protectorate elites were less interested in deconstruction of colonial legal structures, preferring only to replace the colonialists and Krios with their own class of ethnic loyalists under the guise of Africanization. Maintaining the former colony as the seat of administrative and judicial power, the only reconstruction undertaken in the post-colonial era was to ensure that the dominant legal and political institutions serve the interest of a new class of ruling elites. Fueled by more than four decades of patronage and ethnic politics, the new realignment of interest transcended the ideological divided between tradition and modernity, allowing the educated elites to forge alliances with traditional authorities whose support was needed to maintain political power nationwide. Although ethnic politics continued to mediate access to state resources, the fundamental divide bifurcated the dominant oligarchy (protected by inherited state institutions) and the non-elite population whose socioeconomic conditions were based on politicized ethno-regional differences.

Liberia's political history unfolded somewhat differently in that it was ethno-elitist from the onset. As one of the two African countries (in addition to Ethiopia) to avoid formal European colonization, the dominant legal and judicial systems of Liberia are a product of black-settler rule, whose origin is traceable to the activities of the American Colonization Society (ACS). Taking advantage of their exposure to Anglo-Saxon law and relationship with the ACS to develop dominant state systems, the division between "natives" and "civilized people" was constructed by Americo-Liberians, who considered their education and Western-oriented culture as superior. This early discrimination of the modern state was to develop a hierarchy of linguistic and cultural groups, with the Americo-Liberians at the top, establishing dominant legal practices that not only protected their interest but also disciplined indigenous structures and methods. Americo-Liberian rule was to protect the individual human and property rights of the dominant ethno-elite class rather than European merchants and missionaries as in Sierra Leone. There was no political transition in Liberia's so-called independence of 1847 as the True Whig Party hegemony continued until 1980 when the administration of William Tolbert was violently overthrown by Sergeant Samuel K. Doe. But even after the Americo-Liberian oligarchy had been toppled, the ethno-elitist culture was so entrenched that the dominant legal and political institutions were simply reoriented to serve the new powerholders to the exclusion of other indigenes during Doe's almost ten years of authoritarian rule and subsequent civil war.

After a decade-long civil war in Liberia (1989–2005) and Sierra Leone (1991–2002), both countries implemented a post-conflict peacebuilding and reconstruction agenda including reforms designed to rebuild the rule of law: transitional justice, law reform, and justice sector development. These reforms were carried out under international legal tutelage, with their former settler-colonial powers at the forefront of donor assistance. The United Kingdom's interventions in Sierra Leone was part of Prime Minister Tony Blair's "ethical foreign policy" in Africa, which included initiatives such as the African Conflict Prevention Pool (ACPP), Commission for Africa, and the New African Initiative. In Liberia, US-supported rule of law efforts intended to restore political stability in the West African subregion and strengthen national institutions to maintain domestic law and order as part of the Bush administration's war on transnational terrorism. But instead of placing constitutional and institutional limits on executive power, the ruling class has managed to effectively appropriate new legal tools for the consolidation of ruling power and protection of elite interests. Reforms have been welcomed—sometimes promoted by ruling governments—if they provide legal instruments that the ruling class can use to legitimize its rule, legally overpower its opponent, or defend an otherwise controversial state or regime policy.

These findings are consistent with comparative political studies which have posited that legal and judicial institutions are instrumental for the consolidation of power in illiberal democracies and nationalist autocracies around the world. For instance, Moustafa and Ginsburg (2008) assert that courts help regimes to maintain social control, uphold bureaucratic discipline, adopt unpopular policies, and enhance regime legitimacy. Often described as "constitutional authoritarianism," military leaders in Pakistan and elsewhere have repeatedly relied on judges to legalize their authority to rule following a coup d'état. In pre-revolutionary Sudan, legal development has historically provided state elites an instrument to manage grievances against the regime and enforce state's authority to punish, all culminating in reinforcement of an authoritarian regime rather than heralding a new era of democratic rule (Massoud 2013). But contrary to conventional wisdom that judicial systems are fully under executive control, these regimes often allow the courts and law enforcement agencies some autonomy that is useful only to dissociate themselves from controversial political decisions made by the justice system. In other words, these regimes are exercising the rule of law in a circumscribed way, appropriating institutional and legal structures (which have been reinforced by current reform efforts) to ensure that the state law is always applied in favor of the ruling class while projecting an image of fairness and independence.

In terms of the economy, most of the laws and policies passed during the period of war-to-peace transition were intended to enhance the confidence of private capitalists that their property rights would be protected and that there are judicial structures to adjudicate commercial disputes based on international acceptable standards. By establishing a good business environment, the rule of law helps open the local economy to global capital, attracting foreign investors and building confidence in a commercial justice system. In the past twenty-five years of reform, both Sierra Leone and Liberia have become the leading destinations for foreign investors interested in African land and labor for agrobusiness and mining operations just as their predecessors in the early days of colonial and settler rule. Advertised by their own ruling elites, what remains of the natural and human resources of these countries continue to be exploited by corporate agents, aided by rule of law institutions that guarantee individual property rights over communal ownership rights. With their investment and export promotion agencies touting new laws that guarantee concessions and profit, Sierra Leone and Liberia became the new frontier for international interest particularly in palm oil and sugar cane plantation, among other commercial sectors.

It is true that creating a good corporate governance environment elevated both countries among the fastest growing economies in African up to 2014, when they experienced a devastating Ebola outbreak. But most of their populations have been left worse off by this economic boom, just as they were left behind in the settler-colonial economies of the early modern times. Like those times, workers in plantations and mines still have very little protection from capitalist exploitation because the myriad laws that have been passed were first and foremost designed to satisfy the interest of investors and big businesses whose profit depends on exploitation of labor and resources. Land reform policies are still a search for a modern framework to subordinate communal land tenure systems that are inconsistent with international rule of law principles and impede the free market where private individuals must have freedom to buy and sell whatever property. Apart from facilitating dispossession of communal land and resources, new laws have been used to criminalize the informal sector when it is considered an obstacle to global capital, even though informality is often the product of a capitalist mode of production. Not built for them, commercial courts and other formal dispute resolution mechanisms often dismiss social disputes related to the informal economy as inadmissible because they lack proper documentation, do not follow formal due process, and are unrecognized by English law.

At the societal level, the English law has been an instrument for delegitimizing cultural practices in Sierra Leone and Liberia considered repugnant to the conscience of Western civilization. During the era of settler-colonial rule, indigenous laws were separated from the "general" state law because they were deemed antithetical to Judeo-Christian values that shaped the Anglo-Saxon common law tradition. In an ironic twist of legal fate, the personal laws of the English people were elevated to "general" law in both countries while their preexisting indigenous and customary laws were restricted to the personal realm. For certain cultural practices to be elevated to the status of general law, they had to be harmonized with the Western conception of "good conscience, equity, and justice," the disciplinary function of repugnant clauses in colonial laws. It was possible to assimilate into the superior culture established in the settler-colony, provided one denounced indigenous customary practices that conflicted with Judeo-Christian values.

Meanwhile, the legal systems of those outside this culture (who constitute the majority) continue to be disciplined by the English law, which has been upheld as state law, long after the end of settler-colonial rule. Although the majority population in both countries are from rural-indigenous origin, their traditional legal systems remain subordinated to the state system in that customary law is always overruled whenever it clashes with the English law. In the former British colony Freetown, the application of customary law through a tribal court system has long been proscribed, even though the majority population constitutes people of indigenous-rural origin. In Liberia, a recent crackdown on "harmful traditional practices" rendered illegal a host of traditional dispute resolution methods, a move that local communities perceived as creating a justice vacuum, yet applauded by donors, the United Nations, and human rights NGOs.

MULTIPLE COLONIALITIES OF LAW IN AFRICA

The book also examines *why* rule of law promotion has and continues to produce these adverse consequences for the very population reformers purport to help. From a problem-solving perspective, Sriram and others (2011) attribute this phenomenon to the exceptionalism of postcolonial Africa, where state failure and neopatrimonialism have become so normalized that rebuilding the rule of law poses a threat to the personal survival of ruling elites. Among the reasons advanced for persistent rule of law failure, the cultural and political explanations are prominent. Culturally, Sriram argues, the very definition adopted by the UN Secretary-General's (2004) report has a positivist slant because it is premised on assumptions that are generally rooted in the Western human rights traditions, including public creation of laws, private-public distinction, and the operation of state institutions based on a legal-rational logic. Another contributor in the volume, Obarrio, agrees with Sriram when he notes that attempts to overhaul traditional institutions in Africa reflect a "tendency to view 'traditional' justice mechanisms from the perspective of positivist norms associated with Western juridical concepts and [liberal] institutions" (2011, 24). Obarrio contends that in the broad judicial reforms implemented in Africa since the 1990s, the relationship between informal justice actors and public sector institutions has not been addressed in a manner that takes into account the central role of traditional justice mechanisms. Where efforts have been made to recognize traditional values, he argues that there has been "a clear contradictory tendency to idealize, mythologize, and generalize these values while at the same time attempting to bring [them] in line with modern conceptions of human rights" (Obarrio 2011, 24).

In terms of the political implications of institutional change, Sriram and others contend that rule of law reform would be confronted by resistance from authorities who perceive such moves as threat to their political power and interests (Sriram et al. 2011). This argument challenges the idea of an apolitical technocratic reform intervention, warning that "any reforms are both legally and politically contentious and cannot simply be engineered but required political will and consensus" (Sriram 2011, 140). For those concerned with security and justice at the subnational level, they draw attention to the dangers of engaging customary justice systems in the same technical, legal, and apolitical fashion as their formal state counterpart. This work is particularly cognizant of unintended consequences such as a justice or security vacuum where regulation of customary systems is unaccompanied by the necessary state capacity to deliver satisfactory justice. Linked to the state-failure argument, the security vacuum analysis holds that capacity deficit in a formal justice system explains the popularity of informal justice mechanisms. Whereas the formal system continues to grapple with physical and economic inaccessibility, non-state mechanisms deliver relatively cheap, accessible, and expeditious settlement of disputes, this argument asserts (Harper 2011; Isser 2011; Wojkowska 2006).

While these cultural and institutional analyses are undisputable (and confirmed in this book), their preoccupation with problem-solving policy solutions to rebuild the post-colonial state makes them prone to some significant omissions. This book departs from this problem-solving argument by problematizing the modern law itself as an instrument of social domination, insisting that its superimposition, Eurocentrism, and doctrinal legality have outlived the formal end of colonialism. Legal superimposition from this perspective refers to the idea that modern law has always emerged from a particular historical and structural context that it evolves to reflect and serve. In terms of European relations with Africa, this means that international law of the nineteenth and early twentieth centuries was primarily and purposefully designed to serve dominant European foreign policy interest, even when framed as part of the emancipatory "civilizing mission" for Africa. This perspective also sees legal development in Africa as mainly the transplantation of European legal traditions—both the civil and common laws—for the sole purpose of resolving the "native question" in favor of European and Europeanized citizens in colonized territories. Beyond the imposition of European law on pre-existing legal traditions, the coloniality of legal superimposition is its duplicity in that the liberal conception of legality would become premised upon devaluation of other people's cultures and construction of an entity that commands monopoly over the legitimate use of force.

As a logic of domination, the book's conceptualization of legal superimposition is not confined to a specific historical period nor spatially distinguished by race only—in fact, it has outlasted racial colonization. If the socioeconomic and political structures that produce the law remain undemocratic, the law so produced has preservation of the privileges of dominant groups as its foremost priority. This explains why the rule of law mainly applies to the weak and well-behaved states in the international system (Tamanaha 2004) just as the ruling class disproportionately benefits from modern law in domestic jurisdictions. Legal superimposition also does not mean the complete marginalization of laws that purport to protect the weak; on the contrary, the logic presupposes intermittent use of law for counterhegemonic purposes. But the reason for permitting this is that for law to mask dominant interest it must be seen as not entirely unjust or unfair so the weak can obey (Thompson 1975). Meanwhile, any amount of fairness and autonomy exhibited by the law is what the dominant system tolerates and counterhegemonic outcomes ultimately result in strengthening the system's integrity. That African nationalist leaders, who became more adept at applying colonial law, chose to accept the rule of law in form but not its substance is an example of the legal order serving "primarily as a mechanism for asserting, enabling, and legitimating state power not for constraining it" (Prempeh 2013, 168). It must not be surprising that among the post-colonial African regimes that often invoke the rule of law in the name of the state are those that are less tolerant to transparent and accountable governance, human rights, and dissenting opinion.

The other element of coloniality of modern law considered in this book is Eurocentrism. In this respect, rule of law promotion produces adverse consequences not simply because it is rooted in Euro-American cultures and values. In fact, the book acknowledges that the common law for settlers (whether whites, mulatto, or black) was not entirely imposed but emerged to constitute their identities as citizens and subjects of the colonial empire. The problem is that the very identity of the English law required a conceptualization of the "other" (i.e., indigenous Africans) as inferior and primitive, an alterity that enables the dominant group to embark on a civilizing mission. The logic of alterity is so entrenched in the modern law that its very legitimacy as an agent of progress and modernity cannot be divorced from the construction and stability of Africa as premodern, undeveloped, and uncivilized. Defined as "epistemic violence," Mignolo argues that "barbarians, primitives, and undeveloped peoples, and peoples of color are all categories that established epistemic dependencies under different global designs (Christianisation, civilising mission, modernisation and development, and consumerism)" (2002, 84). What makes this epistemic injustice so prevalent in Africa is that the logic has been replicated in relations between "natives" and "nonnatives," meaning that those whose social status depended on Westernization considered themselves closer to the superior identity of the white man than to their indigenous cultures. Differences between the European and non-European became differences between the civilized and non-civilized African, with the Europeanized African assuming the role of regulating, disciplining, and civilizing the population identified as of indigenous/rural descent.

What one customary law officer in Freetown called "an accident of history," often it is the majority or original indigenous groups that Eurocentrism construct as inferior—their laws and social norms become subordinate to the English law that was transplanted to serve a foreign minority. Since the authority of the modern law rests on stabilization of difference, legal bifurcation not only views indigenous African cultures as backward but also contributes to their primitiveness by converting compliant traditional rulers into decentralized despots, utilizing customary practices that generate cheap African labor and resources, and codifying rules of customary law that benefit the imperial project. However, the bifurcation of legal systems is a complicated construction, allowing hierarchies within each social category and an intermediate status. Take, for example, the Krios and Americo-Liberians who became culturally closer to the white man but not at par with him in terms of the full citizenship rights enjoyed by white settlers. Educated protectorate elites soon came to resemble the Krios and Americo-Liberians in terms of embracing the superior Western culture but their indigenous/rural identity was set to complicate their upward social mobility. Regardless, one of the enduring legacies of Eurocentrism is that indigenous legal systems and social norms would remain located in a subordinate position and distrusted by reformers even in the context of post-conflict peacebuilding and reconstruction.

As the third element of the coloniality of law, the book examines doctrinal legality, which manifests itself in both the civil law and common law traditions, although in varying degrees (Merryman and Perez-Perdomo 2019). Here, the doctrine contributes to coloniality by enabling the power-knowledge nexus while restricting subordinate people the ability to freely use law for socially oriented and non-elite courses. If the law emerges from unequal social structures, it is already imbued with the values and interest of the dominant group(s) as sociolegal studies remind us, a reality that the notion of logical formalism enables legal professionals to deny. But in addition to serving an epistemological and methodological function in terms of how law is supposed to work, such denial enables dominant actors to mask politically and ideologically motivated actions under the façade of legal neutrality. By committing to only uphold the formal processes of law, doctrinal legality ends up protecting and defending the current order, producing conservative legal professionals who see themselves as positivist technocrats responsible only for guarding and implementing the law made by the ruling class (Eslava and Pahuja 2012). When these professionals claim separation between the facts of law and their values, they simply reinforce the existing social order because both the law and its dispensers emerge from the dominant culture.

At the same time, this treatment of law as a distinct legal domain separate from the sociopolitical realm prevents the oppressed from using law to challenge the existing system. By failing to accept that law can be unjust, doctrinal legality compels the legal system to constrain or prohibit movements for justice not legally stipulated as permissible such as the right to self-determination, social equality, and distributive justice. The only reform that the system allows are those taking place within and according to the rule of law; anything else is disobedience of the law no matter how legitimate or just it might be. Sometimes, the system produces progressive activists who recognize the disconnect between law and justice and want to use legal instruments to further a just struggle. But the professional commitment to scientific positivism quickly undercuts any sustained effort to overcome the law for the sake of justice (Eslava and Pahuja 2012). While it is tempting to attribute counter-hegemonic results to the emancipatory power of law—from decolonization to the everyday struggle of indigenous communities against global capital—this book has argued that these are political struggles against structural injustice that cannot be substituted by law. The rule of law, as presently constituted and globalized, even serves as a stumbling block in the movement toward a more just and egalitarian society.

In short, *how*, *where*, and *why* does rule of law promotion reinforce social domination in postcolonial Africa have been the questions tackled in this book. I have confirmed that "the claim to a new world order of solidarity and equality" following decolonization "reflected [only] a transition from the imperialistic to liberal worldview of Europe, not the dawning of an emancipatory alternative" (Otto 1996, 354). But in grappling with these questions, the book has also raised further quandaries that are beyond its scope. For instance, one must wonder whether the rule of law would ever guarantee equality for the weak within the existing structures of power and material inequality. Also, can the emancipatory potential of law be realized without a political project of structural equality and social justice? If the rule of law was to become an effective instrument for constructing a more inclusive and just society, what would decolonization of law entail? These questions alert us to the urgent need to deal with what Lu calls "structural alienation" arising from "social and political institutions that define agents' status rights and agency and mediate agents' positional status" (2017, 189). Mutua also suggests radical measures that "disassemble African states" and allow "precolonial entities the right to self-determination as a necessary step to legitimize the African state" (1995, 1118). In what she defines as "decolonizing intervention," Sabaratnam (2017) calls for a rethinking of international relations that requires the recovery of historical presence, politically conscious engagement, and investigation of material realities. In this book, I echo these calls by insisting that structural inequality and social injustices have been reinforced, rather than dismantled, by rebuilding the rule of law in postcolonial Africa.

References

Abraham, Arthur. 2003. *An Introduction to Pre-Colonial History of the Mende of Sierra Leone*. Lewiston, NY: Mellen.

Abraham, Arthur. 1978. *Mende Government and Politics under Colonial Rule*. Freetown: Sierra Leone University Press.

Abrahamsen, Rita. 2009. "Postcolonialism." In *International Relations Theory for the 21st Century*, edited by Kimberly Hudson. New York: Routledge.

Acharya, Amitav. 2004. "How Ideas Spread: Whose Norms Matter? Norm Localization and Institutional Change in Asian Regionalism." *International Organization* 58 (2): 239–275.

Acharya, Amitav. 2009. *Whose Ideas Matter? Agency and Power in Asian Regionalism*. Ithaca, NY: Cornell University Press.

Acharya, Amitav, and Barry Buzan. 2007. "Why Is There No Non-Western International Relations Theory? An Introduction." *International Relations of the Asia-Pacific* 7 (3): 287–312.

Adebajo, Adekeye. 2004. "West Africa's Tragic Twins: Building Peace in Liberia and Sierra Leone." In *Building Sustainable Peace*, edited by Andy W. Knight and Thomas F. Keating. New York: United Nations University Press.

Africa Progress Panel. 2012. "Job, Justice, and Equity: Seizing Opportunities in Times of Global Change." Africa Progress Panel Report.

Ahluwalia Pal. 2001. *Politics and Post-Colonial Theory: African Inflections*. London: Routledge.

Akhavan, Payam. 2001. "Beyond Impunity: Can International Criminal Justice Prevent Future Atrocities?" *The American Journal of International Law* 95 (1): 7–31.

Akuffo, Kwame. 2006. "Equity in Colonial West Africa: A Paradigm of Juridical Dislocation." *Journal of African Law* 50 (2): 132–144.

Alie, Joe A. D. 1990. *A New History of Sierra Leone*. New York: St. Martin's.

Alie, Joe A. D. 2008. "Reconciliation and Traditional Justice: Tradition-Based Practices of the Kpaa Mende in Sierra Leone." In *Traditional Justice and*

Reconciliation After Violent Conflict: Lessons from African Experience, edited by L. Huyse and M. Salter. Stockholm: International Institute for Democracy and Electoral Assistance.

Allott, Antony. N. 1984. "What Is to Be Done with African Customary Law? The Experiences of Problems and Reforms in Anglophone Africa from 1950." *Journal of African Law* 28 (1/2): 56–71.

Amnesty International. 2018. "A Force for Good? Restrictions for Peaceful Assembly and Impunity for Excessive Use of Force by the Sierra Leone Police."

Anghie, Antony. 1999. "Finding the Peripheries: Sovereignty and Colonialism in the 19th Century International Law." *Harvard International Law Journal* 40 (1): 1–71.

Anghie, Antony. 2007. *Imperialism, Sovereignty, and the Making of International Law*. Cambridge: Cambridge University Press.

Autesserre, Severine. 2007. "D. R. Congo: Explaining Peace Building Failures, 2003–2006." *Review of African Political Economy* 34 (113): 423–441.

Autesserre, Severine. 2010. *The Trouble with the Congo: Local Violence and the Failure of International Peacebuilding*. Cambridge: Cambridge University Press.

Autesserre, Severine. 2014. *Peaceland: Conflict Resolution and the Everyday Politics of International Intervention*. Cambridge: Cambridge University Press.

Bamfo, Napoleon. 2000. "The Hidden Elements of Democracy Among Akyem Chieftaincy: Enstoolment, Destoolment, and Other Limitations of Power." *Journal of Black Studies* 31 (2): 149–173.

Bandyopadhyaya, Jayantanuja. 1982. *North Over South: A Non-Western Perspective of International Relations*. New Delhi: South Asian Publishers.

Barkawi, Tarak, and Mark Laffey. 2006. "The Postcolonial Moment in Security Studies." *Review of International Studies* 32: 329–352.

Barnhizer, David, and Daniel Barnhizer. 2009. *Hypocrisy and Myths: The Hidden Order of the Rule of Law*. Lake Mary: Vandeplas Publishing.

Barrows, Walter. 1976. *Grassroots Politics in an African State: Integration and development in Sierra Leone*. New York: Holmes & Meier.

Baxi, Upendra. 2012. "Post-Colonial Legality: A Postscript from India." *Law and Politics in Africa, Asia, and Latin America* 45 (2): 178–194.

Beaulac, Stephane. 2012. "Lost in Translation? Domestic Courts, International Law and Rule of Law a la carte." In *International Law in Domestic Courts: Rule of Law Reform in Post-Conflict States*, edited by Kristjansdotter Edda, Andre Nollkaemper, and Cedic Ryngaer. Cambridge: Intersentia.

Bennet, Trevor W. "Comparative Law and African Customary Law." In *The Handbook of Comparative Law*, edited by Mathias Reimann and Reinhard Zimmerman. Oxford: Oxford University Press.

Benton, Lauren. 1994. "Beyond Legal Pluralism: Towards a New Approach to Law in the Informal Sector." *Social and Legal Studies* 3: 223–242.

Benton, Lauren. 2001. "Making Order Out of Trouble: Jurisdictional Politics in the Spanish Colonial Borderlands." *Law and Social Inquiry* 26 (7): 373–401.

Benton, Lauren. 2002. *Law and Colonial Cultures: Legal Regimes in World History, 1400–1900*. Cambridge: Cambridge University Press.

Berry, Sara. 1992. "Hegemony on a Shoestring: Indirect Rule and Access to Agricultural Land in Africa." *Journal of the International African Institute* 62 (3): 327–355.

Björkdahl, Annika, and Ivan Gusic. 2015. "Global Norms and Local Agency: Frictional Peacebuilding in Kosovo." *Journal of International Relations and Development* 18: 265–287.

Blair, Robert, Sabrina Karim, and Benjamin Morse. 2019. "Establishing the Rule of Law in Weak and War-Torn States: Evidence from a Field Experiment with the Liberian National Police." *American Political Science Review* 113 (3): 641–657.

Boone, Catherine. 2003. *Political Topographies of the African State: Territorial Authority and Institutional Choice*. Cambridge: Cambridge University Press.

Boutros-Ghali, Boutros. 1992. *An Agenda for Peace: Preventive Diplomacy, Peacemaking and Peacekeeping*. New York: United Nations.

Bratton, Michael. 2004. "State Building and Democratization in Sun-Saharan Africa: Forwards, Backwards, or Together?" *Afrobarometer Working Paper* 43.

Bratton, Michael, and Nicolas Van De Walle. 1997. *Democratic Experiments in Africa: Regime Transitions in Comparative Perspectives*. Cambridge: Cambridge University Press.

Brooke, N. J. Esq. 1953. *Report on the Native Court System in Sierra Leone*. Freetown: Government Printing Press.

Brooks, Rosa E. 2003. "The New Imperialism: Violence, Norms, and the Rule of Law." *Michigan Law Review* 101: 2275–2340.

Comaroff, John L. 2001. "Colonialism, Culture, and the Law: A Forward." *Law and Social Inquiry* 26 (7): 305–314.

Carothers, Thomas. 1998. "The Rule of Law Revival." *Foreign Affairs* 77 (2): 95–106.

Carothers, Thomas. 2010. *Promoting the Rule of Law Abroad: In Search of Knowledge*. Washington, DC: Carnegie Endowment for International Peace.

Cartwright, John R. 1970. *Politics in Sierra Leone, 1947–67*. Toronto: University of Toronto Press.

Chabal, Patrick, and Jean-Pascal Daloz. 1999. *Africa Works: Disorder as Political Instrument*. Bloomington: Indiana University Press.

Chalmers, Shane. 2018. *Liberia and the Dialectic of Law: Critical Theory, Pluralism, and the Rule of Law*. Abingdon: Birkbeek Law Press.

Chalmers, Shane. 2019. "The Mythology of International Rule of Law Promotion." *Law and Society* 44 (4): 957–986.

Chandler, David. 2004. "Imposing the Rule of Law: The Lessons of BiH for Peacebuilding in Iraq." *International Peacekeeping* 11 (2): 312–333.

Chandler, David. 2006. *Empire in Denial: The Politics of State-Building*. London: Pluto.

Chandler, David, and Oliver Richmond. 2015. "Contesting Post-Liberalism: Governmentality or Emancipation?" *Journal of International Relations and Development* 18 (1): 1–25.

Chanock, Martin. 1985. *Law, Customs, and Social Order: The Colonial Experience in Malawi and Zambia*. Cambridge: Cambridge University Press.

Chanock, Martin. 1989. "Neither Customary nor Legal: African Customary Law in an Era of Family Law Reform." *International Journal of Family Law* 3 (1): 72–88.

Chanock, Martin. 2001. *The Making of South African Legal Culture 1902–1936: Fear, Favour, and Prejudice*. Cambridge: Cambridge University Press.

Chauveau, Jean-Pierre, and Paul Richards. 2008. "West African Insurgencies in Agrarian Perspective: Cote d'Ivoire and Sierra Leone Compared." *Journal of Agrarian Change* 8 (4): 515–552.

Chimni, Bhupinder. S. 2006. "Third World Approaches to International Law: A Manifesto." *International Community Law Review* 8: 3027.

Chimni, Bhupinder. S. 2017. International Law and World Order: A Critique of Contemporary Approaches. Cambridge: Cambridge University Press.

Chua, Amy. 2004. *World on Fire: How Exporting Free Market Democracy Breeds Ethnic Hatred and Global Instability*. New York: Anchor.

Cohen, Dennis, and John Daniel. 1981. *Political Economy of Africa: Selected Readings*. London: Longman.

Collier, Gershon. 1970. *Sierra Leone: Experiment in Democracy in an African Nation*. London: University of London Press.

Collier, Paul, L. Elliott, Havard Hegre, Anke Hoeffler, Marta Reynal-Querol, and Nicholas Sambanis. 2003. *Breaking the Conflict Trap, Civil War: Causes, Consequences and Aid Policy*. New York: Oxford University Press for the World Bank.

Cooley, Alexander, and James Ron. 2002. "The NGO Scramble: Organizational Insecurity and the Political Economy of Transnational Action." *International Security* 27 (1): 5–39.

Constant, Benjamin. 2003. Principles of Politics Applicable to all Governments. Indianapolis, IN: Liberty Fund Press.

Corbo, Vittorio, and Stanley Fischer. 1994. *Structural Adjustment, Stabilization and Policy Reform: Domestic and International Finance*. Santiago: Agosto.

Cotterrell, Roger. 2006. "Comparative Law and Legal Culture." In *The Handbook of Comparative Law*, edited by Mathias Reimann and Reinhard Zimmerman. Oxford: Oxford University Press.

Cox, Thomas S. 1976. *Civil-Military Relations in Sierra Leone: A Case Study of African Soldiers in Politics*. Cambridge, MA: Harvard University Press.

Courtright, J. "Sierra Leone Small Towns Learn to Fight against Land Grabs." OZY, 6 May 2018.

Cravo, Teresa Almeida. 2016. "Linking Peacebuilding, Rule of Law and Security Sector Reform: The European Union's Experience." *Asia Europe Journal: Studies on Common Policy Challenges* 14 (1): 107–124.

Cresswell, John W. 2008. *Education Research: Planning, Conducting, and Evaluating Quantitative and Qualitative Research*. Hoboken, NJ: Pearson Education Inc.

Dale, Pamela. 2008. "Access to Justice in Sierra Leone." World Bank Justice for the Poor.

Dann, Philipp, and Felix Hanschmann. 2012. "Post-Conflict Theories and Law." *Law, and Politics in Africa, Asia, and Latin America* 45: 123–127.

David, Rene, and John E. C. Brierley. 1968. *Major Legal Systems in the World Today*. London: Stevens and Sons.

Denney, Lisa. 2013. "Liberal Chiefs or Illiberal Development? The Challenge of Engaging Chiefs in DFID's Security Sector Reform Programme in Sierra Leone." *Development Policy Review* 31 (1): 5–25.

Denney, Lisa. 2014. *Justice and Security Reform: Development Agencies and Informal Institutions in Sierra Leone.* London: Routledge.

DFID. 2001. *Making Government Work for the Poor: Building State Capability.* London: Department for International Development.

DFID. 2002. *Safety, Security, and Accessible Justice (SSAJ): Putting Policy into Practice.* London: Department for International Development.

DFID. 2004a. *The Africa Conflict Prevention Pool: An Information Document.* London: Department for International Development.

DFID. 2004b. "Evaluation of the Conflict Prevention Pools: Sierra Leone Report." Prepared by Jeremy Genifer with input from Kaye Oliver.

DFID. 2009a. *Building the State and Securing the Peace.* London: Department for International Development.

DFID. 2009b. "Building the State and Securing the Peace." Policy Paper.

DFID. 2010. "Building Peaceful States and Societies." A DFID Practice Paper.

DFID. 2011. "Project Completion Report for the Justice Sector Development Program." DFID/Sierra Leone.

DFID. 2012. *Operation Plan 2011–2015 Sierra Leone.* London: Department for International Development.

Dicey, Albert V. 1915. *Introduction to the Study of the Rule of Law of the Constitution.* London: Macmillan and Co. Limited.

Donias, Timothy. 2012. *Peacebuilding and Local Ownership: Post-Conflict Consensus Building.* London: Routledge.

Du Bois, W. E. B. 1943. "The Realities in Africa." *Foreign Affairs* 21: 721–732.

Duffield Mark R., and Vernon M. Hewitt. 2009. *Empire, Development and Colonialism: The Past in the Present.* Woodbridge, Suffolk: James Currey.

Dugard, John. 1978. *Human Rights and the South African Legal Order.* Princeton, NJ: Princeton University Press.

Dunn, Kevin C., and Timothy M. Shaw. 2001. *Africa's Challenge to International Relations Theory.* New York: Palgrave Publishers Ltd.

Dyck, Christopher B. 2013. "States of Unrest: Critiquing Liberal Peacebuilding and Security Sector Reform in Post-Conflict Sierra Leone (2001–2012) and Liberia (2003–2013)." Ph.D. Dissertation, University of Alberta.

Elsava, Luis. 2017. "The materiality of international law: violence, history and Joe Sacco's The Great War." *London Review of International Law* 5 (1): 49–86.

Englebert, Pierre. 2000. "Pre-Colonial Institutions, Post-Colonial States, and Economic Development in Africa." *Political Research Quarterly* 53 (1): 7–36.

Eslava, Luis, and Sundhya Pahuja. 2012. "Beyond the Post-Colonial: TWAIL and the Everyday Life of International Law." *Law and Politics in Africa, Asia, and Latin America* 45 (2): 195–221.

Etzioni, Mitchell, and Derek Mitchell. "Corporate Crime." In International Handbook of White-Collar and Corporate Crime, edited by Henry Pontell and Gilbert Geis. Boston, MA: Springer US. 187–199.

Ezeonu, Ifeanyi. 2003. "Structural Adjustment and Stabilization in Sub-Saharan Africa." In *Globalizing Africa*, edited by Malinda S. Smith. Asmara: African World Press Inc.

Fanthorpe, Richard. 2005. "On the Limits of Liberal Peace: Chiefs and Democratic Decentralisation in Post-War Sierra Leone." *African Affairs* 105 (418): 27–49.

Fawole, Alade W., and Ukeje Charles. 2005. *The Crisis of the State and Regionalism in West Africa: Identity, Citizenship, and Conflict*. Dakar: CODESRIA.

Ferencz, Benjamin. 1998. "International Criminal Court: The Legacy of Nuremberg." *Pace International Law Review* 10 (1): 203–235.

Flomoku, Pewee, and Lemuel Reeves. 2010. "Formal and Informal Justice in Liberia." *Accord* 44 (23).

Fordham, Margaret. "Comparative Legal Traditions: Introducing the Common Law to Civil Lawyers in Asia." *Asian Journal of Comparative Law* 1 (1): 1–8.

Fricker, Miranda. 2007. *Epistemic Injustice: Power and the Ethics of Knowing*. Oxford: Oxford University Press.

Fukuyama, Francis. 2012. "Transition to the Rule of Law." *Journal of Democracy* 21 (1): 31–44.

Galanter, Marc. 1974. "Why the Haves Come Out Ahead: Speculations on the Limits of Legal Change." *Law and Society* 9: 95–160.

Gathi, James, T. 2000. "Neoliberalism, Colonialism, and International Governance: Decentering the International Law of Governmental Legitimacy." *Michigan Law Review* 98 (6): 1996–2055.

Gathi, James T. 2006. "Imperialism, Colonialism, and International Law." *Buffalo Law Review* 54: 1013–1066.

Gathi, James T. 2019. "The Agenda of Third World Approaches to International Law (TWAIL)." In *International Legal Theory: Foundations and Frontiers*, edited by Jeffery Dunoff and Mark Pollack. Cambridge: Cambridge University Press.

Galli, Stefania and Klas Ronnback. 2020. "Land distribution and inequality in a black settler colony: the case of Sierra Leone, 1792–1831." *Economic History Review* 0, 0: 1–23.

Gbla, Osman. 2006. "Security Sector Reform Under International Tutelage in Sierra Leone." *International Peacekeeping* 13 (1): 78–93.

Glenn, Patrick, A. 2019. "Comparative Legal Families and Comparative Legal Traditions." In *Oxford Handbook of Comparative Law*, edited by Mathias Reimann and Reinhard Zimmermann. Oxford: Oxford University Press.

Global Witness. 2013. "Logging in the Shadows: How Vested Interests Abuse Shadow Permits to Evade Forest Sector Reforms: An Analysis of Recent Trends in Cameroon, Ghana, the Democratic Republic of Congo, and Liberia." Report.

Gluckman, Max. 1969. *Ideas and Procedures in African Customary Law: Studies Presented and Discussed at the English International African Seminar at the Haile Selassie I University, Addis Ababa*. Oxford: Oxford University Press.

Government of Liberia. 2009. "President Sirleaf Says Traditional Chiefs are Unifying Strength of Liberia." Statement by the Executive Mansion, 21 July.

Government of Liberia. 2010. *Liberia's Truth and Reconciliation Commission Report*.

Government of Liberia. *Liberia's Medium-Term Economic Growth and Development Strategy (2012–2017)—Agenda for Transformation: Steps Toward Liberia Rising 2030*. Prepared by the Ministry of Planning and Economic Affairs.

Government of Sierra Leone. 2002. *National Recovery Strategy of Sierra Leone 2002–2003: le we join an fo mek Salone go bifo: A Framework for Recovery Effort after an Assessment.*

Government of Sierra Leone. 2003. *National Long-term Perspective Studies (NLTPS): Sierra Leone Vision 2025. Sweet Salone—Strategies for National Transformation.* Freetown: Government Printing Press.

Government of Sierra Leone. 2004. *Sierra Leone Truth and Reconciliation Commission Report.*

Government of Sierra Leone. 2005. *Poverty Reduction Strategy Paper (SL-PRSP): A National Program for Food Security, Job Creation and Good Governance (2005–2007).* Freetown: Government Printing Press.

Government of Sierra Leone. 2008. *The Agenda for Change: Government's Policies for Sierra Leone's Poverty Reduction Strategy.* Freetown: Government Printing Press.

Government of Sierra Leone. 2012. *The Agenda for Prosperity: Road to Middle Income Status. Sierra Leone's Third Generation Poverty Reduction Strategy Paper (2013–2018).* Freetown: Government Printing Press.

Graziadei, Michel. "Comparative Law, Transplants, and Receptions." In *The Handbook of Comparative Law*, edited by Mathias Reimann and Reinhard Zimmerman. Oxford: Oxford University Press.

Grenfell, Laura. 2013. *Promoting the Rule of Law in Post-Conflict States.* Cambridge: Cambridge University Press.

Grovogui, Siba N. 1996. *Sovereigns, Quasi-sovereigns, and Africans.* Minneapolis: University of Minnesota Press.

Gutkind, Peter C. W., and Immanuel M. Wallerstein. 1976. *The Political Economy of Contemporary Africa.* Beverly Hills, CA: Sage Publications.

Haggard, Stephen, and Lydia Tiede. 2014. "The Rule of Law in Post-Conflict Settings: The Empirical Record." *International Studies Quarterly* 58: 405–417.

Hanlon, Joseph. 2005. "Is the International Community Helping to Recreate the Pre-Conditions for War in Sierra Leone?" UNU WIDER, Research Paper No. 2005/50.

Harper, Erica. 2011. *Working with Customary Justice Systems: Post-Conflict and Fragile States.* Rome: International Development Organization.

Harrell-Bond, Barbara E., Allen M. Howard, and David E. Skinner. 1978. *Community Leadership and the Transformation of Freetown (1801–1976).* The Hague: Mounton.

Harrell-Bond, Barbara E., and U. Rijnsdorp. 1974. *Family Law in Sierra Leone: A Research Report.* Leiden: Afrika-Studiecentrum.

Harris, Richard L. 1975. *The Political Economy of Africa.* Cambridge, MA: Schenkman Pub. Co.

Hawes, Frank, Ken Lizzio, and Willa Reeves. 2013. "Lessons Learned Evaluation: Access to Justice and Information (Project Implemented by the Carter Center)." Conducted for the USAID/Liberia.

Henderson, Keith, Charles Jakosa, and Charles Gibson. 2009. "Evaluation of Rule of Law Programs in Liberia." Prepared for the USAID.

Herbst, Jeffery. 2009. *States and Power in Africa: Comparative Lessons in Authority and Control.* Princeton, NJ: Princeton University Press.

Herbert Smith Freehills, Standard Chartered, and Prudential Plc. Sierra Leone. "An Investment Guide: A Private Sector Perspective on the Investment Landscape." Freetown: SLIEPA, July 2015.

Human Right Watch. 2014. "Whose Development? Human Rights Abuses in Sierra Leone Mining Boom." Country report.

Hunt, Alan. 1985. "The Ideology of Law: Advances and Problems in the Recent Application of the Concept of Ideology to the Analysis of Law." *Law and Society* 19 (1): 11–38.

Hurwitz, Agnès, and Gordon Peake. 2004. "Strengthening the Security-Development Nexus: Assessing International Policy and Practice Since the 1990s." Conference report, International Peace Academy.

Hussain, Nasser. 2003. *The Jurisprudence of Emergency: Colonialism, and the Rule of Law*. Ann Arbor: Michigan University Press.

Huxley, Elspeth. 1948. "British Aims in Africa." *Foreign Affairs* 28: 43–55.

Ibhawoh, Bonny. 2009. "Historical Globalization and Colonial Legal Culture: African Assessors, Customary Law, and Criminal Justice in British Africa." *Journal of Global History* 4 (3): 429–451.

Ikenberry, John G. 2011. "The Future of the Liberal World Order: Internationalism After America." *Foreign Affairs* 9 (3): 56–86.

Inayatullah, Naeem, and David Blaney. 2004. *International Relations and the Problem of Difference*. New York: Routledge.

International Crisis Group. 2004. "Liberia and Sierra Leone: Rebuilding Failed States."

International Crisis Group. 2006. "Liberia: Resurrecting the Justice System." *African Report*, No. 107.

Isser, Deborah. 2011. *Customary Justice and the Rule of Law in War-Torn Societies*. Washington, DC: United States Institute of Peace Press.

Isser, Deborah, Stephen C. Lubkemann, and Saah N'Tow. 2009. *Looking for Justice: Liberians Experiences with and Perceptions of Local Justice Options*. Washington, DC: United States Institute of Peace.

Jackson, Paul. 2011. "Decentralized Power and Traditional Authorities: How Power Determines Access to Justice in Sierra Leone." *Journal of Legal Pluralism and Unofficial Law* 43 (63): 207–230.

Jackson, Robert H., and Carl G. Rosberg. 1982. "Why Africa's Weak States Persist: The Empirical and the Juridical in Statehood." *World Politics* 35 (1): 1–24.

Joireman, Sandra F. 2001. "Inherited Legal Systems and Effective Rule of Law: Africa and the Colonial Legacy." *The Journal of Modern African Studies* 39 (4): 571–596.

Joireman, Sandra F. 2004. "Colonization and the Rule of Law: Comparing the Effectiveness of Common Law and Civil Law Countries." *Constitutional Political Economy* 15: 315–338.

Joireman, Sandra F. 2006. "The Evolution of the Common Law: Legal Development in Kenya and India." *Commonwealth and Comparative Politics* 44 (2): 190–210.

Jung, Courtney. 2011. "Canada and the Legacy of the Indian Residential Schools: Transitional Justice for Indigenous Peoples in a Non-Transitional Society." In

Identities in Transition: Challenges for Transitional Justice in Divided Societies, edited by Paige Arthur. New York: Cambridge University Press.

Justice Sector Coordination Office. 2007. *The Justice Sector Reform Strategy and Investment Plan 2008–2010*. Freetown: Government of Sierra Leone.

Kandeh, Jimmy. 1992. "Politicization of Ethnic Identities in Sierra Leone." *African Studies Review* 35 (1): 81–99.

Kandeh, Jimmy. 2012. "Intervention and Peacebuilding in Sierra Leone: A Critical Perspective." In *When the State Fails: Studies on Interventions in the Sierra Leone Civil War*, edited by Tunde Zack-Williams. London: Pluto Press.

Kaplan, Irving, M. Dobert, and J. L. Mclaughlin. 1976. *Area Handbook for Sierra Leone*. Washington: Foreign Area Studies of the American University.

Kargbo, M. 2012. "International Peacebuilding in Sierra Leone: The Case of the UK." In *When the State Fails: Studies on Interventions in the Sierra Leone Civil War*, edited by T. Zack-Williams. London: Pluto Press.

Keating, Thomas F., and Andy W. Knight. 2004. *Building Sustainable Peace*. New York: United Nations University Press.

Kelsall, Tim. 2009. *Culture Under Cross-Examination: International Justice and the Special Court for Sierra Leone*. Cambridge: Cambridge University Press.

Kerrigan, Fergus. 2012. "Informal Justice Systems: Charting a Course for Human Rights-Based Engagement." UN report produced for UNDP, UNICEF, and UN Women.

Keukeleire, Stephan, and Kolja Raube. 2013. "The Security-Development Nexus and Securitization in the EU's Policies Towards Developing Countries." *Cambridge Review of International Affairs* 26: 556–572.

Kieh, George K., Jr. 2007. *Beyond State Failure and Collapse: Making the State Relevant in Africa*. Boulder, CO: Lexington Books.

Kilson, Martin. 1996. *Political Change in a West African State: A Study of the Modernization Process in Sierra Leone*. Cambridge, MA: Harvard University Press.

Kissinger, Henry A. 2001. "The Pitfalls of Universal Jurisdiction." *Foreign Affairs* 80 (4): 86–96.

Kotter, Matthias, Tilmann J. Roder, Gunner F. Schuppert, and Rudiger Wolfrum. 2015. *Non-State Justice Institutions and the Law: Decision-Making at the Interface of Tradition, Religion, and the State*. Basingstoke: Palgrave Macmillan.

Kristjansdotter, Edda, Andre Nollkaemper, and Cedic Ryngaer. 2012. *International Law in Domestic Courts: Rule of Law Reform in Post-Conflict States*. Cambridge: Intersentia.

Kritz, Neil J. 1996. "Coming to Terms with Atrocities: A Review of Accountability Mechanisms for Mass Violations of Human Rights." *Law and Contemporary Problems* 59 (4): 127–152.

Kup, Alexander P. 1975. *Sierra Leone: A Concise History*. London: David and Charles.

Kurz, Christof P. 2010. "What You See Is What You Get: Analytical Lenses and the Limitations of Post-Conflict Statebuilding in Sierra Leone." *Journal of Intervention and Statebuilding* 4 (2): 205–236.

Langer, William L. 1986. "Farewell to Empire." *Foreign Affairs* 41: 115–130.

Lapie, P. O. 1944. "The New Colonial Policy of France." *Foreign Affairs* 23: 104–111.

Lesley, Buell R. 1927. "The Struggle in Africa." *Foreign Affairs* 6: 22–40.

Levitt, Jeremy L. 2005. *The Evolution of Deadly Conflict in Liberia: From Paternalism to State Collapse*. Durban: Carolina Academic Press.

Logan, Carolyn. 2013. "The Roots of Resilience: Exploring Popular Support for African Traditional Authorities." *African Affairs* 112 (448): 353–376.

Lowenkopf, Martin. 1976. *Politics in Liberia: The Conservative Road to Development*. Stanford, CA: Hoover Institution Press.

Lu, Catherine. 2017. *Justice and Reconciliation in World Politics*. Cambridge: Cambridge University Press.

Lubkemann, Stephen, Deborah Isser, and Peter Chapman. 2011. "Neither State Nor Custom—Just Naked Power: The Consequences of Ideals-Oriented Rule of Law Policy-Making in Liberia." *Journal of Legal Pluralism* 63: 73–109.

Lugard, Baron. 1930. "Native Policy in East Africa." *Foreign Policy* 9: 65–78.

Mac Ginty, Roger. 2011. *International Peacebuilding and Local Resistance: Hybrid Forms of Peace*. Basingstoke: Palgrave Macmillan.

MacKenzie, Megan, and Mohamed Sesay. 2012. "No Amnesty from/for the International: The Production and Promotion of TRCs as an International Norm in Sierra Leone." *International Studies Perspectives* 13: 146–163.

Maddison, Sarah, and Laura Shephard J. 2014. "Peacebuilding and the Post-Colonial Politics of Transitional Justice." *Peacebuilding* 2 (3): 253–269.

Mahoney, Paul G. 2001. "The Common Law and Economic Growth: Hayek Might Be Right." *The Journal of Legal Studies* 30 (2): 503–525.

Makuwa, Esther, Maarten Voors, Erwin Bulte, and Paul Richards. 2011. "Peasant Grievances and Insurgency in Sierra Leone: Judicial Serfdom as a Driver of Conflict." *African Affairs* 110 (440): 339–366.

Mamdani, Mahmood. 1996. *Citizen and Subject: Contemporary Africa and the Legacy of Late Colonialism*. Princeton, NJ: Princeton University Press.

Mani, Rama. 1998. "Conflict Resolution, Justice and the Law: Rebuilding the Rule of Law in the Aftermath of Complex Political Emergencies." *International Peacekeeping* 5 (3): 1–25.

Manning, Elizabeth R. 2009. *The Landscape of Local Authority in Sierra Leone: How Traditional and Modern Justice Systems Interact*. World Bank: Justice and Development Working Paper Series 1 (1).

Mansfield, Edward D., and Jack L. Snyder. 2005. *Electing to Fight: Why Emerging Democracies Go to War*. Cambridge, MA: MIT Press.

Manteaw, Samuel O. 2008. "Legal Education in Africa: What Type of Lawyer Does Africa Need?" *McGeorge Law Review* 39: 905–970.\

Marshall, David. 2014. *The International Rule of Law Movement: A Crisis of Legitimacy and the Way Forward*. Cambridge, MA: Harvard University Press.

Massoud, Mark F. 2013. *Law's Fragile State: Colonial, Authoritarian, and Humanitarian Legacies in Sudan*. Cambridge: Cambridge University Press.

Massoud, Mark Fathi. 2015. "Work Rules: How International NGOs Build Rule of Law in War-Torn Societies." *Law & Society Review* 49 (2): 333–364.

Mattei, Ugo, and Laura Nader. 2008. *Plunder: When the Rule of Law is Illegal*. Malden, MA: Blackwell Publishing.

Mazrui, Ali. 1983. "Africa: The Political Economy of Nationhood and the Political Economy of the State." *Millennium: Journal of International Studies* 12 (3): 201–210.

McAdams, James A. 1997. *Transitional Justice and the Rule of Law in New Democracies*. Notre Dame, IN: University of Notre Dame Press.

McBride, Keally D. 2016. *Mr. Mothercountry: The Man Who Made the Rule of Law*. New York: Oxford University Press.

McEvoy, Kieran, and Lorna McGregor. 2008. *Transitional Justice from Below: Grassroots Activism and the Struggle for Change*. Oxford: Portland and Hart Pub.

Meierhenrich, Jens. 2008. *The Legacies of Law: Long-Run Consequences of Legal Development in South Africa, 1652–2000*. Cambridge: Cambridge University Press.

Merry, Sally E. 1991. "Law and Colonialism." *Law and Society* 25 (4): 889–922.

Merry, Sally E. 1997. "Global Human Rights and Local Social Movements in a Legally Plural World." *Canadian Journal of Law and Society* 30 (3): 247–274.

Merry, Sally E. 1998. "Legal Pluralism." *Law and Society Review* 22 (5): 869–896.

Merry, Sally E. 2003. "From Law and Colonialism to Law and Globalization." *Law and Social Inquiry* 28 (2): 569–590.

Merryman, John H., and Rogelio Perez-Perdomo. 2019. *The Civil Law Tradition: An Introduction to the Legal System of Europe and Latin America*. Stanford, CA: Stanford University Press.

Mignolo, Walter. 2002. "The Geopolitics of Knowledge and the Colonial Difference." *The South Atlantic Quarterly* 101 (1): 57–96.

Mills-Jones, J. 1988. "Economic Adjustment Programs Understand by Arrangements with the International Monetary Fund: Liberia's Experience 1980–1985." *Liberian Studies Journal* 13 (2): 153–177.

Mokuwa, Esther, Maarten Voors, Erwin Bulte, and Paul Richards. 2011. "Peasant Grievances and Insurgency in Sierra Leone: Judicial Serfdom as a Driver of Conflict." *African Affairs* 110 (440): 339–366.

Moore, Sally F. 1992. "Treating Law as Knowledge: Telling Colonial Officers What to Say to Africans about Running 'Their Own' Native Courts." *Law & Society Review* 26 (1): 11–46.

Moustafa, Tamir, and Tom Ginsburg. 2008. *Rule of Law: The Politics of Courts in Authoritarian Regimes*. Cambridge: Cambridge University Press.

Mutua, Wa Makau. 1995. "Why Redraw the Map of Africa? A Moral and Legal Inquiry." *Michigan Journal of International Law* 16 (4): 1113–1176.

Ndulo, Muna. 2011. "From Constitutional Protections to Oversight Mechanisms." In *Peacebuilding and the Rule of Law in Africa: Just Peace?*, edited by Chandra L. Sriram, Olga Martin-Ortega, and Johanna Herman. Abingdon: Routledge.

Nelson, Harold. 1985. "Liberia: A Country Study." *Global Security*.

Network Movement for Justice and Development and Cord Netherlands. 2013. *Land Rights Project: The Social, Economic, and Cultural Impact of Larger-Scale Land Investment Deals on Local Communities in Sierra Leone*.

Newman, Edward, Roland Paris, and Oliver P. Richmond. 2009. *New Perspectives on Liberal Peacebuilding*. Tokyo: United Nations University Press.

Nobles, Wade W. 1974. "Extended Self: Rethinking the So-Called Negro Self Concept." Paper presented to the National Association of Black Psychologists Convention, August 1974.

Obarrio, Juan. 2011. "Traditional Justice as Rule of Law in Africa: An Anthropological Perspective." In *Peacebuilding and the Rule of Law in Africa: Just Peace?*, edited by S. L. Chandra, O. Martin-Ortega, and J. Herman. Abingdon: Routledge.

OECD. 2009. "Concepts and Dilemmas of State Building in Fragile Situations: From Fragility to Resilience." *OECD Journal on Development* 9 (3): 61–148.

Office of the United Nations High Commissioner for Human Rights (OHCHR). 2006. *Rule of Law Tools for Post-Conflict States: Mapping the Justice Sector*. New York: United Nations.

Orford, Anne. 2013. "On international legal method." *London Review of International Law* 1 (1): 166–197.

Omozurike, Oji U. 1971. "International Law and Colonialism in Africa: Critique." *Zambian Law Journal* 3 (1–2): 95–124.

O'Neill, W. 2003. "The Legacy of the Special Court for Sierra Leone." *United Nations Development Program & International Center for Transitional Justice* (draft): 1–30.

Open Society Initiative for West Africa. 2014. "Sierra Leone Justice Sector and the Rule of Law." Prepared by Mohamed Suma. Freetown.

Orentlicher, D. F. 1991. "Settling Accounts: The Duty to Prosecute Human Rights Violations of a Prior Regime." *Yale Law Journal* 100 (8): 2537–2615.

Otto, Dianne. 1996. "International Law: The Problems of Global Community and the Incommensurability of Difference." *Social and Legal Studies* 5 (3): 337–364.

Paris, Roland. 2002. "International Peacebuilding and the Mission Civilisatrice." *Review of International Studies* 28 (4): 637–656.

Paris, Roland. 2004. *At War's End: Building Peace After Civil Conflict*. Cambridge: Cambridge University Press.

Paris, Roland, and Timothy D. Sisk. 2009. *The Dilemmas of Statebuilding: Confronting the Contradictions of Postwar Peace Operation*. London: Routledge.

Park, Augustine S. J. 2008. "Consolidating Peace: Rule of Law Institutions and Local Justice Practices in Sierra Leone." *Southern African Journal on Human Rights* 24: 536–564.

Pejovic, Caslav. 2001. "Civil Law and Common Law: Two Different Paths Leading to the Same Goal." *Comparative Maritime Law* 40 (155): 7–32.

Peterson, Jenny H. 2010. "Rule of Law Initiatives and the Liberal Peace: The Impact of Political Reform in Post-Conflict States." *Disasters* 34 (1): 15–39.

Pham, John-Peter. 2004. *Liberia: Portrait of a Failed State*. New York: Reed Press.

Pimentel, David. 2010. "Rule of Law Reform Without Cultural Imperialism? Reinforcing Customary Justice Through Collateral Review in Southern Sudan." *Hague Journal on the Rule of Law* 2 (1): 1–28.

Porter, Doug, Deborah Isser, and Louis-Alexandre Berg. 2013. 'The Justice-Security-Development Nexus: Theory and Practice in Fragile and Conflict-Affected States." *Hague Journal on the Rule of Law* 5: 310–328.

Prempeh, Kwasi. 2013. "Neither 'Timorous Souls' Nor 'Bold Spirits': Courts and the Politics of Judicial Review in Post-Colonial Africa." *Law and Politics in Africa, Asia, and Latin America* 45 (2): 157–177.

Pugh, Michael. 2004. "Peacekeeping and Critical Theory." *International Peacekeeping* 11 (1): 39–58.

Pugh, Michael. 2005. "The Political Economy of Peacebuilding: A Critical Theory Perspective." *International Journal of Peace Studies* 10 (2): 23–42.

Rajagopal, Balakrishnan. 2008. "Invoking the Rule of Law in Post-conflict Rebuilding: A Critical Examination." *William and Mary Law Review* 49 (4): 1347–1376.

Reno, William. 1995. *Corruption and State Politics in Sierra Leone.* Cambridge: Cambridge University Press.

Reno, William. 1997. "Humanitarian Emergencies and Warlord Economies in Liberia and Sierra Leone." Working Papers, 149. Helsinki: World Institute for Development Economics Research.

Reno, William. 1998. *Warlord Politics and African States.* Boulder, CO: Lynne Rienner Publishers.

Reno, William. 2011. *Warfare in Independent Africa.* Cambridge: Cambridge University Press.

Richards, Paul. 1996. *Fighting for the Rain Forest: War, Youth, and Resources in Sierra Leone.* Portsmouth, NH: Heinemann.

Richards, Paul. 2005. "To Fight or to Farm? Agrarian Dimensions of the Mano River Conflicts (Sierra Leone and Liberia)." *African Affairs* 104 (417): 571–590.

Richmond, Oliver P. 2005. *The Transformation of Peace.* Basingstoke: Palgrave Macmillan.

Richmond, Oliver P. 2010. *Palgrave Advances in Peacebuilding: Critical Developments and Approaches.* Basingstoke: Palgrave Macmillan.

Richmond, Oliver P., and Jason Franks. 2009. *Liberal Peace Transition: Between Statebuilding and Peacebuilding.* Edinburgh: Edinburgh University Press.

Ryckmans, Pierre. 1955. "Belgium Colonialism." *Foreign Affairs* 34: 89–101.

Sabaratnam, Meera. 2017. *Decolonizing Intervention: International Statebuilding in Mozambique.* London: Rowman & Littlefield International Ltd.

Said, Edward. 1994. *Orientalism* (Rev. Ed.). New York: Random House.

Sawyer, Amos. 1992. *The Emergence of Autocracy in Liberia: Tragedy and Challenge.* San Francisco: Institute for Contemporary Studies.

Sawyer, Amos. 2004. "Violent Conflicts and Governance Challenges in West Africa: The Case of the Mano River Basin Area." *Journal of Modern African Studies* 42 (4): 437–463.

Sawyer, Edward. 2008. "Remove or Reform? A Case for (Restructuring) Chiefdom Governance in Post-Conflict Sierra Leone." *African Affairs* 107 (428): 387–403.

Saylor, Ralph Gerald. 1967. *The Economic System of Sierra Leone.* Durham, NC: Duke University Press.

Seidman, Ann, and Robert B. Seidman. "The Political Economy of Customary Law in the Former British Territories of Africa." *Journal of African Law* 28 (1/2): 44–55.

Sesay, Amadu, Charles Ukeje, Gbla Osman, and Ismail Olawale. 2009. *Post-War Regimes and State Reconstruction in Liberia and Sierra Leone*. Dakar: CODESRIA.

Sesay, Mohamed. 2016. "Harmonizing Customary Justice with the Rule of Law in Liberal Peacebuilding: A Sub-National Comparative Study of Sierra Leone and Liberia." Ph.D. Dissertation, McGill University.

Sesay, Mohamed. 2019a. "Hijacking the Rule of Law in Postconflict Environments." *European Journal of International Security* 4 (1): 41–60.

Sesay, Mohamed. 2019b. "Informal Institutional Change and the Place of Traditional Justice in Sierra Leone's Post-War Reconstruction." *African Affairs* 118 (470): 1–23.

Shamir, Ronen, and Hacker Daphna. 2001. "Colonialism's Civilizing Mission: The Case of the Indian Hemp Drug Commission." *Law and Social Inquiry* 26 (7): 435–461.

Sharon, Assaf. 2016. "Domination and the Rule of Law." In *Oxford Studies in Political Philosophy*, edited by David Sobel, Peter Vallentyne, and Steven Wall, Vol. 2. Oxford: Oxford University Press.

Shaw, Rosalind, Lars Waldorf, and Pierre Hazan. 2010. *Localizing Transitional Justice: Interventions and Priorities After Mass Atrocity*. Stanford, CA: Stanford University Press.

Shilliam, Robbie. 2011. *International Relations and Non-Western Thought: Imperialism, Colonialism, and Investigations of Global Modernity*. Abingdon: Routledge.

Siddiqi, Bilal, and Justin Sandefur. 2009. *Community Based Justice and the Rule of Law in Liberia*. Oxford: Centre for the Study of African Economies (CSAE).

Sillah, Mohammed, B. 2016. "The Lebanese Immigrants in Sierra Leone: A Market Dominant-Minority and Revisiting the Constitutional Statutes for Naturalization and Citizenship." *American International Journal of Social Science* 5(4): 8–16.

Sitze, A. 2013. *The Impossible Machine: A Genealogy of South Africa's Truth and Reconciliation Commission*. Ann Arbour: University of Michigan Press.

Slaughter, A-Marie. 2004. *A New World Order*. Princeton, NJ: Princeton University Press.

Smart, Joko M. 1968. "The Local Courts System in Sierra Leone." *Sierra Leone Studies* 22: 31–44.

Smith, Steve. 2000. "The Discipline of International Relations: Still an American Social Science?" *The British Journal of Politics & International Relations* 2 (3): 374–402.

Snyder, Francis. 1984. "Customary Law and the Economy." *Journal of African Law* 28 (1/2): 34–43.

Sriram, Chandra L., Olga Martin-Ortega, and Johanna Herman. 2011. *Peacebuilding and the Rule of Law in Africa: Just Peace?* Abingdon: Routledge.

Stakes, Robert E. 1995. *The Art of Case Study Research*. Thousand Oaks, CA: Sage Publishers.

Stammes, Eli. 2016. "Values, Context, and Hybridity: Insights of the UN Peacebuilding Architecture." In *Readings in the International Relations of Africa*, edited by Tom Young. Bloomington: Indiana University Press.

Stokes, E. "Riot on the Plantation: In Liberia, Palm Oil has Set Off a Dangerous Scramble for Land." *Al Jazeera America*, 4 October 2015.

Stromseth, Jane, David Wippman, and Rosa Brooks. 2006. *Can Might Make Might? Building the Rule of Law After Military Interventions.* Cambridge: Cambridge University Press.

Subotić, Jelena. 2012. "The Transformation of International Transitional Justice Advocacy." *International Journal of Transitional Justice* 6 (1): 106–125.

Suma, M. 2014. "Sierra Leone: Justice Sector and the Rule of Law." Report for the Open Society Initiative for West Africa (OSIWA).

Tangri, Roger. 1976a. "Conflict and Violence in Contemporary Sierra Leone Chiefdoms." *The Journal of Modern African Studies* 14 (2): 311–323.

Tangri, Roger. 1976b. "Central-Local Politics in Contemporary Sierra Leone." *African Affairs* 77 (307): 165–173.

Tangri, Roger. 1980. "Paramount Chiefs and Central Governments in Sierra Leone." *African Studies* 39 (2): 183–195.

Tetley, William. 1999. "Mixed Jurisdictions: Common Law v. Civil Law (Codified and Uncodified)." *Louisiana Law Review* 60 (3): 677–738.

The Oakland Institute. 2011. "Understanding Land Investment Deals in Africa: Sierra Leone Country Report." The Oakland Institute.

Thompson, Edward P. 1975. *Whigs and Hunters: The Origin of the Black Act.* London: Penguin Books Ltd.

Trebilock, Michael J., and Ronald J. Daniels. 2008. *Rule of Law Development: Charting the Fragile Paths of Progress.* Cheltenham: Edward Elgar.

Trubek David M., and John Esser. 1989. "Critical Empiricism in American Legal System: Paradox. Programme, or Pandora's Box?" *Law and Social Enquiry* 14 (3): 3–52.

Tull, Dennis M. 2003. "A Reconfiguration of Political Order? The State of the State in North Kivu (DR Congo)." *African Affairs* 102 (408): 429–446.

UN Department for Peacekeeping Operations (DPKO). 2008. *United Nations Peacekeeping Operations: Principles and Guidelines.* New York: UN Secretariat.

UN DPKO. 2009. "Methodology for Review of Justice and Corrections Components in United Nations Peace Operations." Prepared by the Department of Field Support.

UN DPKO and OHCHR. 2011. "The United Nations Rule of Law Indicators: Implementation Guide and Project Tools." Endorsed by Members of the Rule of Law Coordination and Resource Group.

UNDP. 2010. "Global Program on Strengthening the Rule of Law in Conflict and Post-Conflict Situations: Building Peace Through Justice and Security." Annual Report.

United Nations. 2004. "A More Secure World: Our Shared Responsibility." Report of the High-level Panel on Threats, Challenges, and Change.

United Nations. 2009. "United Nations Assistance to Constitution-making Processes." Guidance Notes of the Secretary-General.

United Nations. 2010. "United Nations Approach to Transitional Justice." Guidance Notes of the Secretary-General.

United Nations High Commissioner for Human Rights. 2008. *Rule-of-Law Tools for Post-Conflict States: Maximizing the Legacy of Hybrid Courts.* New York: United Nations Publications 08, XIV.2.

United Nations Office of Drugs and Crimes (UNODC). 2006. *Access to Justice: The Independence, Impartiality, and Integrity of the Judiciary. Criminal Justice Assessment Toolkit.* New York: United Nations.

UNODC. 2006. *Compendium on United Nations Standards and Norms in Crime Prevention and Criminal Justice.* New York: United Nations.

UNODC. 2011. "Criminal Justice Reform in Post-Conflict States: A Guide for Practitioners." Developed jointly with the United States Institute of Peace (USIP).

UN Security Council. 1992. "An Agenda for Peace: Preventive Diplomacy, Peacemaking, and Peacekeeping." Report of the Secretary-General.

UN Security Council. 2000. *Report on the Panel on United Nations Peace Operations (Brahimi Report).* New York: United Nations.

UN Security Council. 2004. "The Rule of Law and Transitional Justice in Conflict and Post-Conflict Societies." Report of the Secretary-General, S/2004/616.

UN Security Council. 2006. "The Rule of Law at the National and International Levels: Uniting Our Strengths. Enhancing United Nations Support for the Rule of Law." Report of the Secretary-General.

UN Security Council. 2011. "The Rule of Law and Transitional Justice in Conflict and Post-Conflict Societies." Report of the Secretary-General.

UN Security Council. 2013a. "Measuring the Effectiveness of the Support Provided by the United Nations System for the Promotion of the Rule of Law in Conflict and Post-Conflict Situations." Report of the Secretary-General.

UN Security Council. 2013b. "Strengthening and Coordinating United Nations Rule of Law Activities." Report of the Secretary-General.

UN Security Council. 2014a. "Peacebuilding in the Aftermath of Conflict." Report of the Secretary-General.

UN Security Council. 2014b. "Civilian Capacity in the Aftermath of Conflict." Report of the Secretary-General.

USAID. 2008. "Rule of Law Country Analysis: A Guide for USAID Democracy and Governance Officers."

US Department of State. 2010. "Guide to Justice Sector Assistance." Prepared by the Bureau of International Narcotics and Law Enforcement Affairs (INL).

Van De Walle, Nicolas. 2001. *African Economies and the Politics of Permanent Crisis, 1979–1999.* Cambridge: Cambridge University Press.

Villalon, Leonardo A., and Phillip Huxtable. 1998. *The African State at a Critical Juncture: Between Disintegration and Reconfiguration.* Boulder, CO: Lynne Rienner Publishers.

Wai, Zubairu. 2012. "Neopatrimonialism and the Discourse of State Failure in Africa." *Review of African Political Economy* 39 (13): 27–43.

Wai, Zubairu. 2012. *Epistemologies of African Conflicts: Violence, Evolutionism, and the War in Sierra Leone.* New York: Palgrave Macmillan.

Wai, Zubairu. 2015. "On the Predicament of Africanist Knowledge: Mudimbe, Gnosis and the Challenge of the Colonial Library." *International Journal of Francophone Studies* 18 (2): 263–290.

Waller, Richard. 2018. "Legal History and Historiography in Colonial Sub-Saharan Africa." In *Oxford Research Encyclopedia of African History*. Oxford: Oxford University Press.

Waugh, Colin M. 2011. *Charles Taylor and Liberia: Ambition and Atrocity in Africa's Lone Star State*. London: Zed Books.

Whittlesey, Derwent. 1937. "British and French Colonial Techniques in West Africa." *Foreign Affairs* 15 (2): 362–373.

Wojkowska, Ewa. 2006. *Doing Justice: How Informal Justice Systems Can Contribute?* UNDP, the Oslo Governance Center, and the Democratic Governance Fellowship Program.

World Bank. World Development Report, 2011.

Wyse, Akintola J. G. 1986. *The Krio of Sierra Leone: An Interpretive History*. Freetown: Okrafto-Smart.

Zartman, William I. 1995. *Collapsed States: The Disintegration and Restoration of Legitimate Authority*. Boulder, CO: Lynne Rienner Publishers.

Zolo, Danilo. 2007. "The Rule of Law: A Critical Reappraisal." In *Costa Pietro, and Danilo Zolo, The Rule of Law: History, Theory and Criticism*. Dordrecht: Springer.

Index

www.ingramcontent.com/pod-product-compliance
Lightning Source LLC
Chambersburg PA
CBHW030648270326
41929CB00007B/269